STUDIES IN ETHICS AND THE PHILOSOPHY OF RELIGION

General Editor: D. Z. Phillips

STUDIES IN ETHICS AND THE PHILOSOPHY OF RELIGION

General Editor: D. Z. Phillips

VOLUME I
The Problem of Evil
by M. B. Ahern

VOLUME II
Moral Reasoning
by R. W. Beardsmore

VOLUME III
Theology and Intelligibility
by Michael Durrant

VOLUME IV
Humanism and Ideology
by James R. Flynn

VOLUME V
The Five Ways:
St. Thomas Aquinas' Proofs of God's Existence
by Anthony Kenny

VOLUME VI
Moral Practices
by D. Z. Phillips and H. O. Mounce

VOLUME VII
God and Timelessness
by Nelson Pike

VOLUME VIII
Without Answers
by Rush Rhees

VOLUME IX
Morality and Purpose
by J. L. Stocks

STUDIES IN ETHICS AND THE PHILOSOPHY OF RELIGION

VOLUME III

Theology and Intelligibility

By Michael Durrant

Routledge
Taylor & Francis Group
LONDON AND NEW YORK

First published in 1973
by Routledge & Kegan Paul Ltd.

This edition published 2003
by Routledge
2 Park Square, Milton Park, Abingdon, Oxon OX14 4RN

Simultaneously published in the USA and Canada
by Routledge
270 Madison Ave, New York, NY 10016

First issued in paperback 2010

Routledge is an imprint of the Taylor & Francis Group

British Library Cataloguing in Publication Data
A catalogue record for this book is available from the British Library

Library of Congress Cataloging in Publication Data
A catalog record has been requested

ISBN 978-0-415-31843-3 (hbk) (Volume III)
ISBN 978-0-415-60821-3 (pbk) (Volume III)
ISBN 978-0-415-31840-2 (set)

Publisher's Note
The Publisher has gone to great lengths to ensure the quality of this reprint but points out that some imperfections in the original book may be apparent.

STUDIES IN ETHICS AND THE PHILOSOPHY OF RELIGION

The Series is meant to provide an opportunity for philosophical discussions of a limited length which pursue in some detail specific topics in ethics or the philosophy of religion, or topics which belong to both fields. For the most part, the Series will present work by contemporary philosophers. The contributors, while not representing any single philosophical school, will be in sympathy with recent developments in philosophy. Occasionally, however, unpublished material by earlier philosophers, or works of importance which are now out of print, or not easily accessible, will appear in the Series.

D. Z. PHILLIPS

And by thy wisdom thou formedst man,
That he should have dominion over the creatures
that were made by thee . . .
Give me wisdom, her that sitteth by thee on thy
throne;
And reject me not from among thy servants
(*Wisdom of Solomon*, 9:2,4.)

Contents

Introduction

In this book I shall discuss two items of theological discourse from two different levels of such discourse. My first item is a proposition from natural theology; my second a formula which in the context of sacred doctrine is the doctrine of the Holy Trinity. My reason for including both items in this inquiry is that they both occupy a fundamental position in traditional Christian theology. The first is the foundation of any corner-stone of revealed theology; the second a corner-stone of much revealed theology itself.

Within the context of the discussion and extent of Sacred Doctrine in the *Summa Theologica* (Ia,q1,a1), Aquinas presents us with the thesis that it is necessary to man's salvation that there should be knowledge revealed by God besides that yielded by 'philosophical science' built up by human reason. His argument for this thesis has as its first premiss: 'Man is directed towards God as an end that surpasses his reason'. However God is not simply an end in traditional Christian thought but is the last end of rational creatures (IIa,q1,a8): so I examine first the conjoint proposition that man is directed towards God as an end that surpasses his reason and that God is the last end of rational creatures. I have taken this conjoint proposition as the first subject of my investigation since, according to Aquinas (Ia,q1,a1), upon the truth of at least the first part depends the possibility of the necessity of a knowledge revealed by God. However, a condition of such a proposition's being either true or false is that it is a possible, that is a sensible one. My inquiry will concern the sense of such a proposition. Upon the issue of this proposition being possible, that is sensible, depends the possibility of a revealed theology—at least as understood by St Thomas—hence the importance of an investigation concerning the sense of this proposition.

My second item, the discussion of which will occupy the greater part of this book, clearly comes under the heading of revealed theology—namely the doctrine that God is three persons in one substance. Here again I shall be concerned with the question of sense and for the purposes of this book I shall limit myself almost exclusively to St Augustine's *De Trinitate* as the classical discussion of the matter. I take it that an examination of the Trinitarian formula needs no justification; the doctrine of the Trinity is a central feature of orthodox Christian doctrine, yet as far as I am aware it remains undiscussed in the recent literature of philosophical theology—as does the first subject of my inquiry. My conclusions that

(a) God cannot sensibly be spoken of as an end or as the one and only last end

(b) the Trinitarian formula is an impossible one and hence that the doctrine of the Trinity is an impossible one

are not to be thought to commit me to the view that it is not possible to speak of God at all or that every theological remark, as opposed to any religious one, is in some way impossible. That I am not so committed I am keen to point out at the end of Chapter 5. Each theological remark must be investigated in its own right. Wittgenstein does put forward the suggestion that theological sentences have the role of 'grammatical remarks'. I have had recourse to some which do seem to perform such a role in the course of this book. It might be suggested that it is the character of theological sentences to be grammatical in Wittgenstein's sense, namely that they set forth the conditions of sense for religious belief and hence determine what religious propositions are possible: they are not to be thought of as expressing propositions themselves or as expressing that which is true or false. This is an interesting suggestion which I am not able to pursue in this present work. However, as regards the first item for discussion such a suggestion is open to the initial and strong objection that such sentences are regarded by Aquinas as expressing propositions which are eternally true, for as forming part of natural theology such items must meet with the requirements of an Aristotelian science. Further, Aquinas puts it forward as a thesis to be established by an argument based on eternally true premisses that God is the last end of rational creatures; if this were simply to be construed as a 'grammatical remark' then it is quite unclear why he needs to defend it and argue for it. Further, on the 'grammatical' construction of the Trinitarian formula it is difficult to see how the doctrine of the Trinity can be said to form part of the content of the faith to be affirmed in credal affirmations such as that of St Athanasius or how heresies concerning the Trinity can be regarded as false doctrine. But even if it can be plausibly argued that sentences expressing (i) the tenets of natural theology (ii) the doctrines of revealed theology, cannot be properly regarded as expressing that which is either true or false at all, the issue of sense still arises since the question of whether such sentences, which on a 'grammatical' account purportedly set out the rules for possible religious discourse, themselves have sense. This issue could only fail to arise if one maintained the philosophical position that a sentence has sense in that it has a use. This position is however highly controversial and I see no good reason for subscribing to it; indeed if some of the arguments presented in this book are correct then there is a good case for maintaining that this position is false, for at some places in this book we are presented with sentences which do *prima facie* have a use but which turn out to have no sense.

My discussion of the first item will necessitate some extended discussion and interpretation of some passages in both Aquinas and Aristotle. I hope this will encourage students of philosophy (at least) to read these passages for themselves and cast more light on them than I have been able to do. In relation to the Trinitarian formula it has been necessary to discuss Aristotle on 'substance' at some length, and once again I hope this discussion will encourage non-classical students to extend that general interest in Aristotle already much kindled by Professor Anscombe's contribution in her essay in *Three Philosophers*. I further hope that my necessarily limited discussion of ὀυσία and ὑπόστασις in some of the writings of the Greek Fathers of the Church will kindle philosophical interest in an area which, as far as I can judge, is sadly in need of revitalizing. There is much more to be said here than I have been able to say.

I have supplied Latin and Greek texts where I have thought it necessary or desirable and I have either supplied a translation or provided a gloss. In Chapter 1 I have in most cases used the translation of the *Summa Theologica* provided by the Dominican Fathers (Burns Oates & Washbourne), with alterations and amendments where I have thought necessary. Appendix C to Chapter 2 was presented as a chapter in its own right in the original draft, but in the light of its nature the editor has persuaded me to include it as an appendix to Chapter 2. I have attempted to provide the relevant texts in full as these are not easily obtainable; I have supplied reference to the appropriate column in Migne's *Patrologia Graeca* as I have found that scholars in this field often fail to do so, with the result that a very great deal of time can be spent tracing the original text. Apart from an attempted initial translation I have left Aristotle's phrase τὸ τί ἦν εἶναι untranslated, for I know of no uncumbersome English phrase to translate it and have been unable to provide one myself; as I point out, 'essence' as customarily understood will not do.

I am much indebted to Professors MacKinnon and Phillips for their critical comments on the original draft; to Professor J. L. Evans for his comments and persistent encouragement; to Professor T. H. McPherson and Mr J. A. Brunton for their critical comments on individual chapters and to Mr R. Attfield for some advice on the translation from the Greek. Finally I should like to express my appreciation of the facilities offered me at St Deiniol's Library, Hawarden. My wife has been a constant source of encouragement and has had to bear with me during the period through which this book has been written; my debt to her is indeed great.

Michael Durrant
Cardiff

Summary

Chapter 1

I first examine Aquinas's thesis that it 'belongs to man to act for an end', with a view to determining what kind of thesis is being put forward. I contend that the thesis being advocated is best understood as a conceptual one and that Aquinas's inquiry is an inquiry into the concept of human operation. To understand what it is for φ, where φ is an activity, to be a human operation is to understand that there is an end in that the question of an end is necessarily relevant. I likewise contend that the thesis that there is a last end to human life is best understood as a conceptual thesis. It is the thesis that we must posit the concept of a last end in the sense that we must allow that there be some (at least one) situation in which the form of question: 'For the sake of what (With a view to what) are you pursuing x?', where x is an end, necessarily has no application. In other words there must be at least one replacement for x such that understanding what this signifies entails that one cannot raise this form of question to that x. I go on to consider whether God can be spoken of as an end by considering a case in favour of the thesis and then what I regard as crucial objections against such a thesis, which leads me to the conclusion that God cannot be so sensibly spoken of and that there are special difficulties arising from the contention that God is 'an end which surpasses the grasp of human reason'. Finally I turn to the question of whether God can be said to be (i) a last end (ii) the one and only last end, and I consider possible interpretations of both these propositions.

Chapter 2

I discuss various senses of οὐσία introduced by Aristotle in his 'philosophical dictionary', which senses of οὐσία act as a backcloth and indeed a framework for later discussions in theology, in, for example, the Greek Fathers of the Church. I argue that 'God', in its Christian use, does not exhibit the features or play the roles which terms falling under the various senses of οὐσία exhibit or play and that therefore God cannot be said to be 'substance' in any of these senses. In Appendix A to this Chapter I cite evidence of Aristotelian influence on the thought of the Greek Fathers: in Appendix B, I argue that God in the Christian conception cannot be regarded as *a* god, or as *one* god, in contrast to a line of thought put forward by Professor Geach. In Appendix C, I investigate some of the writings of the Greek Fathers of the Church on the topics of οὐσία and ὑπόστασις. In section A of this Appendix I consider cases of the use of οὐσία which might be thought to reflect one or more of the Aristotelian senses of that term discussed in the main body of the chapter. These cases turn out to be more problematic than one might initially suppose. An impossible conception of 'substance' as a characteristic or property of individuals emerges with a correlative doctrine of 'simple' individuals. In section B, I argue that there is a confusion in the thought of certain scholars in this field as concerns οὐσία and ὑπόστασις. They introduce a misguided, indeed impossible concept of 'substance' in their appreciation of those writings of the Greek Fathers which they regard as central to the doctrine of the Trinity. I produce textual evidence that such an impossible doctrine is to be found in my Section B.2. In Section C, I argue that in many cases cited by scholars the correlative notion of ὑπόστασις is an illegitimate one. I consider cases in which the use of this term is problematic, giving special consideration to the notion of οὐσία ὑποστατή as introduced by St Hippolytus. Finally I argue that scholars in this field are also open to the charge of perpetrating an unintelligible concept of ὑπόστασις, concluding that the backcloth against which St Augustine's discussion of God as substance and his subsequent discussions of correlative notions is set is a patchwork of confusion.

Chapter 3

I examine St Augustine's case for saying that God is *substantia* : *essentia*. I maintain that his argument breaks down and I consider some reformulations. I contend that these reformulations fail, since one can only offer a plausible account of his case as an argument if one introduces an illegitimate concept of substance which is taken over from the writings of the Greek Fathers discussed earlier.

Chapter 4

I examine St Augustine's use of the phrases 'of the same substance'; 'in the same substance'; 'in one substance'. I claim that the concepts which such phrases express can have no intelligible use in the contexts in which St Augustine attempts to employ them and that indeed their use in such contexts is necessarily unintelligible. They are only thought to have an intelligible use on account of certain errors—errors deriving from the writings of the Greek Fathers and ultimately, I suggest, from some of the earlier writings of Plato.

Chapter 5

I consider St Augustine's thesis that 'Three persons' can answer the question 'Three *what*?' when it is asserted that the Father, Son, and Holy Spirit are three. I argue that one cannot get as far as formulating St Augustine's question and hence his problem, but that even if one could, 'person' in his use could not supply an answer, for 'person' in such a use cannot furnish us with a term which can in turn provide us with a unit of counting. Indeed I contend that there is no use in which 'person' exhibits those features which would enable it to be introduced as a unit of counting. I then turn to *prosopon* and examine the various senses in which it was understood in early thought: I argue that in none of those senses is it able to furnish a unit of counting in its own right and hence be preceded by a number. Further, I press that there seem to be insuperable difficulties in introducing the various senses of *prosopon* in connection with God. I maintain that neither ὑπόστασις in the sense of Aristotle's τὸ ὑποκείμενον or in that illegitimate sense I traced in the writings of the Greek Fathers can provide us with a unit of counting. After a brief return to St Augustine to consider a well-known passage in which he does not, as formerly, treat 'person' as a generic term, I consider some difficulties which might be levelled against some supposed consequences of what has been advocated so far, and consider the suggestion that what is required is a reinterpretation of the Trinitarian formula. I examine one such reinterpretation. Finally I discuss some points St Augustine makes about the possibility of formulating a doctrine of the Trinity. I conclude with some comments on what my discussion implies and is intended to imply.

I

God as an End and as the Last End of Rational Creatures

A In my investigation of the two fold proposition I introduced in my 'Introduction', namely that man is directed towards God as an end that surpasses his reason and that God is the last end of rational creatures, I shall first raise the question of what it is to say that man has ends, or as Aquinas puts it, 'that it belongs to man to act for an end'. To do this I shall consider what kinds of consideration Aquinas allows in favour of the proposition or against it and the kind of consideration his central thesis is. These are set out in the *Summa Theologica* (IIa,q1,a1). I shall not investigate all the considerations in detail, but I shall supply an illustrative list to substantiate my point that St Thomas is pursuing a conceptual inquiry here, an inquiry into the concept of human operation.

A.1 Aquinas, in his customary manner, proceeds by enlisting objections to the thesis in question. The first objection has two contentions:

(1) that an end is not a cause (. . . finis non habet rationem causae).

(2) that on account of ('for', 'from', 'because of') which (*propter*), a man acts is the cause of his action since this preposition (*propter*) indicates a cause. (Sed propter illud agit homo quod est causa actionis cum haec praepositio *propter* designet habitudinem causae.)

Now it is clear that Aquinas in enlisting this objection is not putting forward an empirical or factual objection, for he is not concerned with any particular end or any particular cause or series of such ends or causes. The question 'Which end?' makes no sense whatsoever in connection with (1) above and it would be equally senseless to raise the question 'Which man?' in connection with 'a man' or the question 'Which cause?' in connection with 'cause' or 'action' in (2) above. These comments are intended to apply to anything which is correctly described as an end and as that for (on account of, from, because of) which (*propter*) a man acts; both comments could be rendered in terms of the universal quantifier, it being left an open question as to whether there did actually exist any end. The objector's argument in favour of the first contention above is as follows:

> It seems unfitting for a man to act for an end. For a cause is naturally prior to its effect. But an end in its very name implies something last. Therefore an end is not a cause. (Videtur quod homini non conveniat agere propter finem. Causa enim naturaliter prior est sub effectu. Sed finis habet rationem ultimi, ut ipsum nomen sonat. Ergo finis non habet rationem causae.)

Here also the questions 'Which man?' asked of 'a man'; 'Which one(s)?' asked of 'a cause' or 'an end' respectively make no sense, yet only upon the condition of these questions having sense can the possibility of an empirical or factual inquiry or argument be entertained. The objector's argument can be expressed as follows: 'To speak of A being the cause of B necessarily implies that A is an event or state of affairs or substance (following Aristotle) which precedes B in time, whereas to speak of A being the end of B necessarily implies that A is an event or state of affairs which postdates B and has yet to come about or be brought about. Therefore an end is not a cause.' What we have here is an argument to the effect that the concept of 'end' necessarily precludes any *x* which is said to be an end from being a cause (which is correct).

I have designated the objector's second contention as (2) above. Here again we are not faced with an empirical or factual contention for the same reasons as expressed above. I construe (2) as a contention to the effect that if it is said that a man acted on account of (for, from, because of) (*propter*) such and such, then a cause of his action is offered. This contention reports or purports to report what is necessarily implied by the use of *propter*. So in the first objection we have reports or at least purported reports on what is necessarily written into the concepts of 'cause', 'end', and the use of *propter*.

I now turn to objection 3 to further support my claim that a conceptual inquiry is being pursued here and not any kind of factual or empirical inquiry—not even a 'psychological' one. I shall not investigate objection 2 since such investigation would involve detailed exegesis on Aristotle's *Magna Moralia* 1211b27 and parallel passages in the *Nicomachean Ethics*, and, as I shall have to do some detailed exegetical study later, I shall not trouble the reader with any such study now. Objection 3 has two contentions:

(i) A man does not seem to act for an end when he acts deliberately (. . . tunc videtur homo agere propter finem, quando deliberat).

(ii) Man does many things without deliberation, sometimes not even thinking of what he is doing—for instance moving the foot or hand or scratching the beard whilst intent on something else. Therefore man does not do everything for an end. (Sed multa homo agit absque deliberatione, de quibus etiam quandoque nihil cogitat: Sicut cum aliquis movet pedem vel manum aliis intentus, vel fricat barbam. Non ergo omnia agit propter finem.)

It is clear that (i) is not intended to be an empirical or factual remark about any given man, for the objection is in terms of a man—any man—and in connection with the phrase 'any man' one cannot sensibly ask 'Which man?'. The inapplicability of the question 'Which man?' rules out any construction of (i) in terms of the proper names of individual men standing proxy for 'a man' in that proposition, which in turn rules out any possibility of (i) being taken as a factual proposition concerning individual men.

Further, to construe this as a factual proposition would make the relation between deliberation and acting for an end a merely contingent relation. In the light of these considerations I construe (i) as a remark on the concept of 'acting deliberately'—that is, for any action which is deliberate we can always ask the question: 'For the sake of what did A do Y?' or 'With a view to what did A do Y?', where the answers to these questions is taken to specify an end. Nor can (ii) above be regarded as a piece of factual reasoning, for the question: 'What tokens of those type actions have you in mind?' is here inappropriate. Aquinas and his objector are not concerned with given token instances of the type 'moving one's hand', 'scratching one's beard', as can be seen by the fact that questions appropriate to token actions are beside the point (for instance 'Did he move his hand jauntily or smoothly?'; 'Did he scratch his beard after the clock struck ten or as it struck?'). Further, 'that there are many actions which are not deliberate' cannot, in this context of its use, be regarded as a general empirical (psychological) proposition, for the question, 'How many?' clearly makes no sense here. I thus construe the objector to be making the point that having an end in view is not necessary to the concept of deliberate action. In his reply to objection 3 Aquinas says that such activities as the objector cites cannot properly be regarded as human actions 'since they do not proceed from deliberation of the reason' (quia non procedunt deliberatione rationis). I support this view on the following grounds—they cannot be regarded as actions, since in relation to them whilst the question: 'With a view to what are you φing?' (where 'φ' is a verb of action) can sensibly be raised, it admits of no answer. These cases of scratching our beards or moving our hands whilst intent on something else are cases of things we find ourselves doing. They are doings as opposed to actions on the one hand and doings as opposed to occurrences or happenings on the other, for in the case of the latter (i.e. occurrences or happenings), the question 'With a view to what are you φing?' cannot be sensibly raised at all—not that it can sensibly be raised, but that an answer cannot be supplied, as in the former case. Thus the debate between Aquinas and the objector is a conceptual one concerning the relation of 'end' to the concept of action.

A.2 Thus far I have contended that the type of objection Aquinas raises against the thesis that it belongs to man to act for an end is conceptual: granted that a similar case can be made out for the 'replies' to the objections, as I contend it can, then for Aquinas to be consistent the thesis itself must be a conceptual one. Can this be substantiated? It is my case that Aquinas's principal reply so substantiates. The mainstay of his principal reply is that the end is the principle in human operations (Sed finis est principium in operabilibus ab homine). Now to say that the end is the principle in human operations is certainly not rewritable as: 'The end is the principle in particular operations A_1 A_2 A_3 ... A_n (where 'A_1' etc. are token instances of a type action A), for Aquinas is saying that the end is the principle of *any* human operation, and as I have previously commented in connection with 'any', one cannot ask, 'Which one?', and hence get the possibility of an answer in terms of a set of token operations. Further, Aquinas produces nothing which could constitute *evidence for* some empirical thesis of the form:

The end is the principle in every human operation, namely, in A^1, A^2, A^2, ... A^n (where 'A' with a superscript denotes a *type* of human operation) or

The end is the principle in every human operation—namely, in A_1, A_2, A_3, ... A_n (where 'A' with a subscript denotes *token instances* of types of human operations)

We have nothing here which could be regarded as a *survey* of either (a) types of human operations or (b) tokens of such types, purporting to reveal how people actually act. Again, a remark about 'the end' cannot be conceived of as a remark yielding a factual truth since, for such a conception to be possible, Aquinas's remark would have to be renderable in the form 'Some end . . .' and the sense of 'some' so employed would have to be that sense which gives sense to the question 'Which?'. However, 'The end is the principle in human action' is only exponible in terms of 'some end' in the sense of '*some end or other*', so that we might have:

'Some end or other is the principle in human operations'

but in connection with this use and sense of 'some', the question 'Which end?' is not raisable. That use and sense of 'some' concerning which the question 'Which one?' has application clearly cannot express the sense of 'the end' here, for (i) 'The end is the principle in human operations (namely in any human operation whatsoever)' is not the equivalent of and not expressible by (ii) 'Some end (namely x) is the principle in any human operation whatsoever'; not equivalent since (i) might be true and yet (ii) be false; not expressible by, since no *particular* human end can be the principle in *any* human action whatsoever, as opposed to its possibly being the case that a particular human end can be the principle in *every* human action.

For these reasons Aquinas's remark that it belongs to man to act for an end must be construed as a remark which yields us a truth about human operations in general, namely a truth about the concept of 'human operation'. To understand what it is for φ, where φ is an activity, to be a human operation is to understand that there is an end in that the question of an end is necessarily relevant—namely, for any φ, if φ is a human operation, then one can always ask: 'For the sake of what is A φing?' or 'With a view to what is A φing?'—even though one might sometimes get the answer: 'He has no particular end in mind.'* The end is the principle

* It is necessary to introduce the form of question, 'With a view to what . . .?' as well as the form, 'For the sake of what . . .?' since it might be objected that this latter form naturally takes as an answer the name of a state which it is reasonable to suppose will be brought about by the φing in question. But not only such states can constitute ends: one may have a quite particular end in mind—for example, to cross the Atlantic by 'Concorde' or to play the organ in St Paul's Cathedral. Such cases are more naturally covered by the form of question, 'With a view to what are you φing?'

in human operations in that what differentiate human operations from other operations (such as operations in the animal world) is that the questions, 'For the sake of what is A φing?', 'With a view to what is A φing?' can always properly be asked and answered. Human operations are purposive, goal-directed operations.*

Someone may object that what we have in Aquinas is not a truth about the concept of 'human operation' but about human operations. It seems immaterial which way we express the matter: if what we have is a truth about the concept of 'human operation', then we do have a truth about human operations in general; we have a truth about the nature of human operations.

B.1 I now turn to the contention that there is a last end of human life. My investigation will take the same form as that above, with the same aim in mind. As above, I shall not investigate all the considerations in detail. The relevant passage is IIa,q1,a4. Objection 1 reads:

> It would seem that there is no last end of human life but that we proceed to infinity. For it is the *ratio* of good to be diffusive as Dionysius states (*Div. Nom.* iv). Consequently if that which proceeds from good is itself good the latter must needs diffuse some other good, so that the diffusion of good goes on indefinitely. But good has the nature of an end. Therefore there is an infinite series of ends. (Videtur quod non sit aliquis ultimus finis humanae vitae, sed procedatur in finibus in infinitum. Bonum enim secundum suam rationem est diffusivum sui, ut patet per Dionysium . . . Si ergo quod procedit ex bono, ipsum etiam est bonum, oportet quod illud bonum diffundat aliud bonum: et sic processus boni est in infinitum. Sed bonum habet rationem finis. Ergo in finibus est processus in infinitum.)

What is it to say that it is the *ratio* of good to be diffusive? This cannot be construed as some kind of factual remark, since it is not writable in the form: 'Every case of good diffuses good', where this in turn is writable as, 'All observed cases of good . . .', for the objector is talking about *good* here, not about all observed cases of good. The question, 'Which cases of good are you referring to?' is equally out of place here as 'Which end?' was in the earlier discussion. On

* See Notes at the end of this Chapter.

the other hand, what is being put forward cannot be regarded as an analytic truth, for one cannot write the point as, 'For any *x* if *x* is good or a good, then there is some *y* produced by *x* such that *y* is itself good', claiming this to be an analytic truth concerning 'good', without being open to the charge of perpetrating a falsehood. Again, we cannot write the point as: 'For any *x* if *x* is good or a good, then it always *makes sense to say* that there will be some *y* produced by *x* such that *y* is itself good', for this is not strong enough to convey the point in question. An objector might press that 'For any *x*, if *x* is evil or an evil, it *always makes sense* to say that there will be some *y* produced by *x* such that *y* itself is good.' However, in order for the thesis here to be regarded as a conceptual truth, it is not necessary that it either be an analytic truth or be writable solely in terms of what it makes sense to say. As Professor Geach has pointed out* a proposition specifying the *ratio* of something gives us a conceptual truth about that thing, even though the proposition expressing the *ratio* is not an analytic truth. What the objector is claiming, in claiming that it is of the *ratio* of good to be diffusive, is that it is *normally* the case that the following rule holds: 'For any *x*, if *x* is good or a good, then there is some *y* produced by *x* such that *y* is itself good.' It is claimed that if this rule did not *normally* or for the most part hold, then the concept of what it is for *x* to be good or a good would break down—as the concept of what it is for S to be a statement or I an intention would break down if the following rules did not normally or for the most part hold respectively: (i) 'For any *x*, if *x* is an intention, then *x* is carried out' (ii) 'For any *x*, if *x* is a statement, *x* is veracious.'

However, the objector's contention that it belongs to the *ratio* of good or a good to be diffusive only has application to a limited class of cases, namely those cases in which to say that *x* is good or a good is to allocate or entails allocating a disposition to *x*, such as 'X is a good man', 'Wine is a good'; and even within such a class of cases there are prob-

* P. T. Geach, 'Good and Evil', reprinted in *Theories of Ethics*, ed. P. Foot, *Oxford Readings in Philosophy*, O.U.P., 1967.

lems.* There are other types of case to which the thesis appears to have no application, e.g., 'X is a good marrow': 'X is a good piece of marble'. As this is so, the regress mentioned in objection 1 above does not follow.

B.2. I now turn to the second major contention in objection 1 above, namely that good has the nature of an end. I shall not repeat objections to the construction of this thesis as a possible factual thesis; any such construction is open to the same type of objection as I have raised earlier. The proposition has the form 'For any x, if x is a good...'. The account I offer is as follows: to say that good has the nature of an end is to say that anything which is a good (like health or honour) can sensibly answer the question, 'For the sake of what (With a view to what) are you φing?' (where φ is a verb of action) and not only sensibly answer this form of question but constitute the primary type of answer to this form of question. The specification of some good is the primary type of answer to this form of question, since other types of answer are dependent for their sense upon this type of answer. Consider the case in which someone asks 'Why (in the sense of 'For the sake of what', 'With a view to what') are you publishing those incriminating letters?' and gets the answer, 'To ruin my political opponent'. Here we might think we have a counter-case, but this is not so, for the condition of this answer being intelligible is that we can provide an answer to the 'Why (For the sake of what)' question which would specify some good or benefit. I only know what will constitute a harm for my political opponent if I already know what will constitute a good or benefit for him. We could not introduce the notion of a harm being the end of our action unless we could introduce the notion of a good being so, for a harm is the destruction either of a human flourishing or something conducive to the destruction of human flourishing. If I harm a man, for example, by discrediting him, then I either destroy his flourishing as a

* 'A is a good man' might hold true under some conception of what it is to be a good man, and yet no further (positive) good be produced. A might simply be a good man in that he pays his debts and fulfils his obligations.

human being or do something which is conducive to the destruction of such flourishing. On the contrary, a good or benefit is not the destruction of some harm. Health, for example, is such a good or benefit, but health cannot be explained or analysed in terms of the destruction of disease or the absence of disease, for the very concept of disease itself cannot be understood without reference to the concept of health. Disease is a derivative concept in the way in which health is necessarily not. This is not to deny the obvious truth that some people have evil ends, but only to contend that the possibility of their having evil ends depends upon there being good ends, that is upon there being 'goods' which are aimed at and striven for, of which evil is the privation or possibly annihilation. For example, murder is evil since it is the wanton destruction of the possibility of human well-being or flourishing, that is of the possibility of certain 'goods' being attained. In such a case it seems possible and pertinent to speak of evil as the annihilation of good.

Thus what we have in this remark that good has the nature of an end, is, I contend, a correct conceptual thesis to the effect that the name of some good can (a) sensibly (b) primarily form an answer to the form of question mentioned. In answer to the objection that Aquinas is talking about good whereas I am talking about the concept of 'good', I reply as formerly, for what holds of the concept of 'a good' holds of a good.

B.3 Objection 2 reads: 'Further, things pertaining to reason can be multiplied to infinity; thus mathematical quantities have no limit . . . But desire of the end is consequent on the apprehension of reason. Therefore it seems that there is also an infinite series of ends.' For my present purposes I shall only be investigating the second contention in this objection—namely, that the desire of the end is consequent upon the apprehension of reason (Sed desiderium finis sequitur apprehensionem rationis).

Again this is not a contention about some particular end or about each and every individual end; the question 'Which end or ends?' is inapplicable here. Neither can we write 'some end' for 'the end', where 'some end' gives rise to the question 'Which one?' What we have here is a contention about any end whatsoever and hence, as in previous cases, I contend that what we have is a conceptual contention. The point being made is that the condition of the possibility of our desiring certain *x*s which can constitute ends is that we understand what is involved in them. For example, one can, logically can, desire wealth or honour because one understands what having money or honour involves; one can give an account of what it means to have money or honour. It would not be intelligible for anyone to say that he desired money or honour if he did not know what having money or honour involved and could involve for him. This is in contrast with a case of mere wishing; one can wish for the stars or the moon even though one does not know what having the stars or having the moon involves or could involve; but one cannot *want* or *desire* the stars or the moon. Wanting and desiring entail setting about to get what one wants or desires, but in order to set about getting what one wants or desires one has to understand what would constitute getting what one wants or desires and this in turn supposes that one knows what is involved in what one wants or desires.* Hence what we have here is a point about what is necessarily involved in the concept of desiring or wanting—a point about the condition of the sensible employment of these concepts. This can be equally expressed by saying that it is a point about desiring and wanting.

B.4 As my last example from the objection Aquinas brings against the thesis that there is no last end of the human will, I consider the first contention of objection 3 which reads: 'the good and the end is the object of the will' (bonum et finis est objectum voluntatis). It would be tedious to reiterate reasons against saying that what we possibly have here is a statement of supposed psychological fact concerning the wills of a number of people, so I refrain. The account I offer is as follows: the good and the end is the

* Cf. Anthony Kenny, *Action, Emotion and Will*, London, Routledge & Kegan Paul, 1963, p. 115.

object of the will in that the specification of some good and some end answers the form of question, 'For the sake of what (with a view to what) is A φing?', and the answer to this form of question is the object of the will in that it tells us what a man's aims and intentions are.* It might be objected that it is not necessary that some good should answer the above form of question; some evil might do so. To this it can be replied as above (p. 9), that unless the form of question could take as an answer some good it could not take as an answer some evil. Evil is the privation or possibly annihilation of good. What we are presented with here is a point about the concepts of 'good (a good)' and 'end'—or, if you prefer it, a point about the nature of good (a good) and an end.

It is therefore my case that the objections brought against the thesis that there is one last end of human life are conceptual—or at least I put it in this way to avoid confusion. In the light of this it is reasonable to expect that Aquinas's main contention here that there is one last end to human life will also be a conceptual contention, or, if you prefer it, a contention concerning what is essential to our having ends. I shall now investigate this main contention in detail.

B.5 His counter-argument to the objections raised is:

> The Philosopher says (*Metaphysics* II, 8) that to suppose a thing to be indefinite is to deny that it is good but the good is that which has the nature of an end. Therefore it is necessary to fix one last end. (Sed contra est quod Philosophus dicit 2 Metaph. text. 8, quod qui infinitum faciunt, auferunt naturam boni. Sed bonum est quod habet rationem finis. Ergo contra rationem finis est quod procedatur in infinitum. Necesse est ergo possere unum ultimum finem.)

To appreciate what is involved here it is necessary to consider what Aristotle says at *Metaphysics*, 994b9ff. Commenting on τὸ οὗ ἕνεκα,† he says that it is a τέλος and

* Or in some contexts, motives. Motives can be regarded as reasons specifying aims (cf. R. S. Peters, *The Concept of Motivation* (second edn), London, Routledge & Kegan Paul, 1960, pp. 35, 38).

† ἕνεκα translates as either 'For the sake of . . .' or 'on account of . . .' depending on the context. 'On account of . . .', in turn, is renderable as 'With a view to . . .' The point to be noted here is that ἕνεκα introduces explanation of action—an explanation in terms of a forward-looking reason; it does *not* introduce a cause.

is such a sort of thing that it is not done for the sake of (on account of) something else but other things for the sake of (on account of) it; if there is not a τέλος then there will be no τὸ οὗ ἕνεκα, and that those who introduce τὸ ἄπειρον (infinity) do not realise that they are destroying the nature of the good.

To expound on Aristotle's position here: the question 'For the sake of what (on account of what) are you risking your life?' can take as answers for instance, 'glory', 'honour', 'wealth', 'my country' (patriotism). These are τέλοι in the sense that they *need not* be pursued for the sake of something else, whereas the action specified in a particular application of the form of question 'For the sake of what are you φing?', in order to be the action of an intelligent human being, must be done for the sake of something else. For example, in order for your action of risking your life to be an intelligible action the question 'For the sake of what . . .?' (or its variants) must be answered. A man who risks his life for no purpose whatsoever is doing something which is unintelligible. In contrast, in connection with 'honour', 'glory', 'wealth' etc., whereas it seems possible to raise the question 'For the sake of what (on account of what) are you pursuing honour, glory, wealth, etc.?' it is not *necessary* in order for us to understand a man's actions that we should raise it, or if we do raise it then it is perfectly possible for the man to say that he is not pursuing wealth, honour, glory, etc. for the sake of anything else. A man's action of risking his life is intelligible to us if he says he is doing it for the sake of honour or glory, even though we may think he is misguided.* We have an explanation of his action here—we may even have *the* explanation of his action, though not necessarily: and we have no need, as thus understanding his action to raise the further question, though we might.

However, Aristotle in this passage obviously wants to say that there must be a final τέλος (ἔσχατον 994b11), namely that there must be some answer to the form of question 'For the sake of what (On account of what) are you pursuing *x*?'

* Cf. Notes at the end of this Chapter.

(where x is a τέλος), such that this form of question itself is not possibly applicable to *this* answer. We have seen that it is possible (but not necessary) to raise the question 'For the sake of what (With a view to what) are you pursuing honour, glory, wealth, etc.?', but Aristotle argues that there must be some situation in which the question 'For the sake of what (With a view to what) are you pursuing X?' has no *possibility* of application, *not* simply that it has the possibility of application and that it is not necessary in order to understand the activity in question that there be an answer, *and* he says, unless there *is* some such situation you destroy the nature of the good. What is the rationale behind this thought? It is this—that unless there is at least one situation in connection with which the form of question was inapplicable and necessarily inapplicable, then there could be no situation in which the form of question was applicable and answerable, for a condition of the form of question having sense and being answerable in connection with some situation, is that it has no sense (has no application) in at least one other. This is a particularization of the general thesis that a condition of the possibility of a form of question having sense is that it be applicable in some circumstances but not in all. And this is surely correct, for a form of question which purportedly had application to all situations whatsoever is a necessarily nonsensical form of question since in such a purported circumstance the notion of 'application' would lose its sense and one could not introduce the distinction between a possible answer and an impossible one, let alone that between a correct answer and an incorrect one. We have a parallel situation in the notion of a statement. A statement is only meaningful if something is necessarily excluded, for if nothing is necessarily excluded, then we could not specify *what* is stated.

Why would denial of the thesis that there must be (at least one) last end entail the destruction of the nature of the good? The answer to this is that for Aristotle the good of φ (where φ is an action) is that for the sake of which the action is done; but there could be no concept of 'that for the sake of which some action is done' if one denied the above thesis, for denial of the above thesis would entail denial of the possibility of the question 'For the sake of what are you doing φ?', upon which the concept of 'that for the sake of which something else is done' depends for its possibility. Acceptance of the correctness of the Aristotelian thesis does not, of course, entail acceptance of the view that the question 'For the sake of what is *everything* else done' makes sense or acceptance of the view that the question 'For the sake of what does a man do *everything* he does?' makes sense. The second question here clearly does not make sense; that it supposedly *does* rests on the fallacy of thinking that, since it is perfectly possible to ask of any *given* action 'With a view to what (For the sake of what) is A φing?', we can equally ask it of the sum total of a man's actions taken as a whole; but from the fact that a question makes sense when asked of a given member of the class it does not follow that it makes sense when asked of the sum total of those members taken as a whole; indeed it necessarily does not follow, since the sum total of members of that class is not itself a member of that class. The first question above assumes the fallacious position that 'Every action' is itself a member of the class of actions.

To return to Aquinas. In so far as he is following Aristotle in the *Metaphysics* passage, his contention against the objectors is that it is necessary to introduce the concept of a last end in the sense that there must be some answer to the question 'For the sake of what are you φing?' (With a view to what are you φing?) concerning which it makes *no sense* to ask this question. Someone will object that Aquinas is not concerned simply to introduce the concept of a last end here, but to say that there must be a last end. As against this one must ask: 'What would it be to assert that there must be a last end *other than* to assert that it must be the case that in at least one case the form of question, "For the sake of what . . . (With a view to what . . .)?" has no application to something which has already formed an answer to this form of question?' It might also be objected that Aquinas's question is not in the form of whether there must be one last end, but whether there *is*. In reply one must ask the objector to turn to the text to see what it is that Aquinas turns to for support. As we have seen, he turns to the Aristotelian contention discussed above—and indeed at the end of his main argument to answer the objectors he concludes 'it is *necessary* to fix one last end' (Necesse est ergo ponere unum ultimus finem).

B.6 It is now necessary to turn to Aquinas's own defence of the thesis that there must be at least one last end. He says:

> Absolutely speaking, it is not possible to proceed indefinitely in the matter of ends, from any point of view. For in whatsoever things there is an essential order of one to another, if the first be removed, those that are ordained to the first must be removed also. (Respondeo dicendum quod per se loquendo, impossible est in finibus procedere in infinitum ex quacumque parte. In omnibus enim quae per se habent ordinem ad invicem, oportet quod remoto primo, removeantur ea quae sunt ad primum.)

What is it to maintain that there is an essential order of ends? His point, I think, can be expounded as follows: the condition of our being able to raise the question 'For the sake of what (With a view to what) are you *x*-ing or pursuing *x*?' (where '*x*' here is a τέλος) is that we should be able to raise this form of question of other αs (actions which we attempt to explain) which yield an answer in the form of a τέλος. There is an essential order of ends in that the condition of the possibility of having an *x* which can constitute a final end, is that one has *x*s concerning which the question yielding an answer in the form of a final end has application. That is, we could not have the concept of a final end unless we had the concept of ends which were not such, namely ends concerning which the form of question, 'For the sake of what?' (With a view to what?), *did* have sensible application. And this, to put the matter generally, is the point that a condition of the possibility of the form of question—'For the sake of what (With a view to what) did you pursue *x* or are you pursuing *x*?' (where *x* is a τέλος)—failing to have sense on at least one occasion, is that it has sense on at least one occasion, which point is correct. As thus understood, I see nothing inherently objectionable in the thesis that there is an essential order of ends and in this context I do not see what other account would be pertinent. Objection may be offered here on the grounds that Aquinas offers in adumbration of his point Aristotle's purported proof that there must be a first mover. The particular point stands irrespective of the adumbration, but lest anyone should have qualms, an account can be offered of Aristotle's argument which would at least make it intelligible to modern ears. What Aristotle is saying is that in our explanation of motion we cannot have an infinite series of explanations; the question διὰ τί which gives rise to an ἀρχή τῆς μεταβολῆς* cannot be raised of *every* answer given to this question itself: there must be at least one case in which this question cannot sensibly be raised. The rationale behind this is exactly the same as that behind the doctrine of the last end. To say there is a first mover is to say that there must be at least one case in which a certain form of the διὰ τί question necessarily has no application. To say that without the first mover none of the others can move, since they only move through being moved by the first mover, is to make the point that unless there is at least one circumstance in which the appropriate form of the διὰ τί question necessarily fails to have application, then such question cannot have sensible application, for the necessary failure in at least one case is a condition of the possibility of the question having sense. It might be objected that Aquinas and Aristotle are talking about entities, movers, not the condition of the possibility of certain questions. I think this objection too crude; Aristotle at least is not talking about entities pushing one another (on a mechanistic model basis) as can be seen from his discussion of αἴτια (*Physics* 194b24ff.). He is concerned with the giving of certain types of explanation—explanations which take the form of different types of answer to the διὰ τί question and the condition for the introduction of those types of explanation.

B.7 Aquinas also maintains that if there were no last end nothing would be desired (*quia si non esset ultimus finis, nihil appeteretur*) (IIa,q1,a4). His argument is that if there

* Cf. *Physics*, 194b16ff.

were no last end nothing could be intended and if nothing could be intended then nothing could be desired, since in the order of intention that which is first is the principle, as it were, moving the appetite, and if you remove this principle then there will be nothing to move the appetite, and the principle in the intention is the last end (. . . Id enim quod est primum in ordine intentionis, est quasi principium movens appetitum: unde subtracto principio appetitus a nullo moveretur . . . Principium autem intentionis est ultimus finis). What is it to maintain that if there were no last end nothing could be intended? I offer the following account. If the form of question 'For the sake of what (With a view to what) are you φing?' necessarily did not have application in at least one case, then this would not be a sensible form of question; but if this is not a sensible form of question then nothing *could* be intended, for one's intention is what answers this form of question. Intentions are forward-looking reasons for action,* and answers to this form of question supply such reasons for action. What we have here in the thesis that if there were no last end nothing could be intended is a truth about the concept of intention—the condition of its intelligible introduction. But why, it might be asked, is it that if nothing could be intended then nothing could be desired? Surely there can be desiring (wanting) without intentions? Cannot I be said to want something and yet *not* have the intention of getting it? This suggestion is open to the crucial difficulty that it does not allow for the distinction between wanting (desiring) and wishing. I can certainly wish for *x* and not intend to get *x*—my wishing that I had £25,000 does not entail that I intend to get £25,000; but the test as to whether I want or desire that sum of money as opposed to simply wishing I had it is precisely whether I intend to get it. I could not consistently

* Cf. Anthony Kenny, op. cit., p. 92. It might seem a little strained to say that one's intentions answer the form of question 'For the sake of what . . .?'; the strain is eased if we precede answers by 'to obtain or to get', which it is quite natural to do; for example, 'For the sake of what are you taking a bath?', 'For the sake of health—in order to get (obtain) health'. We could equally say here 'What is your intention in taking a bath? and get the answer 'to get (obtain) health'.

say that I want £25,000 but that I have no intention of getting it. If I did make such a remark, then I can be rightly accused of not really wanting at all but simply expressing a wish. In the light of this, Aquinas is correct in maintaining that if nothing could be intended nothing could be desired and that to maintain this is to maintain a truth about the concept of desire. However, how does this fit in with the point that in the order of intention that which is first is the principle, as it were moving the appetite, and that if you remove this principle then there will be nothing to move the appetite and the principle in the intention is the last end? I construe his point that in the order of intention that which is first is the principle, as it were moving the appetite, as follows:

(i) the principle of the intention is that which forms the possibility of the intention—namely the form of question 'For the sake of what (With a view to what) are you φing?'

(ii) this is first in the order of intention in that unless this form of question has sense (has application), then there is no possibility of there being a situation in which it would make sense to say that the form of question had *no* application.

(iii) this principle, *as it were*, moves the appetite in the sense that one could not have the possibility of wanting or desiring something unless this question were a possible question—since one cannot, as argued above, want something and not intend to get it.

(iv) if you remove this principle, that is do not allow this form of question 'For the sake of what (With a view to what) are you φing?' then there would be nothing, *as it were*, to move the appetite in the sense that one could not in such circumstances have the possibility of wanting, since for this possibility to arise there must be the possibility of intending.

(v) To turn to Aquinas's last comment in the passage under discussion—that the principle in the intention is the last end. The principle which, *as it were*, moves the appetite is the form of question I set out above; and this is first in the order of intention as explained in (ii) above; but this principle is not the principle *in* the intention—*principium inten-*

tionis. The principle *in* the intention is the condition of the possibility of forming the concept of an intention—namely the necessary inapplicability in at least one case of the form of question 'For the sake of what (With a view to what) are you *x*-ing or pursuing *x*?' where '*x*' is a τέλος. This is the condition of the possibility of forming the concept of an intention, since this is the condition of the possibility of the concept of an end, and the concept of an intention is not logically separable from that of end in that a specification of one's intention answers the form of question 'For the sake of what (With a view to what) are you φing?'

What Aquinas is doing here is putting forward the conditions which must be met if the concept of 'intention' and that of 'forming an intention' are to be intelligibly introduced. As a result of this investigation I contend that Aquinas's inquiry as to whether there is a last end of human life is an inquiry which can, in terms intelligible to the modern reader, be expressed as a conceptual inquiry, and the thesis that there is a last end to human life is the thesis that we must posit the concept of a last end in the sense that we must allow that there must be some situation in which the form of question 'For the sake of what (With a view to what) are you pursuing *x*?' (where *x* is a τέλος) necessarily has *no* application, namely there must be at least one replacement for *x* such that understanding what such a replacement is and involves, entails that one cannot raise this form of question. It is contended by Aristotle and Aquinas that εὐδαιμονία: *felicitas*—approximately 'happiness', more strictly 'well-being'—is such a sort of thing (Aristotle, *Nicomachean Ethics*, 1097b1; Aquinas, IIa,q3,a1). 'Happiness' is said to be αὔταρκες, self-sufficient; and by αὔταρκες Aristotle means that which of its own accord makes life desirable and lacking in nothing.

C.1 I maintained earlier (Section A) that to say that it belongs to man to act for an end is to maintain a conceptual thesis to the effect that for any φ if φ is a human operation, then one can always ask 'For the sake of what (With a view to what) is A φing?' and for *x* to be an end is for *x* to be an answer to this form of question. For God to be an end therefore is for 'God' to be an answer to a question of this form. And, it might be argued, the condition of God being an end is that 'God' is a possible answer to this form of question in the culture in which this form of question has its life, and whether 'God' is a possible answer is decidable by whether people actually speak like this in the culture. For example, it can be argued that 'wealth' is a possible answer to this form of question precisely because it is allowed to count as an answer in our culture as it did in ancient Greece: indeed it can be maintained that in the *Nicomachean Ethics*, 1097a25, Aristotle is reporting on what, in ordinary Greek ways of thinking, is allowed to count as an answer to the 'For the sake of what . . .' question (cf. also *N. Ethics*, 1097b1–21). So it might be said, to say that God is an end, as to say that wealth is an end, is to report on what is the case in a given culture, in a given 'form of life'. Someone might object here, 'We want to know whether it is *true* that God is an end, not simply that "God" is allowed to constitute an answer to a certain form of question. We know it is *true* that wealth is an end.' To this it must be replied: 'What is it to know that it is true that wealth is an end *other than* to know that people do certain things for the sake of (with a view to obtaining) wealth?' Similarly in the case with God, to know that it is true that God is an end is to know that people do certain things for the sake of God, with a view to fulfilling his will. It might be further pressed by an objector that that God is an end is held to be an *objective* truth—a truth independent of our culture or of any culture whatsoever. But what *could* be intended by 'objective truth' here *other than* this is what actually counts as an end—other than what is the case in the culture, in the form of life? It cannot be maintained, that is, there could be no sense in the contention that by 'objective truth' could be meant a truth *independent* of a culture, of a form of life, for any truth is of necessity expressed in a language and a language is part of a culture, a form of life. Indeed Aristotle's own inquiry at *N. Ethics*, 1097a25 ff., shows that what constitutes an end for the Greeks is determined by Greek culture. The objector may further persist, he may press that when Aquinas talks of God as an end, he intends that this proposition shall be objectively true in the sense that it is true *independently* of what Christian theology allows—independently of how Christians speak of God. I do not think that this position can be sustained as far as Aquinas is concerned, since the proposition itself occurs in a theological context, but on general philosophical grounds such a position cannot be maintained. To maintain it would entail maintaining the view that it would make good sense to speak of a proposition being true independently of and external to that conceptual scheme of which it forms a part. This would commit one to the implausible view that one could sensibly speak of (for example) the propositions of mathematics being true without reference to the axioms and rules of mathematics: that one could sensibly speak of propositions in physics being true independently of the concepts of physics: that one could sensibly speak of propositions in a material object language being true without reference to the concepts of material object language. Such a position would also commit one to the possibility of saying that propositions in a scheme of thought A (say propositions about particle motion) could not be said to be true since they did not satisfy the requirements for truth in a scheme of thought B (say propositions about material bodies)—which rightly strikes one as preposterous.

The objector may take up another line of attack at this point, namely that in Aquinas's formulation as originally mentioned, we have the statement that man is *directed* towards God as an end. Surely, the objector will press, such a proposition is not exponible as: ' "God" can (and does) form an answer to the form of question "For the sake of what are you φing?".' In reply to this, one must ask what account would be offered by Aquinas of the proposition 'Man is directed towards something or other as an end'. Aquinas has no explicit discussion of such a proposition, but it is obvious that the relevant discussion is his discussion on whether it belongs to man to act for an end, which I have already discussed earlier. Further, Aquinas could not maintain that a man's actions are literally directed towards God, such that man had no choice, for this would (a) destroy the concept of human action—for an action is something one can at least be said to choose to do or refrain from doing and this possibility is not open on a straight interpretation here; (b) it would destroy the very concept of 'end' as that for the sake of which something else is done. For God to be thought of (even analogically) as an end, it must at least be possible to speak of *something being done*, but if man is directed towards God (literally), then it is not possible to speak of a man *doing* anything as opposed to *finding himself doing something*. In the light of this, to maintain that a man's actions are directed towards God can only be to maintain that man has God as an end, which thesis is exponible as above.

C.2 In the last section I have offered an account of what it is to say that God is an end and to consider some objections. I shall now consider another line of objection which takes as its starting-point the view advocated at the beginning of that section, namely that it was perfectly intelligible and indeed true to say that God is an end since 'God' can answer the form of question 'For the sake of what are you φing?' and 'God' can so answer this since 'God' *does* answer it in our culture, namely in that part of our culture which is constituted by religious belief. An objector may strongly protest at this line of argument on the grounds that, from the fact that a certain part of our culture allows 'God' to answer this form of question, it does not follow that 'God' can properly form an answer to this form of question; it may be *quite illegitimate* for 'God' to form such an answer since God does not exhibit those features which an end exhibits. Such an objector will reject the principle that if a form of words has a use in a system of discourse, then such a form of words has a meaning, and he is right in rejecting this principle in this case if it can be shown that God does not exhibit those features which an end exhibits, and that in this case theology has taken over the notion of 'end' from another culture and tradition in which this concept has its natural home. I shall be having more to say on this later.

C.2 (a) The objector proceeds as follows. Although 'God' is a perfectly possible answer to the form of question 'For the sake of what are you φing?' as far as Greek and English grammar go, God nevertheless cannot be sensibly spoken of as an end for the following reasons:

(i) If x is an end, like 'wealth' or 'health', then if I am φing for the sake of x, this is always exponible as 'I am φing in order to become x-ly', for example, if I am digging for the sake of my health, this is exponible as 'I am digging in order to become healthy', but in the 'God' case there is no such exposition possible without a radical change of sense—'I am φing for the sake of becoming godly' does not express the original 'I am φing for the sake of God'. It will be countered that this is not a telling objection since in cases where I say 'I am φing for the sake of man' or 'I am φing for the sake of (a particular man) Jones', the proposed exposition does not work either, namely, 'I am φing for the sake of man' is not renderable as 'I am φing for the sake of becoming manly' and it is impossible to draft any such exposition in the case of Jones, since 'Jones' is a proper name—yet I can still φ for the sake of man or the sake of Jones. However, this counter-objection cannot sustain its initial force, for in cases where 'man' or 'Jones' answers the above question, 'man' or 'Jones' is elliptical for a phrase of the form 'the ψ— of man' or 'the ψ— of Jones', where the ψ— is replaceable by an abstract noun signifying something which is conducive to the well-being of man or Jones—for example, the betterment, welfare, happiness or health of man or Jones; hence one's ends here are only man or Jones in the sense of the ψ— of man or Jones. This can be seen by the consideration that we should not understand anyone who said that he was φing for the sake of man but that he was not to be taken as φing for the sake of the ψ— of man, for example, someone who said that he was giving his money to UNESCO for the sake of man (mankind) but not for the betterment, welfare, development, happiness, of mankind. In the 'God' case, however, 'I am φing for the sake of God' is certainly not exponible in the form 'I am φing for the ψ— of God': it would be absurd to say that 'I am feeding these hungry people for the sake of God' can be written as 'I am feeding these hungry people for the sake of the betterment (happiness, welfare, development, etc.) of God'. Someone might say that it is possible for the assertion in question here to be read as 'I am feeding these hungry people for the sake of the glory of God', but in this case we should not have a parallel with the items specifiable in the original list, for it cannot be maintained that to do something, for example, to build a temple for the sake of the glory of God, is to do something conducive to the well-being of God, whereas it could be maintained that this is the case if we do something for the glory of man or Jones. Indeed, it might be urged, to say that A built a temple for the glory of God is to comment on the *character* of what A does, not to specify the purpose for which A did it.* Equally, if someone says he is doing something for the sake of God in the sense of doing something with a view to doing the will of God, it is difficult to maintain that to do the will of God is to contribute to the well-being of God, as it can be maintained that to do the will of a certain man might at least in some cases be to contribute to the well-being of that man. Here again it might be urged that to say that I am doing something with a view to doing the will of God, is not to specify an end, but to comment on the character of what I do.

(ii) An end is a state of affairs or state or possibly (though not in Aristotle's use) an eventuality, which (a) one can bring about; (b) one can intend to bring about either for oneself or for others. However, it will be argued, God is not a state of affairs or an eventuality: not a state of affairs since (1) any state of affairs has existence in a spatio-temporal scheme or at least a temporal scheme (2) God's existence must in any case be distinguished from the existence of states of affairs.†

* I owe this comment to Professor Phillips.

† Cf. D. Z. Phillips in 'Faith, Scepticism and Religious Understanding' in *Religion and Understanding*, Oxford, Blackwell, 1967, pp. 66 ff.

Further, God is not a state parallel to health, say, for the reason that whilst for health to exist is for there to be men who are healthy, for God to exist is not for there to be men who are godly. Again, God is obviously not an eventuality like winning the Grand National, since God cannot be said to exist at any particular moment in time as opposed to any other moment in time.

(iii) Since God cannot be meaningfully spoken of as a state of affairs, state, or eventuality, God cannot meaningfully be said to be something one could bring about or intend to bring about; indeed God's existence is not something which a man *can* bring about or intend to bring about or set about bringing about—as one can bring about, intend to bring about and set about bringing about health, wealth, or even happiness. Indeed, it will be pressed, it makes no sense to say that God's existence is *brought about by anything*—God's existence is prior to that of the world. It might be countered that 'man' or 'mankind' or 'Jones', whilst they might be something for the sake of which something else is done, cannot be spoken of as states of affairs, states, or eventualities which can be brought about or which one can intend to bring about. This counter-move cannot be sustained, since as I argued above, for 'man', 'mankind', or 'Jones' to be ends was for the ψ— of man or Jones to be ends, and the (for example) betterment, welfare, happiness, etc., of man or Mr Jones is certainly a state of affairs or a state which (a) can be (b) can be intended to be (c) can be set about being, brought about.

C.2 (b) Have we then crucial objections to speaking of God as an end in that God does not satisfy the requirements of being a state of affairs, a state, or an eventuality, which can be thought of as being able to be brought about or which one can intend to bring about or set oneself about bringing about and in that no statement to the effect that God is an end can be shown to be the equivalent of a statement which specifies something which can be brought about, or which one can intend to bring about, or set oneself to bring about? Only if we regard it as a necessary condition of anything being an end that it be a state of affairs, a state, or an eventuality which it is sensible to speak of as being brought into existence by our activity and hence that it is sensible to speak of our intending to bring it about or set about bringing it about. But how is it decidable that such requirements are necessary conditions for speaking of something as an end? We must look to the context in which the concept of 'end' has its natural habitat. This concept has such habitat and has its origin in the field of explanation of human activity and in a certain kind of explanation, namely in the explanation of human action by reference to what human beings could bring about.* To speak of God as an end is to take over a concept which was part and parcel of one conceptual scheme—namely the scheme for the intelligibility and explanation of human actions by reference to what human beings could be said to bring about and attempt to transfer it to another in which the fundamental concept of that scheme, 'God', cannot be said to signify anything which human beings can be meaningfully said to bring about. Hence propositions only having the appearance of sense ensue. This is not to say, of course, that there cannot be explanations of human activity in terms having reference to God—there can be such explanations in terms of doing God's will, but such explanations will not be explanations in terms of God as an end but in terms of doing of God's will as an end; and the doing of God's will is certainly an end, for it can be brought about. However it is not stated here that the doing of God's will or the keeping of the divine commandments is an end, but simply that God is an end, and 'God' is obviously not exponible as, for example, the doing of the divine will or the keeping of the divine commandments.

Against the above contention it might be replied: ' "End" has a use in theological discourse and in Christian talk about God, and in such a use it has sense.' I have already touched on this line of thought and I shall now adumbrate further. The consideration that people talk like this, even that a

* This is clear from Aristotle's examples of ends. Cf. *N. Ethics*, 1097a26ff.

whole system of discourse employs such talk, that a whole 'language game', to use Wittgenstein's term, employs such talk is not itself a sufficient condition of such talk being meaningful: it is only a sufficient condition of sensible discourse when the concepts employed are those which have their natural home in the discourse and are not taken out of some other system of discourse (conceptual scheme) in which they have their home and subsequently dislodged. As pointed out above, however, the case in hand does not meet this sufficient condition. To this it might be objected: 'Are you saying that it is never possible for concepts to be transferred from one scheme to another?' No, but in those cases where we get a meaningful transference, the rules for their operation must be clearly specified in their new context and they must not rely for their intelligible introduction upon their old use and 'grammar'. These conditions are precisely *not* met here, for Aquinas offers us no new rules for the operation of 'end' in connection with God, and our understanding of the notion of God as an end, in his use, is clearly dependent upon our understanding the concept of an end in a context external to that of religious belief or theological doctrine—namely understanding the concept of an end in the explanation of human action, which understanding necessarily precludes God from being an end. If anyone should think that a mere linguistic quibble is what is involved in my present discussion, then he must also say that Aquinas's contention that God is an end is *also* a mere linguistic quibble.

It seems therefore that the only sense in which God can be meaningfully said to be an end is the sense in which *either*:

(1) such things as the doing of God's will or the keeping of God's commandments can be said to be an end—in general, the sense in which the *x*-ing of the divine ___ is an end (where *x* is replaceable by such verbs as 'doing'; 'keeping' and the blank by 'will' or something pertaining to the will), but as above argued these are not equivalent to God being an end; *or*

(2) the *y*-ing of God can be said to be an end, where *y* here is replaceable by such verbs as 'worshipping', 'praising', 'blessing', 'glorifying', 'adoring': in general verbs signifying the worship of God. It is clear that the activities signified by such verbs can be ends, for the worshipping, glorifying, praising, etc., of God is something we can bring about and intend to bring about, and it is also clear that the question 'For the sake of what are you worshipping, glorifying, praising, etc., God?' has *no* sense. In this way the worshipping, etc. of God are final ends. However we cannot get out of the above difficulty by saying that for God to be an end is for the *y*-ing of God, in the above explained sense, to be an end, since for God to exist is not for the *y*-ing of God to exist; God might exist even though the *y*-ing of God did not exist. This objection might be challenged in the following way: 'We can only speak of God existing in that people worship, praise, glorify, etc., Him: whether God exists cannot be decided *independently* of whether people carry out certain religious practices, such as praising, adoring, glorifying, etc.' Our challenger might go even further and assert that for God to exist *is* for these activities to be in operation: hence, he might continue: 'For God to exist is for the *y*-ing of God to exist, hence for God to be an end is for the *y*-ing of God to be an end.' It is only if such reasoning is permissible that it is possible for God to be spoken of as an end: but there are strong objections to such reasoning. Taking the stronger position first, it has to be noted that the verbs which can replace '*y*-ing' are all 'intentional' verbs, and hence if this position is at any stage of an argument going to amount to the position that for God to exist is simply for certain religious activities such as worshipping to exist, the position is a non-starter. If the stronger position does not have such overtones, it is still open to crucial objections. First, if for God to exist *is* for the *y*-ing of God to exist, then the very idea of an argument for the existence of God would be unintelligible. All the heathen would have to do would be to join in the religious practices; but the idea of an argument for the existence of God is certainly not unintelligible in at

least the present context of discussion. Secondly, if for God to exist is for the *y*-ing of God to exist, then to believe that God exists is to believe that the *y*-ing of God exists, which is patently absurd. Thirdly, if the above thesis holds, then to believe in God is to believe in the *y*-ing of God, which is false; the *y*-ing of God is part of what *constitutes* belief in God. Finally, if the above thesis holds, then to worship God or to praise God, etc., is to worship or praise the *y*-ing of God, which is manifestly absurd. To worship God is not to worship the worshipping of God. In relation to the weaker thesis, all it is necessary to comment here is that, in the tradition I am at present considering, whether God exists is an independent issue from the consideration that people carry out certain religious practices, and if God's existence were not so independent it is not clear how one could introduce the notion of the Christian God being the true God, namely the true object of worship.

C.2 (c) At this point a more radical type of reply might be brought against the objections to saying that God is an end. It will be said that all along it has been assumed that an end is something which can be spoken of as being brought about by human agents (or achieved by human agents); but, if we take into consideration Aquinas's discussion at IIa,q3,a1, this is not the case, for we must bear in mind a distinction Aquinas introduces between:

(i) the thing itself which we desire to obtain (ipsa res quam cupimus adipisci),

(ii) the attainment, possession, use or enjoyment of the thing desired (ipsa adeptio, vel possessio, seus usus, aut fruitio ejus rei quae desideratur).

So, to give examples, we must distinguish between:

(iii) the end—for example wealth, health, happiness,

(iv) the attainment, possession, use or enjoyment of these.

Thus Aquinas argues that ends in one sense, namely (ii), are states or states of affairs which are attainable by human effort, can be brought about by human endeavours; but ends in the sense of ends in themselves, ends in sense (i), are not so attainable. Ends in sense (i) are *increatum*; and

God in this sense is an end—indeed man's last end in that he is the uncreated good. So, it might be pressed, granted this distinction, God is properly an end. What can be said for this distinction? We might press that 'happiness' or 'wealth' of themselves cannot be brought about and are not themselves states or states of affairs, as opposed to someone's possession of happiness or wealth, but that they are indeed ends in that they can properly form an answer to the form of question 'For the sake of what are you φing?' and hence the same applies in the God case. Here I think any defence of the distinction must stop, for an objector will reply that the distinction is bogus on the following grounds. First, it rests in part on a category mistake—namely that of treating 'achievement' verbs as themselves denoting states of affairs, for example it treats the *attainment of* wealth or happiness as *itself* a state—which commits one to the absurdity that one can seek to attain the attainment of happiness, etc., that one can bring about the attainment of wealth or happiness, etc. Further, it seeks to distinguish between, for example, happiness and possession of happiness as regards ends; but if a man has happiness as his end, then he has possession of happiness as his end, and if he has the possession of happiness as his end, then he has happiness as his end. The possession of happiness cannot be a separable end from happiness, for a man cannot sensibly say he wants to possess happiness but that he does not want happiness. To treat the possession of happiness as *itself* an end disparate from happiness is to misconstrue the phrase 'possession of happiness' as a combination of two elements 'possession of' and 'happiness', whereas 'possession of happiness' must be construed as 'possession of —' (parallel to a function), with 'happiness' standing in the argument place.* Indeed I do not think it extravagant to say that misconstruction of phrases like 'the possession of', 'the use of', 'the enjoyment of' is basically responsible for the distinction introduced here. To get the

* It is odd that Aquinas does not see this as he himself introduced such a point in connection with the concept of 'Form' (cf. P. T. Geach: 'Aquinas', in G. E. M. Anscombe and P. T. Geach, *Three Philosophers*, Oxford, Blackwell, 1961).

distinction Aquinas has to construe such phrases as having independent sense when they are not so construable—as can be seen from the fact that such phrases require completion in the form of an abstract noun. Further, it will be objected, how can happiness, for instance, be said to be an end, if it is logically impossible that one should attain it? And how can happiness (for instance) itself be that which we desire to obtain if nothing whatsoever in the nature of the case could count as our attaining it? If it is logically impossible that we should attain happiness in the sense of happiness itself, then it is logically impossible that we should desire it, for, as previously argued, an object of desire must be something it is *possible* for us to *attain*.

C.2 (d) Here it might be pointed out that, strictly speaking, in the proposition I am investigating Aquinas never actually says that God is an end, but that man is directed towards God as an end. If however anyone thinks he can build up a case on this point, he will be quickly disillusioned, for in the above-discussed passage (IIa,q3,a1), God is said to be an end. This consideration apart however, an objector may press that even if it is the case that God is only spoken of *as* an end, it is not possible that there be an analogical extension of the concept of 'end' such that God can be spoken of as an end, since in order for God to be so analogically spoken of there must be (i) some further classification under which both God and end can be subsumed—which is impossible, for as Aquinas himself argues (Ia,q3,a5) God is not in a genus, (ii) there must be some logical parity between the concepts of 'God' and 'end', but there is no such parity. The set of 'formal' predicates which it makes good sense to use in connection with ends, it makes no sense to use in connection with God—for example, such predicates as 'can be brought into existence by human effort', 'can be set about being brought about by human effort', 'can occupy a given time in the temporal order'. In short, 'God' and 'end' do not exhibit the same 'grammar'.

C.2 (e) Finally, it will be pointed out by an objector, that it is not simply the case that God is said to be an end, or even spoken of as an end, but that God is an end which surpasses the grasp of human reason (qui comprehensionem rationis excedit), so we have to raise the question of whether this is an intelligible notion. It is unfortunate that St Thomas does not expand on this notion at Ia,q1,a1 and gives us no example or parallel case. We may consider the following as interpretations for 'an end surpassing the grasp of man's reason'.

(1) An end which necessarily cannot be specified. This interpretation leaves us with a concept which has no sense. There cannot be an end which is necessarily inexpressible, for in such a putative case nothing *could* constitute our striving towards or aiming at such a supposed end—let alone our bringing it about. We could not sensibly be said to strive towards or aim at such a supposed end, for in order to strive towards something or aim at something, *some* account of what one is supposedly striving towards or aiming at must be possible in order for one to be sensibly said to decide that one's present action *constitutes* a striving towards or an aiming at *that* thing as opposed to some other. We could not speak of bringing the supposed end about here, for as it necessarily cannot be specified, nothing could sensibly be said to count in favour of its being brought about or its failure to be brought about. Granted this interpretation of 'end', an end so understood is not a *special sort* of end; it has no possibility of being an end at all.

(2) An end which whilst in principle specifiable, is not in fact so specifiable—on account of human limitations, say. On this interpretation, whilst in theory something *could* constitute our setting about trying to get this end, our striving towards this end, our bringing about this end, etc.—these notions have the *possibility* of application here, we do not know what *would constitute* our setting about trying to get this end, our striving towards this end, or our bringing this end about. To this it will be righly replied that if we cannot in fact give any specification of what this end is, and cannot in fact give any account of what would constitute our setting about getting this end (as we cannot if we cannot in

fact specify what this end is) and cannot give any account of what would constitute striving towards this end or bringing this end about (as we cannot granted the hypothesis here), then it is unintelligible to speak of 'end' here, though not necessarily unintelligible as in the former interpretation. The point being made here is that in order for *x* to be an end we must be able to give at least *some* account of what constitutes *x*, what constitutes setting about bringing it about that *x*, what constitutes striving after *x*, achieving *x*: indeed being able to give some specification of what constitutes *x* is a prior condition of giving an account of what constitutes setting about bringing it about that *x*, or what constitutes achieving *x*. For example, unless I am in fact able to give some account of what happiness is, I cannot be said to have happiness as my end, since having happiness as my end supposes that I can say what would constitute my setting about getting happiness and what would constitute my achieving happiness, but I precisely cannot say these things on the present interpretation of 'an end beyond the grasp of man's reason'; on this account I should have no possibility of knowing that I had attained the supposed end. Hence this interpretation too fails to make sense of 'an end which is beyond the grasp of man's reason'.

(3) Aquinas may well intend by 'beyond the grasp of man's reason', 'beyond the grasp of philosophical science built up by human reason' in the sense mentioned in this opening section of the *Summa Theologica*, for what would be required by such a science is a formal definition *per genus et differentia* in the Aristotelian sense. Now it seems perfectly possible for *x* to be an end and yet be beyond the grasp of man's reason in *this* sense, for whilst it is necessary in order for *x* to be an end that we should be able to give *some* account of *x*—namely, some account of what *x* comprises (as previously argued)—it is not necessary that we be able to give a strict definition, an account such that its denial is a self-contradiction; indeed such an account may not be possible. But if this is the sense in which we are to take 'beyond the grasp of man's reason', then we are up against an old prob-

lem in a new form. The old problem is, 'How is it decidable that the truths of "natural reason" and the truths of revelation concern one and the same *x*?' In its new form the problem is: 'How is it decidable that, granted "natural reason" gives us *part* of the essence of God, that truths of revelation complete the list? What is the rule for completion here?' It would only be intelligible to speak of God as an end *beyond* the grasp of man's reason in the present sense if we know what could *possibly* be candidates for an account of God's essence; but this is precisely what we do not know.

D. I now turn to the question of whether God can be said to be (i) a last end (ii) *the* last end. From what I have argued earlier (Section B) the thesis that there is a (viz., at least one) last end to human life is the thesis that we must introduce the concept of a last end in the sense that we must allow that there is some state of affairs concerning which the form of question: 'For the sake of what (With a view to what) are you pursuing *x*?' (where *x* is a τέλος) necessarily has no application—namely, there must be some replacement for *x* such that understanding what *x* involves entails that one cannot raise this form of question. On such an account, for God to be a last end is for it to be impossible to raise the question 'For the sake of what are you pursuing God? ('With a view to what are you pursuing God?'), where God is a τέλος. It might be objected that it is very queer indeed to talk of pursuing God, whilst it is perfectly unqueer to talk of pursuing wealth or happiness. It may well be thought that this objection is of no substance, for we can easily substitute 'seeking after' for 'pursuing', without any radical or relevant change of sense and there is nothing odd in the notion of seeking after God. So, it might be said, for God to be a last end is for it to be impossible to raise the question 'For the sake of what are you seeking after God?', where 'seeking after God' is already a τέλος. *And*, someone might say, it *is* so impossible, granted what God is. However, this line of thought will not do, for the change from 'pursuing' to 'seeking after' *does* involve a relevant and radical change of sense. Ends are pursued after, striven for, in that they are brought about by human effort—as opposed to being sought after and found, for although we can set about seeking after something, that which we seek is not something brought about by our own effort. We can only speak of seeking after God and finding Him—certainly not of bringing it about that we find Him; possession of God is God—given, not something we can achieve and can be spoken of as achieving by our own efforts, as we can of any end.

Can any sense be attached then to saying that God is a last end of rational creatures, let alone the last end? It might be said that if God cannot be spoken of as an end, it follows that He cannot be spoken of as a last end and hence as the last end. This does not so follow, for we may consider the following objection—if God is spoken of as the last end, then the proposition 'God is the last end' cannot be taken as a proposition in which 'is the last end' expresses a predication of God, any more than 'is the last Prime Minister' in 'Harold Wilson is the last Prime Minister' expresses such a predication; rather we have a proposition of identity. Thus, whereas to say that God is *a* last end is exponible as expressed earlier and open to the objections raised to that expression, to say that God is *the* last end is to say that God is identical with whatever it is concerning which the question 'For the sake of what (With a view to what) are you pursuing *x*?' (where *x* is a τέλος) has no sense—it being assumed that this form of question has no sense *both* in at least one case and at the most one case. Both Aristotle (*N. Ethics*, 1097b1ff.) and Aquinas (IIa,q1,a7) contend that if 'happiness' (εὐδαιμονία: *felicitas*), replaces the *x* here, then the question has no sense, so, it might be said, to say God is the last end has perfectly good sense—God is identical with happiness as things turn out, for happiness is the last end. It will be clear to the reader that all is not well here. First, whereas an argument has been produced for saying that the form of question mentioned must have no sense in at least one case, no argument has been produced to show that such form of question must have no sense in at the most one case;

neither *could* any such argument be produced for the very notion of 'failing to have application' entails that whatever fails to have application (fails to have sense) must fail to have application *in theory* to more than one case. A form of question which *necessarily* failed to have sense in more than one case would not be a form of question at all, any more than a form of question which necessarily only had application (only had sense) in one case would be a sensible form of question at all. Thus God cannot be said to be identical with the one and only last end, for the concept of 'the only and only last end' as above construed has no sense. *All* that can be said here is that the form of question mentioned has no application in at least one case and that it is claimed by both Aristotle and Aquinas that it has no sense in that case where it is applied to happiness. Secondly, the problem arises as to whether it is possible for God to be identified with happiness. The strong objection to such an identification is that happiness is a state which man can acquire, work towards, strive after, and achieve by his own efforts; whereas, as previously argued, God is not such a state or even a state at all. The only way in which identity would be possible here would be to allow Aquinas's distinction between the end itself and the attainment, possession, enjoyment, etc., of the end; but this distinction cannot be substantiated. It should be added here that Aquinas himself does not say that God is identical with happiness or is happiness itself, as Boethius does, but only that happiness is of the essence of God (IIa,q3,a1). Thus this attempt to give an intelligible account of 'God is the last end' fails.

One final account may be attempted. It may be said that we must distinguish between:

(1) 'God is the last end' = 'God is identical with whatever it is that is the last end',

(2) 'God is the last end' = 'God is to be *identified as* whatever it is that is the last end.'

Whereas (1) yields an identity proposition, (2) gives us a rule for the use of 'God'—or in more traditional terms, tells us what God's nature is. The second objection raised against

(1) does not hold against (2); it is misguided here to object that if God is to be identified as, for example, happiness, then the 'formal' predicates which can sensibly be attached to happiness must be sensibly attachable to God, for (2) has the force: 'Whenever the word "God" occurs, one can substitute whatever is at the most and at the least such that it makes no sense to ask "For the sake of what (With a view to what) are you pursuing *x*?", where *x* is a τέλος.' As this is so, it might be pressed, it is not the case that predicates which can sensibly be applied to whatever it is that is at the least and the most such that it makes no sense to ask the above form of question (for example happiness) must also be sensibly applicable to God, any more than (to draw an analogy) what is sensibly predicable of a value for a variable is sensibly predicable of that variable. God is not to be thought to be *identical with* happiness or anything else concerning which the above form of question cannot sensibly be raised, any more than a value or set of values can be thought to be identical with the variable for which they are values. Further, it might be said, since God is not so to be thought of, (2) cannot be open to the charge of reductionism; to make such a charge would be to confuse (2) with (1). However, this account does not answer the *first* objection raised to (1) above; indeed it supposes that the concept of 'whatever is at the most and the least such that it makes no sense to ask "For the sake of what (With a view to what) are you pursuing *x*?" . . .' is a possible concept, whereas it is not so *vide* my argument in the first objection to (1). 'Happiness' could not, logically could not, be such as to fall under *this* concept; all that could so fall, one might surmise, would be some entity signified by a logically proper name, some logically unique individual; but this supposed possibility is ruled out by the introduction of 'whatever': 'whatever' demands that a general term be introduced. It might be suggested that the only sense in which God can be said to be identified as the last end is the sense in which God is said to be identified as whatever it is which is such that *in fact* the form of question 'For the sake of what (With a view to

what) are you pursuing *x*?' has at the least and at the most no application. Even here however we are faced with an impossible formulation, since in order to maintain the specification 'in fact' it is necessary that we deal not with a form of question, but with a *particular instance* of such a form of question—yet the whole argument for the necessity of positing at least one last end was that there be at least one situation in which the form of question 'For the sake of what (With a view to what) are you pursuing *x*?' (where *x* is a τέλος) has no sense. A parallel point here is that the question of *application* relates to the question of *sense*; it cannot relate to the question of *fact*.

The impossibility of giving sense to 'the one and only last end' renders it impossible to give an account of what it is to say that God is the one and only last end of rational creatures. The only proposition of which a sensible account could be offered is that God is *a* last end, and crucial difficulties have already been raised to this proposition. One may however offer another account of such a proposition which would dispense with those difficulties. In the former account it was assumed that to say that God is a last end can only be construed in one way, namely that 'is a last end' is a predication of God; but it might be pressed there are other possibilities—the possibilities suggested by (1) and (2) above. Following (1) above, to say that God is a last end is to say that God is identical with whatever it is which is such that the form of question 'For the sake of what (With a view to what) are you *x*-ing?' (where *x* is a τέλος) necessarily has no application. This account runs into several difficulties. First, there might be several such entities exhibiting incompatible characteristics. Secondly, it will be objected that God cannot be said to be identical with any such entities without the charge of reductionism resulting. Thirdly, and more importantly, if God is identical with any such entities (for example happiness), then for any proposition in which the word 'God' occurs we can substitute the name of such an entity and obtain an equivalent proposition, but this is not possible. For example, 'God is infinitely loving' is not the equivalent of 'Happiness is infinitely loving', for there is a problem as to whether the latter even makes sense, let alone that it is true for all the possibilities for which the former is true. Following (2) above, to say that God is a last end is to say that God is to be *identified as* whatever it is that is such that the above form of question necessarily has no application. This account also runs into difficulties. First, parallel to the first difficulty above, there might be several such entities, exhibiting incompatible characteristics, with which God would have to be identified. Secondly, whilst the charge of reductionism fails on this account, it seems at best simply false and at worst unintelligible that one can make the substitutions permitted by the rule: 'Whenever the word "God" occurs one can substitute the name of whatever it is which is such that the form of question "For the sake of what (With a view to what) are you *x*-ing?" (where *x* is a τέλος) necessarily has no application', for this would permit us to write for such examples as 'God created the heavens and the earth' and 'God created man in his own image', that 'Happiness created the heavens and the earth' and 'Happiness created man in its own image' respectively. The only substitution for 'God' here which would yield sense and retain the truths of the Christian faith would be 'love' in the sense of ἀγάπη. Now it certainly can be maintained that 'love' is *a* last end in the sense that the question 'For the sake of what (With a view to what) are you pursuing (striving after) love?' is unintelligible; if someone persists in asking this question this shows they do not understand what love is. But it cannot, logically cannot, be shown that love is the *only possible* case in which the above question is unintelligible; and it is false that 'love' is the only case where the above question fails to have sense.

E. I thus conclude as follows:

(1) that God cannot be sensibly spoken of as an end;

(2) that there is a sense in which the proposition 'God is a last end' has sense—namely the sense discussed immediately above, but that such a construction leads at the best to false results, at the worst to unintelligible ones.

(3) that God cannot be said to be the one and only last end, in that no sense can be attached to this concept in the context of its introduction in this discussion. This, of course, is not to say or to be committed to the absurd position that any phrase of the form 'the one and only . . .' is a nonsensical form of expression.

NOTES

p. 7 It might be objected that the question of an end is not necessarily relevant in regard to any and every human operation: actions which involve moral and aesthetic considerations might be put as cases in point. Professor Phillips has raised this difficulty and referred me to J. L. Stocks, *Morality and Purpose*, London, Routledge & Kegan Paul, 1969. In the paper 'The Limits of Purpose', Stocks claims that 'As soon as purpose is precisely defined it becomes clear that it accounts for none of the highest human activities: that on the contrary, the very existence of art, of morality, of religion, of genuine thought and knowledge depends on the ability of man to rise above that of purpose' (p. 17). Stocks's actual argument, however, depends on his acceptance of what he describes as 'two features of the purposive attitude which show its essential incompleteness' (p. 19). These are:

(i) that the effort and energy spent on fulfilling a purpose are not self-justifying, but only, as it were, excused by the result produced;

(ii) that there is a faulty abstraction in the purposive view of a situation and of the changes made or proposed to be made in it (pp. 19–20).

On (i), one might aptly comment that *of course* the effort and energy spent on fulfilling a purpose are not self-justifying, but what is objectionable about this? Not everything can be self-justifying and indeed there is a problem as to whether anything can; cases in which it makes no sense in the nature of the case to ask for a justification are not cases of self-justification. Further, such effort and energy are not *excused* by the result, but justified by the end aimed at and we must not confuse 'end' and 'result' as Stocks does here and in other places throughout the paper.

On (ii) Stocks claims that on the 'purposive' account there is no room for the individual. The point about there being no room for the individual seems to be that the value of each feature of a situation is its actual or possible contribution to a single result; each feature in a situation only has value in that it contributes to a single result. The implication of this is that there are many features in a total situation which do not have value because they contribute to a certain result. To see what Stocks has in mind we turn to his examples. Take his case of riding a bicycle (p. 22). He admits that when I ride a bicycle I normally have a purpose in riding and hence that the form of question I have been discussing has possible application here, but, he presses

> I may also feel an affection for the machine I ride and delight in the expertness with which I manage it. Such feelings do not in any way conflict with or prejudice any purpose I may have in riding . . . What enters here is not a new or further purpose; it is the conscious enjoyment of the means and methods by which the work is done; and it is this that I regard as the distinctively artistic contribution.

Now even if one agrees with Stocks that the artistic contribution is that we enjoy doing something or enjoy a means or way of doing something, this is of no consequence for the above contention, for the enjoyment of something is not itself an operation but something one gets out of an operation.

However, even if the bases of Stocks's argument are open to such objections, it might still be pressed that we cannot raise such questions as: 'With a view to what' or 'For the sake of what are you painting this picture? (where the painting of the picture is a genuine artistic activity as opposed to being a means to financial reward) or the question, for example: 'With a view to what are you defending the innocent?' (where the action of defending the innocent is a genuinely moral one as opposed to one done for what one might get out of it). I fail to see why *not*. Why cannot the answer to the first question be (for example): 'With a view to creating an object of beauty?' (even Stocks allows for this (p. 24). 'The effort must no doubt be fruitful, it must be successful in producing something worth having . . .') and as regards the second we might answer: 'With a view to upholding justice'. I find no argument in Stocks which shows that we cannot in principle raise such questions, namely that it is a misunderstanding to think that we can ask for purposes or goals in connection with a genuinely moral or aesthetic action. From the consideration (p. 24) that the artist 'cares nothing for money, little even for the pictures he has made', that he does not paint pictures with a view to financial gain or with a view to just doing a job, it does not follow that he paints pictures with *no* end in mind, let alone that we cannot even raise the question of an aim or end. Indeed if artistic activity consists in simply 'the exercise of artistic gifts' for no purpose, then artistic activity becomes a mere pastime and we cannot distinguish between the professional and the amateur. Again, from the consideration that a man may be barred at any moment from pursuing his moral end by 'the most promising avenue' (p. 29) by the consideration that he cannot use any and every means to that end, it does not follow from this that there cannot be moral ends; indeed it seems that Stocks's very case here depends for its intelligibility on such a possibility. The most that could be claimed here is that an account in terms of purpose cannot give us a *complete* account of moral activity: there are some aspects of moral situations which might lead us to say that 'Morality. . . must operate by giving significance to detail by setting a different value on features which to purpose were indifferent or equal in value', but from this it does not follow that it can offer us *no* account—which would be required in order to show that the questions I interpret Aquinas as raising cannot in principle be raised of actions which involve moral considerations. If we follow Stocks we shall have to say

(a) that there can be no good reasons for acting morally and that this is necessarily the case. We shall be reduced to saying (p. 28) 'The moral contribution seems to be a mere negation. At a certain point, without rhyme or reason, it makes a man see a barrier he cannot pass: he can only say that he does not consider himself free to improve on the situation in just that way'—which is indeed a reduction. Professor Phillips (*vide* his introduction, ibid., p. 4) would doubtless comment that this is no reduction but the truth of the matter. 'If one asks why men should have a regard for such ideals and standards of behaviour one can only reply that they do, that is all.' This is quite unsatisfactory. If I hold certain ideals I hold them as worth while and I can be called upon to give reasons as to why they are held to be worth while. If it is in principle impossible for me to give such reasons, then the holding of moral ideals or standards of behaviour differs not logically from my doing something simply because I enjoy it or get pleasure from it. I cannot in principle justify my enjoyment of something, as opposed to explaining it, for my enjoyment of something is something that happens to me, not something I do. Yet one cannot say that having regard for certain ideals or standards of behaviour is like enjoyment, that it calls for explanation but necessarily not for justification, since my having regard for such ideals or standards *is* something I do, not something I feel or something that just happens to me. In this way, to revert to Stocks, even if we were to accept his account of the 'artistic contribution', the analogy between art and morality in this respect at least is dangerous.

(b) that 'Morality, like art, cares nothing for results. To morality it does not matter what the results may be so long as they are practically acceptable'—on which view it is a matter of no moral consequence if my action on a given occasion brings about untold human misery, so long as it is 'practically acceptable'. This is an easy way of dispensing with one's conscience over, for instance, Hiroshima.

(c) that morality, like art, 'is an embroidery on the fabric of human purposes' and hence, to pursue the analogy, is like embroidery, dispensable, an agreeable and pleasurable 'extra'.

p. 13 It may be denied that it is possible to raise the question 'For the sake of what are you pursuing honour?', since the notion of pursuing honour is a distortion either in the sense that someone who pursues honour for the sake of something else does not perform honourable deeds, or in the sense that it is a misunderstanding of what honour is to think that one can raise the question of a further end. On the contrary, a deed is an honourable one irrespective of whether a man does it for example for the sake of fame or reputation or, for that matter, the honour that he will get from it. It is an honourable deed to pull a child out of a blazing house even if you do it for the sake of fame, and it is honourable because of the value we set on human life. The second sense of 'distortion' mentioned above relies on the principle that morality is not pursued for further ends and hence that we cannot for instance raise the question 'Why pursue honour?' To maintain this line leads to the difficulties mentioned in (a) above, and it could in any case be replied that one pursues honour, for example, since in general the pursuance of honour leads to at least a less miserable state of affairs in general than the pursuance of its contrary. It may also be objected that it is a distortion to speak of pursuing honour as an end in itself such that if a man claims that he is doing something for the sake of honour, he is a morally distorted person. Now it may be held that it is morally objectionable to do something with a view to getting honour, but this does not entail that it is morally objectionable to pursue honour or have honour, as opposed to your being honoured, as your end.

2

Precursus to the Doctrine of the Trinity in St Augustine: Aristotle on Substance (οὐσία)

Introduction

At *De Trinitate* V, ii, St Augustine says: 'Est tamen sine dubitione substantia vel si melius hoc appellatur essentia quam Graeci οὐσίαν vocant'; by 'the Greeks' here is meant the Greek Fathers of the Church. To understand the framework in which they wrote and to offer any critical appreciation of their writings on this matter, as I shall attempt to do in an appendix to this chapter, it is necessary to start one's investigation of οὐσία in classical Greek philosophy. For this purpose I shall investigate what Aristotle says on the matter at *Metaphysics*, Δ 8, 1017b10 ff. My reason for selecting this passage as the basis of my investigation is that it occurs in Aristotle's 'philosophical dictionary' and purports to cover not only his own uses and senses of this term, but those uses and senses which had been handed down to him or were in operation at the time of his writing. In this way the passage provides us with a useful compendium of the uses and senses of οὐσία for discussion in their own right and which act as an essential background to the later discussions of the Greek Fathers of the Church. It is customary to stress that the main philosophical influence upon the Greek Fathers is that of

Plato and the Stoics;* I do not dispute the influence of Plato and the Stoics, but this is not to say that the philosophy of Aristotle, as they understood it, did not influence their writings; indeed that it did so can be well supported.† In fact I think it can be maintained that it influenced their writings to a much greater extent than is customarily acknowledged. The important consideration for my present purposes is that we have a relevant framework within which to work and the Aristotelian discussion provides such a framework. I shall investigate the above-mentioned passage from the *Metaphysics* with a view to answering the question of whether there is a sense in which God can be said to be substance in the senses of 'substance' provided by the framework. If upon investigation it turns out that God cannot be so said to be, then the question arises as to how the Greek Fathers, at least in writings regarded as central by authorities in this field, can maintain the contrary. In an appendix to this chapter I shall attempt an explanation of this, claiming that it is only as a result of certain errors, a fundamental misinterpretation of the framework within which they were writing and subsequent variants on an impossible doctrine of substance, that they were able to speak of God in the language of substance.

A.1 Aristotle enlists the various senses of οὐσία as follows:

(1) οὐσία he says, means the simple bodies—earth, air, fire, water and the like; and in general bodies and things animal and divine which are composed of bodies. All these are called substances because they are not 'καθ' ὑποκειμένου λέγεται, ἀλλὰ κατὰ τούτων τὰ ἄλλα'—not *said of* a subject but other things are *said of* them.

(2) οὐσία in another sense means whatever partakes in those things which are not said of a subject which is such that it is the explanation (αἴτιον) of those things being the things that they are, for example, the soul of the animal.

* Cf. J. N. D. Kelly, *Early Christian Doctrines* (third edn), London, A. & C. Black, 1965, p. 10.

† Cf. Appendix A to this Chapter.

(3) οὐσία = whatever partakes in those things which are not said of a subject which is such as to determine and indicate the individuality of those things and whose destruction brings about the destruction of the whole.

(4) οὐσία = τὸ τί ἦν εἶναι (usually translated 'essence'), the formula of which is the definition.

And then Aristotle adds, by way of summary (but which in fact is no summary): 'Thus it follows that οὐσία has two (main) senses (i) τὸ ὑποκείμενον ἔσχατον—ultimate subject of predication; (ii) that which has individual and separate (χωριστὸν) existence.'

I shall not pursue a detailed study of all these uses; that would take a work in itself. I shall limit myself to investigating those uses which had a decided influence on later thought and which are philosophically interesting; this will leave me with a discussion of (1), (4), (ii) and (2) in that order.

A.2 As regards (1), it is first necessary to pass a comment on the notion of 'said of' a subject. This notion is introduced at *Categories*, 1a20. 'Said of a subject' cannot without restriction be interpreted as 'predicated of' a subject *if* by 'predicated of' one means 'description of what is referred to by the subject term'; 'characterization of what is referred to by the subject term'; 'saying something about what is mentioned by the subject term' (I take these accounts from Strawson's list—*Individuals*, p. 139).* 'Said of' cannot be interpreted solely in this sense, since what Aristotle designates as 'second substance' words are 'said of' a subject, but a predication in the category of second substance is not specifiable in any of the above ways. Rather we should take the sense of 'said of' here in the sense of the reference of a grammatical predicate. Secondly, it must be noted that 'substance' here is a logical concept, not a physical one; the 'simple bodies' are not said to be substances because they have a certain physical composition which renders them elementary, but because they can occur solely as the subjects of propositions and never as predicates.

* P. F. Strawson, *Individuals—A study in Descriptive Metaphysics*, London, Methuen, 1959.

To turn to a consideration of 'simple bodies': Aristotle's point is that, whilst 'fire', for example, can replace '__' in the propositional formula '__ is productive of heat' and yield a proposition of a subject–predicate type, 'fire', for example, cannot replace the blank in either of the following propositional formulae and yield such a proposition.

(i) 'This gaseous substance is __'.

(ii) 'Water is __'.

To be sure, 'fire' can replace the blank in either of the above formulations and yield a proposition, but, Aristotle would argue, in both cases what we have are not instances in which something is 'said of' a subject, but propositions asserting identity. It will not do (for Aristotle) to say that, in the case of the proposition 'This gaseous substance is fire', 'fire' here says what this gaseous substance is, for two reasons, I think. First, a word which specifies what something is certainly can be 'said of' a subject (as witness the case from *Categories*, 1a20, mentioned above): secondly, to get parity with the rest of Aristotle's list of 'things not said of a subject' here, it would appear that 'fire', 'water', etc. are taken to be the proper names of the elemental substances, and granted 'fire', etc. *are* such names, then 'fire,' etc. certainly cannot be *said of* a subject. Any proposition in which such a name occurred in the putative predicate place would rightly be said to be a proposition of identity; we must make a radical distinction between names and predicates.* Now Aristotle's account of what is covered by οὐσία in his statement 'and in general bodies . . .' is ambiguous as to whether he means '*men*', '*horses*' or particular men or horses; is Aristotle talking about the *kinds* or the *particulars of those kinds*? He certainly means at least the latter (cf. *Categories*, 2a11) and his point certainly holds in relation to these cases. 'Socrates' (as the name of a particular man) can replace the blank in '__ is white' and yield a proposition in which something is 'said of' a subject; 'Socrates' (in this use) cannot replace the blank in the formula 'This man is __' and yield a proposition in

* Cf. P. T. Geach, *Reference and Generality*, Cornell University Press, 1962, Chapter 2.

which something is 'said of' a subject. Indeed 'Socrates' (in this use) can replace the blank in such a formula, but what is yielded is an identity proposition. By contrast Aristotle cannot intend that the *kinds* 'man', 'horse' shall be substance in this present sense, for, as has already been indicated, 'man' ('men') most certainly can be 'said of' a subject. Hence one must conclude that when Aristotle says 'and in general bodies . . .', intending to talk of *particular* horses, men, animals, etc., such are what he designates 'first substances' at *Categories*, 2a11.

Can God be said to be substance in this first sense or rather senses? It might be pressed that there are certain features of 'God' which would stand in support of a positive contention: 'God' like 'Fire' does not admit of a plural form—'Gods' is the plural of *a* god, not of 'God' and that 'God', like 'Fire' cannot be used as a unit of counting.* We certainly cannot ask 'How many?' in connection with the use of 'Fire' under consideration, or speak of one Fire or one Water in this use, for 'Fire' and 'Water' are (in this use) the proper names of elemental substances. Neither can we in the case of 'God', it might be claimed; we can speak of 'many gods', ask how many gods there are, but we cannot do this in the case of 'God', for 'God' is not the singular of the plural form 'gods'. But at this point any further parallel between the two cases breaks down, since it seems that 'God' *can* replace the blank in the formula 'Jesus Christ is __' 'and yield a proposition in which 'God' is said of a subject, for in the proposition 'Jesus Christ is God' we do not have an identity proposition as we do in the case where 'Fire' replaces the blank. To say 'Jesus Christ is God' is not to say nor can it be to say that Jesus Christ is identical with God, for this would be to say that Christ was identical with the Godhead. With this breakdown is ruled out any claim that God can be said to be substance in the sense that 'simple bodies' are.

Can God be said to be substance in the in which a τόδε τι is a first substance, namely in the sense that particular men

* I am aware that some people might object to this; the case in support of such contentions is argued later (p. 58) and in Appendix B to this chapter.

or particular horses are such? Particular men and particular horses are said to be substances in that they are never 'said of' a subject, but everything else is 'said of' them. It is clear that God cannot be said to be substance in this sense either, for the same reason as presented above. It might be further said that it cannot possibly be maintained that God is substance in the way in which τὸ τόδε τι is substance, for τὸ τόδε τι is a body or a part of a body which, of necessity, exists in space and time. Yet, as Aquinas has argued (Ia,q3,a1), God is not a body. This observation is correct, but it is not of relevance in the immediate context, for all we are concerned with here is Aristotle's criterion for substance in the first sense.

An objection may be made at this point to my method of treatment of Aristotle's list at 1017b10–13, namely that this list presents us with entities of various kinds, and surely entities can never be predicated in the sense of 'said of'. What is 'said of' a subject, is not, surely, an entity but an expression or at least something linguistic as opposed to something non-linguistic. So, it will be said, there is a category confusion in my account. Professor Ackrill* has pointed out that what is 'said of' a subject is not something linguistic: the relation of 'said of ... as subject' holds between things, not words. Indeed it was for this reason that I earlier suggested that we should take what is 'said of' a subject as the reference of a grammatical predicate and not as the predicate expression. This consideration however does not produce a serious objection against my treatment of the items in Aristotle's list, since it is clear from what he says here and at *Categories*, 2 that his concern is with what can occur as a subject and never as a predicate, and there seems to be little to choose between whether we say that certain types of expression can occur as subjects and never as predicates, or the references of such expressions, for the

* Aristotle's *Categories* and *De Interpretatione* in the Clarendon Aristotle Series, Oxford, Clarendon Press, 1963, p. 82. Aristotle however is not always so clear as Ackrill on the point that the 'said of' relation is not linguistic. Cf. *Categories*, 1a20ff. and Ackrill's hedging in his comments on 2a31–4, namely where Aristotle does not clearly support Ackrill's account he is accused of being careless.

important point is that our decision (and Aristotle's) that certain entities are substance is determined in the immediate context by the role which expressions standing for them can play as regards the subject-predicate form of proposition.

A.3 As a preliminary to the question of whether God can be said to be substance in sense 4 above, it is necessary to raise the question whether this sense of οὐσία is one with which Augustine was acquainted, for *this* sense of οὐσία is a technical sense introduced by Aristotle, possibly for the purposes of overcoming certain difficulties in formulating a problem granted the presence of Platonic metaphysics (cf. Professor Anscombe's illuminating conjecture in *Three Philosophers*).* A case in favour of answering in the affirmative has recently been put forward by Professor H. A. Wolfson in his book, *The Philosophy of the Church Fathers*.† Wolfson claims that all five of Aristotle's kinds of relative unity as put forward in *Metaphysics*, Δ 6 are to be found in the post-Apologetic Fathers, and produces evidence to this effect. Unity in respect of τὸ τί ἦν εἶναι is one of the senses mentioned in the *Metaphysics* passage. Granted this, we cannot dismiss substance in this sense as being one of the senses in which God might have been thought to be substance; on the other hand we cannot say that *essentia* is a direct translation of Aristotle's τὸ τί ἦν εἶναι; this would be a crass error.‡

Aristotle's phrase 'τὸ τί ἦν εἶναι' is quite hideous Greek, as Miss Anscombe has pointed out. The phrase is usually but misleadingly translated into English as 'essence'. Misleadingly, since those who use the term 'essence' in the British tradition mean by it 'those qualities a thing must have in order for it to remain the same thing throughout a period of time', whereas as Miss Anscombe (op. cit.) has argued, and I shall further argue, that the phrase and what Aristotle

* G. E. M. Anscombe and P. T. Geach, *Three Philosophers* (Aristotle, Aquinas, and Frege), Oxford, Blackwell, 1961.

† H. A. Wolfson, *The Philosophy of the Church Fathers*, Cambridge, Mass., Harvard University Press, 1956.

‡ Cf. C. C. J. Webb, *God and Personality*, London, Allen & Unwin, 1918, p. 25 ff.

intends by it cannot be so translated. Indeed, if we were to take it that what Augustine might have in mind by *essentia* is 'essence' and the account offered of 'essence' is that just given, this would render Augustine's argument that God is *essentia* (*De Trin.*, V, ii) nonsensical at one short blow. God could certainly not be a set of *qualities* which something else has in order for that *x* to remain the same *x* throughout a time period, since (a) 'God' as a single word cannot designate a set of qualities (as opposed to what 'God' designates being *analysable* in terms of a set of qualities); (b) God could not be said to be a quality *at all* either in some general philosophical sense deriving from eighteenth-century British philosophy or in the special sense Aristotle introduces at *Categories*, 8b25. Not in some such general philosophical sense, for in such a sense a quality is something an individual is supposed to *have* or *exhibit*, but to say (for instance) that Jesus Christ is God is *not* to say that Jesus has or exhibits God or even has or exhibits God-like qualities; *prima facie* it is to say *what* Christ is. Not in the special Aristotelian sense of 'quality', for an expression which is a predicable only signifies in the category of 'quality' (ποιόν) if it answers the question ποῖον; ('How is it?', 'What is it like?)' when asked of an already identified individual. As concerns Jesus Christ, 'God' does not (nor cannot) answer the ποῖον; question, for all that can answer that question is an adjective of a certain sort, and 'God' is not reducible to any such adjective —we cannot write 'divine' for 'God'.

Aristotle's τὸ τί ἦν εἶναι cannot be given the customary account mentioned above for the following reasons, and seeing this will help us to get clear what it would be to say that God is substance in this sense. At *Metaphysics*, 1029b14 Aristotle says that τὸ τί ἦν εἶναι of each thing is that which is said καθ' αὑτὸ (*per se*) of each thing, with the restriction at 1029b17 that not all that comes under the heading of a *per se* predication is included in τὸ τί ἦν εἶναι of a subject. We need not concern ourselves directly with this restriction. Aristotle only introduces it here to exclude one sense of *per se* which he has previously introduced (*Meta.*,

1022a31–3), namely the sense of *per se* in which λευκόν (white, transparent) is said of a surface—namely, a surface is the prime subject of transparency. The senses of *per se* which are central here are the first two senses introduced at 1022a25ff., but unfortunately the first of these senses is explicated in terms of τὸ τί ἦν εἶναι. However, one can glean from Aristotle's discussion of the 'transparency' case that τὸ τί ἦν εἶναι is not to be given the customary account. The sense in which τὸ τί ἦν εἶναι is *not* something which is said *per se* is the sense in which transparency is said of a surface. A surface is the prime subject of transparency, but (i) to be a surface is not to be transparent, (ii) not every surface is transparent: whereas τὸ τί ἦν εἶναι is *per se* of its subject in the sense that it is identical with what it is said to be the 'essence' of, namely τὸ τί ἦν εἶναι of *x* is what it is to be *x*, but 'what it is to be *x*' cannot possibly be a set of qualities which *x* has, for the very introduction of the notion of 'a set of qualities which *x* has' presupposes the identification of *x* which demands that we can already specify what it is to be *x*.

Further, Aristotle says in several places, including his second account of *per se* predication at *Meta.*, 1022a29, that the λόγος (formula) of τὸ τί ἦν εἶναι is a definition (*Meta.*, 1017b23; 1043a22; 1029b22), but a definition, in Aristotle's sense at least, does not and cannot state the characteristics or qualities of what is defined. Further evidence can be offered for my contention concerning 1029b15ff., but I shall not pursue this; for present purposes it would be otiose.

Granted that the formula of τὸ τί ἦν εἶναι of *x* is a definition, it would seem to follow that the formula of τὸ τί ἦν εἶναι must be a set of words, at least a phrase as opposed to a single word; hence God can never be substance in this sense, for 'God' is not such a formula. However, in certain cases it is not necessary that the λόγος (formula) of τὸ τὶ ἦν εἶναι be a set of words as opposed to one word. It is not necessary in those cases in which Aristotle makes no distinction between τὸ τί ἦν εἶναι and τὸ__εἶναι, where the blank is filled out by the dative case of a noun, personal pronoun, or proper name. A passage in which Aristotle appears to make no distinction between these concepts is at *Metaphysics*, Z1029b13ff. Having said that τὸ τί ἦν εἶναι of each thing is that which is said *per se*, he continues: οὐ γάρ ἐστι τὸ σοὶ εἶναι τὸ μουσικῷ εἶναι. From the fact that the phrases τὸ τί ἦν εἶναι and τὸ σοὶ εἶναι occur in consecutive sentences and Aristotle moves straight from one to the other without any apology or comment, one can conclude that, although in other places he keeps the two notions distinct, here at least he equates them or at least regards them as alternatives. What he says in the passage mentioned is that τὸ σοὶ εἶναι ('the-to-be-you'; 'what it is to be you') is not to be musical and at least one natural interpretation of this is that what it is to be you, namely *man* does not include being musical (cultured)—for to be man (a man) does not entail being cultured. On this account 'the-to-be-you' is the specification of a second substance; hence as Aristotle makes no clear distinction here between τὸ τί ἦν εἶναι and τὸ__εἶναι, nor considers it necessary to explain the move, on this account τὸ τί ἦν εἶναι will be a second substance too. In consequence we have a case for saying that a single expression, if it be an expression for a second substance, can express τὸ τί ἦν εἶναι of something or other. Thus God is not ruled out as substance in this sense of substance, if it can be shown that 'God' is a second substance term. (One might additionally comment here that, in view of the importance Aristotle gives to second substance at the beginning of *Metaphysics* Z and in the *Categories*, it is odd that he does not consider this category formally in his list at Δ 8; this omission would also lead one to suppose that second substance *is* to be included under τὸ τί ἦν εἶναι in this list. Further, a case can be made out for saying that in those influenced by Aristotelian philosophy, such as the Greek Fathers of the Church, there was no rigid distinction drawn between τὸ τί ἦν εἶναι and τὸ__εἶναι (cf. Wolfson, op. cit., p. 316).)

I now turn to the question of whether 'God' can be regarded as a second substance term. According to Aristotle, for *x* to be an expression signifying a second substance, *x* must be able to answer the τί ἐστι; (What is it?) question when asked of an individual of a certain sort; a second substance word tells you *what* something is, as opposed to how it is or what it is like (cf. *Categories*, 1b13, *Topics*, 103b22, *Metaphysics*, 1028a12). A second substance word signifies a genus or a species; 'man' and 'animal' are given as examples (*Categories*, 3a10ff.). As this is so, it is incorrect to hold that a second substance is introduced to make a prime substance determinate or to bestow on prime substances a certain quality, as Professor Mackinnon argues.* Second substances are the kinds to which first substances belong, but Aristotle's first substances are not 'simple individuals' but individuals of a certain kind or sort, for instance a particular man or a particular horse. What then is the special role and importance of second substance words? Miss Anscombe (op. cit., p. 8) has offered an account of the role of second substance words in terms of the conditions necessary for the introduction of proper names into a language and for the understanding of the reference of proper names. Her account, as I understand it, is that words which indicate second substances are necessary, for without them we could not sensibly introduce the notion of '*the same*' (for, concerning 'the same' we can always ask and necessarily have to ask: 'the same *what*?'), and unless we are able to introduce the notion of 'the *same x*' we cannot allocate a proper name to a particular. To quote Miss Anscombe (op. cit., p. 8):

> Aristotle's 'second substance' is indicated by the predicate, whatever it is, say '*x*', that is so associated with the proper name of an individual that the proper name has the same reference when it is used to refer to the same x, with the restriction that the individual is not such as to exist in a subject.

Now whilst it is the case that for any expression 'A' to be a proper name, it must be the proper name of something or other, such that we can sensibly say that the name refers to

* In 'Aristotle's Conception of Substance' in *New Essays on Plato and Aristotle*, ed. Renford Bambrough, London, Routledge & Kegan Paul, 1965, p. 97 ff.

the *same* individual on different occasions of use and, for *this* requirement to be met, 'same' must take as a completion some word which will allow us to refer to the continued identity of the individual, I do not think it can be claimed (as I think Miss Anscombe here is claiming) that what determines whether any predicate is a predicate in the category of 'second substance' is whether it can be sensibly prefixed by 'the same' and can be used as a principle of continued identity for particulars. Aristotle has no contention to this effect; indeed he is singularly silent on the issue at *Categories*, 3a10ff.; and strictly speaking he does not discuss proper names here at all, but only what Strawson calls 'referring expressions'. 'Same' and 'the same' can sensibly prefix words which come under the heading of 'matter words' in Aristotle's philosophy ('mass' terms) such as 'gold', 'bronze', 'silver'. In his discussion of 'the same' at *Topics*, A7, whilst putting a premium on what seem to be second substance words* he does not restrict the sensible use of 'the same' to these. Further, such words as designate what comes under Aristotle's heading of 'matter' *can* indicate *x*s which can be used as principles of continued identity for individuals (cf. P. T. Geach, *Reference and Generality*, pp. 39–40). On these grounds I do not think it can be maintained that the distinguishing feature of second substance words is that set out above; rather, from the examples Aristotle gives it would seem that such a feature is that such words can and do function as principles of continued identity for individuals *and* can and do function as units of counting *in their own right* (as opposed to other generic and specific words which *cannot*) and that in order to introduce counting *at all* for individuals falling under the other Aristotelian categories, terms exhibiting such a feature must be introduced (cf. *Categories*, 4a10; 4a18). However, second substance terms do not exhaust the class of terms which must be introduced for counting to take place *period*: or the class of terms which can provide units of counting in their own

* The actual example used here is 'cloak', which is not strictly a second substance word, but a general word amenable to number.

right (cf. terms which come under the heading of εἶδος at *Metaphysics*, 999b17; *De Caelo*, 278a1; *Metaphysics*, 1033a4). In connection with the use of second substance words one can sensibly ask 'How many?' and get the answers 'twenty', 'three', etc. In connection with the use of 'matter' words, such questions do not make good sense without further ado. Matter is not, as such, enumerable; one cannot raise the question 'How many gold(s)?'; 'How many silver(s)?', etc. are there present on a given occasion in the way in which one can ask 'How many men?' 'How many horses?'; 'How many animals?' To put the matter succinctly for our present purposes, second substance words furnish us with a class of terms which can provide us *both* with a criterion of continued identity (in Professor Geach's sense) *and* with units of counting in their own right; they are to be differentiated from 'matter' terms in this respect, but they do not exhaust the class of terms exhibiting such a characteristic.

A.3 I now turn to the question of whether 'God' can be regarded as a second substance term, and hence whether God can be said to be substance in this sense. There are some initial objections to an affirmative answer. I enlist them as follows:

(1) 'God' (as opposed to 'god') cannot be prefaced by the indefinite article, as any second substance word (in English) can.

(2) 'God' (as opposed to 'god') has no plural form as second substance words have; 'gods' is the plural of 'god', not of 'God'.

(3) 'God' (as opposed to 'god') is not enumerable; we can talk of 'One (many) god(s)', but not of 'One (many) God(s)'. We cannot form a question 'How many __ are there?' using 'God'; of course we can ask 'How many *gods* are there?', but 'gods' is not the plural of 'God'. On the contrary any second substance word can take a number.

Against such initial objections it may be replied that (a) whatever the supposed virtue and illumination of (1), it clearly depends for its point upon the contingency that certain languages possess the indefinite article form; others equally do not, so it is not a point of substance.* (b) The Christian asserts that he believes in one God and that his God is the one and only true God, thus 'God' *is* an enumerable term and to this we may add the support of Aquinas, who says that 'the term "God" agrees with common nouns in that the form it signifies is found in several subjects (*supposita*)' (Ia, q 39 a4 ad 1 um). Professor Geach has argued:† 'It is important that for Aquinas "God" is a descriptive predicable term (*nomen naturae*—Frege's *Begriffswort*) and not a logically proper name. Only because of this can the heathen say his idol is God and the Christian contradict him and both be using "God" in the same sense'.‡ As against this it can be argued that these comments hold true as concerns 'god' but *not* as concerns 'God',§ and even if considerations (1)–(3) above *hold* concerning 'God' it does *not* follow that 'God' is a *nomen individuis* (a proper name), for these considerations hold of general terms which are not enumerable—such as 'gold' or 'copper' (Aristotle's 'matter' terms). Indeed 'God' cannot be regarded as a proper name, for if that were the case the proposition 'Jesus Christ is God' could only be construed as an identity statement, which I have previously argued is impossible. Granted 'God' is a *nomen naturae* in the sense of a general term like 'gold' or 'bronze' then Aquinas's point still holds, for the form of 'gold' or 'bronze' can be said to be found in many subjects and both the heathen can assert and the Christian deny that the idol is God, using the term 'God' in the same sense. What is impossible on such a construction is the use of the term 'God' in connection with number—as it is with the term 'gold'. I do not think any clear decision can be taken as to whether when the Christian speaks of God he can be thought of as using 'God' as an enumerable general term or as a non-enumerable one. When he says 'I believe in one God' or 'Our God is the one and only true God', then 'God'

* There is much more to be said on this; I return to it in Appendix B to this Chapter.

† P. T. Geach, *God and the Soul*, London, Routledge & Kegan Paul, 1969, p. 57.

‡ I discuss this case in Appendix B to this Chapter.

§ Cf. Appendix B.

on these occasions of use certainly seems to be an enumerable general term. On the other hand, in such statements as 'Jesus Christ is God' or 'The Holy Spirit is God', 'God' does not seem to be such an enumerable general term, for 'Jesus Christ is God' or 'The Holy Spirit is God' are not respectively writable as 'Jesus Christ is one God' ('Jesus Christ is a God'), 'The Holy Spirit is one God' ('The Holy Spirit is a God'). Clearly however in these uses 'God' is not a proper name. Yet again in such a proposition as 'God is merciful' or 'God is powerful' we have in 'God' as thus occurring a type of general term which cannot be prefaced by 'a' or 'one'.* It might be counteracted that in such a use we can write 'The one and only God is merciful'—so that here 'God' goes proxy for a definite description. This suggestion has been put forward by Geach (*God and the Soul*, p. 58).† This supposes that 'God' can either be regarded as *a* god or that 'God' is prefaceable by a number—which contentions I hope to counter in Appendix B to this chapter. For the moment suffice it to say that such an account of 'God' as Geach puts forward will not do for 'God' in such a proposition as 'Jesus Christ is God' (not that he would claim this).

As things stand at the moment, without any further argument to show that the uses of 'God' as a general term are all reducible to one use in which 'God' is an enumerable general term, it cannot be claimed that 'God' is a second substance term, for a second substance term *is* a certain type of enumerable general term. There are in any case more specific reasons why 'God' cannot be said to be a second substance term. A second substance term can be said to refer either to some one individual or some set of individuals. In the case of the proposition 'Socrates is (a) man', Aristotle holds that 'Socrates' and 'man' have identity of reference; in the case of 'Man is animal', Aristotle parallels this to 'Socrates is (an) animal' (cf. *Categories*, 2a35ff.) and 'man' in this use refers to all men viewed as a conjunction (cf. Aristotle's points at *Physics*, 218a7; 239b8). Even if 'God', in its use in Christian

* Cf. my paper 'God and Analogy' in *Sophia*, vol. VIII, no. 3, pp. 18–19, and the implications of Appendix B to this Chapter. † See Notes to this Chapter.

thought, can be said to refer to all, it cannot be regarded as referring to some one spatio-temporal particular or set of such particulars, for God is said to be 'outside' space and time: yet it is no contingency that second substance terms do so refer. Further, whether *x* is a second substance is not *solely* determinable by the kinds of logical consideration raised above. Second substance terms present us with units of counting and criteria of continued identity as concerns things of natural origin—things which are generated as opposed to things which are created or manufactured, which suffer corruption or decay as opposed to destruction. But God is not of such natural origin. It does not make sense to say of God that He was generated or created or that He will suffer corruption or decay, but for any second substance it makes perfectly good sense to say these things.

On these grounds I contend that it is not possible for God to be thought of as second substance, and hence *vide* my earlier argument for God to be thought of as substance in the sense of τὸ τί ἦν εἶναι.

A.4 As I commented above, from the fact that 'God' in some uses at any rate is not an enumerable general term, it does not follow that 'God' is a *nomen individuis.* In these uses 'God' seems to resemble non-enumerate general terms like 'gold' or 'silver'. Whereas if *x* is a second substance word it follows that *x* can answer the 'What-is-it?' question; this feature is not a defining characteristic of second substance words. 'Gold', 'silver', 'bronze', etc. can answer the 'What is it?' question asked of an individual substance already identified under some other description. We might ask this question of the yellow dust in this pan and get the reply 'Gold', 'Gold' here tells us what the substance is; it does not name the substance. Similarly 'God' answers the question 'What is Jesus Christ?': we get the reply 'Jesus Christ is God': 'God' in this use does not name Christ. Further, in answer to the objection that 'God' can provide us with a criterion of identity—namely that Jesus Christ can be said to be not the *same* God as the Jesus of Mohammed, or that the pre-existent Christ is the same God as the

Christ who was crucified on Calvary, it must be replied that it is not the prerogative of second substance terms to act as criteria of identity for individuals—as I have pointed out above (p. 56) (cf. also *Reference and Generality*, pp. 43–4). Hence failure to be a second substance term or an enumerable general term does not entail failure to act as a criterion of identity. A parallelism in some uses of the term 'God' and non-enumerable general terms like 'gold' or 'silver' may tempt one to press the point that God can be said to be οὐσία in the way in which gold, silver, bronze, etc. can—in the sense that 'God' exhibits the formal features that those terms do. Indeed, that God is οὐσία in this sense has been put forward in the past.* There are however differences between 'God' on the one hand and such terms as 'gold', etc. (matter terms) on the other. In the case of gold and bronze, for gold and bronze to exist it is not necessary for there to be *x*s which *are* gold or bronze: the metals 'gold' and 'bronze' exist independently of there being gold or bronze things: it is not the case that for gold and bronze to exist *is* for there to be *x*s which are of gold or bronze. It might be argued that in the 'God' case the matter is different, namely that for God to exist *is* for there to be *x*s of which 'is God' is truly predicable.† Further, God does not have the feature of τόδε τι (particularity) in the sense that 'gold' or 'bronze' does, for whereas we can speak of 'This (lump of) gold', there is no such formulation that we can use in connection with 'God'. We cannot draw up any formulation of the kind: 'This (_ of) God', where the blank here can take the *same kind* of filling as in the 'matter' case. We can, of course, draw up a formulation of the kind 'This (_ of) God' where the blank can take as a filling such terms as 'son', 'law', 'act', but we have not a parallel in these cases to 'lump', 'piece of', 'chunk', for these terms divide arbitrarily, whereas the former do not divide at all. Again, whereas in the 'matter' case, *x*s which are gold or bronze are *of* gold or bronze (golden or 'bronzen'), in the 'God' case, if some individual is said to be God,

* Cf. St Basil's reference at *Contra Eun.*, 1.19; Athenagoras, *De Resurrectione*, 6.
† Cf. Professor Geach's argument in 'Aquinas', op. cit., p. 89.

this is not exponible in terms of that individual being *of* God. Obviously A can be said to be *of* God and in no way *be* God —for instance some action or prophet; and to say 'A is God' is not exponible as 'A is divine' (to make a contrast with the 'A is golden' case), for clearly A can be divine without being God. It is also the case that whilst 'God' in the proposition 'Jesus Christ is God' exhibits some similarities to non-enumerable general terms which can form a criterion of continued identity, it is unlike such general terms as far as the question of reference is concerned. If we say 'The powder in this box is gold', someone can ask what 'gold' refers to in this use and get the answer 'The powder in this box'; but if we say 'Jesus Christ is God' it seems we cannot ask what 'God' refers to in this use. We cannot say that 'Jesus Christ' and 'God' have the *same* reference, for in order so to say we have to specify what that reference is—we have to say they both refer to one and the same *x*; but it is just this specification which seems impossible. We cannot say that both 'Jesus Christ' and 'God' refer to one and the same *man*, for 'God' cannot refer to some man; and to say 'Jesus Christ' and 'God' refer to one and the same individual is useless unless we are prepared to specify what that individual is. It might be suggested that in this proposition both 'Jesus Christ' and 'God' refer to one and the same *person*, but this suggestion is only possible if 'person' can provide us with a term which can act as a principle of continued identity and individuation for individuals—a thesis I shall later contend is impossible (Chapter 5). Finally, 'God' cannot be said to be a substance term in the sense of an Aristotelian 'matter' term, for in the case of the latter the question of a reference to spatio-temporally determined objects can sometimes arise: in the case of 'God', if the question of reference can arise at all, the question of reference to spatio-temporally determined objects or object cannot arise *at all*.

A.5 I shall now consider whether God can be said to be substance in the sense in which that which has 'individual and separate' existence is said to be substance (. . . ὃν ἂν τόδε τι ὂν καὶ χωριστὸν ᾖ.) (A.1(4) sense (ii) above). Aristotle says that the μορφή and εἶδος of each particular sort of thing comes under this category. For these purposes Aristotle seems to be equating μορφή and εἶδος (form), which is unfortunate for there is a distinction to be drawn. At *Metaphysics*, 1029a3–8, Aristotle says that the μορφή of the statue is τὸ σχῆμα τῆς ἰδέας: the 'arrangement' of what is signified by, to invoke a contemporary term, 'characterizing universals'* in their use as predicates of a statue. (That ἰδέα covers 'characterizing universal', cf. *Physics*, 193b36; *Metaphysics*, 1036b13; 1073a19.)† Here, I take it, the arrangement of the properties signified by such characterizing universals would be for example 'manly shape'. But not every εἶδος term has reference to what is signified by characterizing universals in their use as predicates, nor is every such term of the form '__shape' writable in such a form. Indeed at *Metaphysics*, 1029a31 Aristotle dismisses an account of substance in terms of a combination of 'matter' and μορφή, but this is not to reject an account of substance in terms of 'matter' plus εἶδος. An account of substance in terms of 'matter' and μορφή is rejected, I take it, since an account in terms of its matter plus the properties signified by the characterizing universals which hold true of it is unsatisfactory in that such an account cannot tell you *what* something is. Indeed you have to know the answer to this question in order to identify the particular parcel of matter and the particular properties signified by the characterizing universals as the matter it is and the properties they are. This is why Aristotle says that an account of substance in terms of a combination of matter and μορφή is to be dismissed since it is 'posterior'.

Miss Anscombe (op. cit., p. 49) says:

> The form, then, is what makes what a thing is made *of* into that thing. It may be literally a shape, as it is the shape that makes the bronze into a statue: or again an arrangement e.g. letters to make a syllable; or a position, as the position of a beam makes it a threshold, or a time, as the time of eating food makes that food breakfast.

* As introduced by Professor Strawson, *Individuals*, p. 168.

† I am here indebted to Mr A. Spangler, formerly of the University of Nebraska.

I find Miss Anscombe's account helpful and perceptive, but there are difficulties. (a) She does not distinguish between μορφή and εἶδος. (b) It cannot be maintained that it is the shape, in the sense of μορφή, which makes the bronze into a statue, for as we have seen above Aristotle rejects this, and as a general thesis it cannot be maintained that what makes any given lump of bronze into a statue is solely its shape. (c) Whilst it must be agreed that the position of a beam is what makes it a lintel and that the time of eating food is what makes that food breakfast, is it clear that Aristotle would regard such items as an εἶδος? Miss Anscombe supplies no references, but from the examples she gives I take it that she has implicit reference to *Metaphysics*, H2, 1042b15ff. and 1043a1ff. In these passages Aristotle does not explicitly invoke his concept of εἶδος, but in so far as he is putting up (in the latter passage) definitions of various kinds, it is reasonable to say that a reference to 'form' is implicit. However, it becomes clear from 1043a6ff. that, whilst 'being in a certain position' or 'eaten at a certain time' might be forms in that they signify the actuality (ἐνέργεια) of something or other, in that they do not signify the actuality of substances, they do not signify 'actuality *per se*' (αὐτή ἡ ἐνέργεια, 1043a7), namely such forms are in some way deficient. It is only in the case of 'substantial' definitions that we get a reference to a non-deficient central case of a form. To keep this discussion relatively short I shall only investigate the question of the sense in which a substantial form has individual and separate existence: indeed this is the sense of 'form' relevant to our present discussion.

In what sense does the substantial εἶδος of something or other have *individual* existence? At *Metaphysics*, 1035a1ff., Aristotle says that we may speak of το εἶδος and of the thing having a form as an individual thing, but that we may never so speak of τὸ ὑλικὸν καθ' αὑτὸ (matter in itself). I construe this as follows. An εἶδος has individual existence in that any term falling under this category can be sensibly preceded by 'one' and can be sensibly combined with a demonstrative to make identifying reference to some individual. Such a term can be so preceded and used, since it can provide a principle of continued identity and individuation for individuals. For example, 'rational animal' or 'animal' (the 'form' of man) can be so preceded and used; so can 'man' as designating the thing which *has* the form. By contrast, τὸ ὑλικὸν καθ' αὑτὸ cannot, for this is unspecifiable: it only becomes specifiable by the introduction of some form. At *Metaphysics*, 1043a33, Aristotle presents us with a clear example of the type of concept he has in mind by 'form', in the sense of a substantial form, in his more worked out thought. The example here is 'shelter', and 'shelter' can be preceded and used in the way I have set out. 'Shelter' exhibits those formal features which second substance terms exhibit, though it is not itself a second substance term and strictly speaking no second substance term is an εἶδος: rather, an εἶδος, in the sense of a substantial εἶδος, is the εἶδος *of* some second substance or of something falling under an analogical extension of that category—as, for instance a house, which is not strictly speaking a second substance. 'God' in its Christian use cannot be preceded by 'one', as I shall further argue later. Further, in such a use it cannot form part of an expression which can be used to refer to some individual—not simply or solely in the sense that 'shelter' can be so used, that is to refer to a spatio-temporal individual, but in the sense that in order for 'God' to be so used, 'God' must be a term which can furnish us with a criterion of continued identity and a principle of individuation for individuals, and this is only possible if one can construe 'God' as 'a god', a thesis about which I have already raised some difficulties, and to which I shall be returning later (Appendix B to this chapter).

The feature of 'separation' is even more difficult to explain and grasp, and as far as I am able to ascertain there are at least two senses in which a form, in the sense under discussion, may be said to be 'separate'. In the first sense the form has separate existence in the sense that it has separate existence from the particulars which fall under it. Whilst it is necessary that any particular must be a particular of some kind or sort and hence must fall under some form either directly in that the sort under which it falls is its form (as with the 'shoe' example at *Metaphysics*, 1016b16), or indirectly in that a definitional account of the sort under which it falls will specify its form (as at *Metaphysics*, 1013a27ff.; 1043a12ff.), it is *not* necessary that any form be the form of some particular. There can be, and presumably are, some non-instantiated forms. To allow however that there are some non-instantiated forms is not to allow that there are some *non-instantiable* forms: indeed it can be argued that this is one very important difference between Aristotle's concept of 'form' and Plato's concept, for Plato's 'Forms' *are* non-instantiable. According to Aquinas, God is not simply a non-instantiated form, but a non-instantiable one. He says (*Summa Theologica*, Ia, q3, a2 ad 3 um) that God is a form which cannot be received in matter but is self-subsisting and is individualized precisely because it cannot be received in a subject (Sed illa forma quae non est receptibilis in materia, sed est per se subsistens, ex hoc ipso individuatur quod non potest recipi in alio; et hujusmodi forma est Deus; unde non sequitur quod habeat materiam.) Hence God cannot exhibit that feature of 'separation' which Aristotle's substantial forms exhibit in at least one sense of 'separation'.

There is another sense in which a form, in the sense under discussion, has 'separate existence', namely in the way in which a 'sortal universal' in Professor Strawson's sense does.* It supplies a principle for distinguishing and counting the particulars it collects; it presupposes no antecedent principle or method of individuating the particulars it collects. In contrast, other types of universal which apply to and collect particulars—Strawson's characterizing universals, Aristotle's μορφή terms, where μορφή is distinguished from εἶδος, and Aristotle's ἰδέας, do not exhibit this feature of separation, for whilst they can, as Strawson says, supply principles of grouping, even counting particulars, they supply such principles for particulars *already distinguished* or

* *Individuals*, p. 168.

distinguishable in accordance with some other principle or method. In order for 'God' to exhibit the feature of 'separation' in this sense, 'God' must be a universal which can apply to or collect particulars, but just this seems to be ruled out in the Christian use of 'God' in that 'God' is said to signify a self-subsistent non-instantiable form. It might be countered that all Aquinas's statement need be taken to imply is that the form 'God' cannot be said to have instantiation in *material* particulars, but that nevertheless it can be said to have instantiation in and apply to or collect *non-material* particulars in the sense of 'persons' and more particularly non-material particulars in the sense of ὑποστάσεις. For this counter-claim to be taken seriously, it is necessary that 'persons' are cases of non-material particulars and that the relevant sense of ὑπόστασις is a coherent one. I shall be arguing in my Appendix C to this chapter that the relevant sense of ὑπόστασις is incoherent and the thesis that persons are non material particulars is dependent on the thesis that 'person' is a term which can supply us with a unit of counting—a thesis I shall be arguing against in my last chapter in this book.

It might be contended that 'God' can be said to be an εἶδος in the sense in which the soul is said to be an εἶδος in the *De Anima*. For Aristotle a soul is necessarily the soul of some body of a certain kind, and to make identifying reference to a soul necessarily involves making identifying reference to that of which it *is* the soul. God can thus only be thought to be an εἶδος in this sense if it is necessarily the case that God is the God of some sort or type of thing and if, viewed as an individual soul, He acquires His identity from that of which or of whom He is the God. Neither of these conditions seems to hold. It is only a contingency that God is the God of, for instance, men or of any particular group of men; indeed I take it that it is only a contingency that God is the God of *anything*, for it is not necessary to God that He created anything. Further, if it were necessarily the case that God is the God of some type or sort of thing or of all types or sorts of thing, then His existence would depend upon the existence of such types or sorts of thing, as the existence of the soul does; but God's existence does not depend upon any other existence. Again, it cannot be claimed that God, viewed as an individual εἶδος (soul), acquires His identity from that of which or of whom He is the God. It cannot be said, for instance, that He acquires His identity from being the God of the Christians, since if this were the case it would not even be possible to raise the question of whether the Jews and the Christians worship one and the same *x*. Yet again, whereas on Aristotle's account to say that A has a soul is to say that A is a living F, where F designates a body of some type or kind, it is impossible to draw up any such formulation in the God case, for as Aquinas has argued (*Summa Theologica*, Ia,q3,a1), God is not a body.

On these grounds it is my contention that God cannot be said to be substance in the sense in which a form is said to be substance.

A.6 Finally I turn to οὐσία in the sense of whatever partakes in those things which are not predicated of a subject and which is such that it is the αἴτιον of those things being the things they are (sense (2) in A1 above). Here αἴτιον must be rendered as 'explanation', not as 'cause', for we get the αἴτον of something in response to a question which falls under the general form of question διὰ τί;—On account of what? Why? (cf. *Physics* 194b16ff). What constitutes an αἴτιον in the relevant sense here is some predicate or set of predicates which is such that it produces a sufficient condition of an individual being the sort of thing it is or of a sort of thing being of that sort.

There are difficulties in maintaining that 'God' can perform such a role since

(i) at *Metaphysics*, 1044a36-b1 Aristotle states quite clearly that the formal αἴτιον of *x* is τὸ τί ἦν εἶναι of *x* but, as I have previously argued, God cannot be such in the sense of the denotation of the definition of *x*, for 'God' cannot be a definition; neither can 'God' be part of the definition of *x* in Aristotle's sense of definition, for to be so 'God' would either have to indicate a genus or differentia, but no noun can indicate a differentia and it does not seem possible that 'God' in its Christian use could indicate a genus. According to *Topics*, 102a32ff. a genus is predicated in the category of τί ἐστι (What-it-is) of several things which differ in kind, and predicates falling under the category of τί ἐστι are those which are 'fittingly' contained in the reply of one who has been asked 'What is this object before you?'. Aristotle gives as his example the case of a man—someone is asked 'What is this object before you?' and the 'fitting' reply is that it is an animal. Thus in order for 'God' to be a genus by this account, 'God' must be a 'fitting' reply to the question 'What is this before you?' where the object before you already falls under some species. But it seems that 'God' in the Christian use could never answer such a question, for *what* is the species under which some individual must fall in order for 'God' to provide such an answer? That is, what are the species of which 'God' is the genus? Further, the Christian concept of God is such that 'God' could never answer the 'What is this before you?' question asked of some perceptible individual, for God is eternal and a-spatial which no perceptible individual ever is.

(ii) It seems that we can ask for the formal αἴτιον of God in the sense of τὸ τί ἦν εἶναι of God, even though we cannot know the answer in this life (cf. *Summa Theologica*, Ia,q6,9,10,11) hence God Himself cannot be τὸ τί ἦν εἶναι or a part thereof. 'God' designates something for which we can seek a 'formal explanation', but cannot itself *be* or be part of such an explanation.

(iii) It might be argued that after all there is a use of 'God' in which 'God' presents us with the formal αἴτιον of something, namely when it is said that Jesus Christ is God. The following problems arise in connection with this contention. A formal αἴτιον produces an explanation (or purports to produce an explanation) in the sense of an account of an individual being the sort of thing it is. Now if 'God' answers the τί ἐστι; (What is it?) question of Christ, such that God is the sort of thing Christ is, then 'God' itself cannot be a 'formal explanation', but itself requires such an explanation in the way that 'man' does. If 'God' does *not* answer the τί ἐστι; question of Christ, but is regarded as potentially a 'formal explanation' of Christ, then it is necessary that Christ be an individual of a certain sort, the 'formal account' (explanation) of which sort will contain 'God'. On this account the following difficulties arise: (a) in order for 'God' to be part of such 'formal account', 'God' must indicate a genus, which seems impossible *vide* (i) above: (b) What is the sort of which Christ is a member and which stands in a species–genus relation to God? Whatever answer we produce here we are fraught with difficulties. If we give the answer 'man', then 'God' cannot be the formal αἴτιον of Christ or a part thereof, for man is not a species of God. If we answer 'person', then apart from difficulties which arise specifically in this connection, which I shall be discussing in a later chapter, it cannot in any case be maintained that 'person' is a species of God. 'Spirit' cannot provide any such answer either, for to say, '*x* is (a) spirit' is not to say *x* is a sort of thing.*

It might still be pressed that there is nevertheless a sense in which God can be said to be a 'formal explanation' *vide* Aristotle's discussion at *Metaphysics*, 1043a10ff., where we are faced with a different kind of example, namely where the individual for which we seek a 'formal explanation' is not a__ (where the blank takes as a replacement either a second substance term or a term which can be a unit of counting) but a __, where the blank is filled out with a phrase such as 'a piece of' or 'a bit of' completed by a mass word such as 'ice', so that we have as our individual, for example, a given piece of ice. Now 'ice' is defined as 'frozen water', hence either 'frozen water' or possibly 'water' is the αἴτιον of this piece of ice. Take it that 'water' is.† Now someone might press that 'God' could be said to be the formal αἴτιον of Christ under the description 'This particular animated

* Cf. C.4, pp. 130–1.

† It is possible to take either here owing to the fact that Aristotle sometimes does equate τὸ τί ἐστι and τὸ τί ἦν εἶναι and a formal αἴτιον is τὸ τί ἦν εἶναι.

lump or mass of flesh and bones', as 'water' is of this particular piece of ice. The difficulties in maintaining such a view are pretty clear. First, we have the difficulty that 'God' is not a genus, as 'water' is; secondly, in order for 'God' to be a formal αἴτιον parallel to 'water', 'God' must exhibit those logical features which matter terms do—which is not the case, as I have argued above. Further, God is not related to lumps of animated flesh and blood in the way in which water is related to a piece of ice. A piece of ice is properly defined in terms of 'frozen water', but a lump of animated flesh and bones cannot be defined in terms of '__God'; what on earth or in heaven could fill out the blank here! In any case, it may be added, in the light of *Metaphysics*, 1043a19ff., it is clear that Aristotle wants to rule out the kind of definition which invokes matter terms as being genuine definitions expressing τὸ τί ἦν εἶναι and hence of being genuine cases of formal ἀιτίαι.

A.7 I thus conclude that 'God' cannot be said to be a substance term in the sense that, granted its use in Christian thought, it cannot perform those rules or exhibit those features which Aristotle's substance terms do in any of the senses of substance above discussed, and hence I conclude that God cannot be substance in any of the above senses. It might be commented that this conclusion is hardly surprising, since one would hardly expect 'God' in its Christian use to perform those roles or exhibit those features which such substance terms exhibit, for God is not part of that scheme of which such terms are an integral part, namely the scheme of material bodies and spatio-temporal existents—which some may be tempted to call 'our ordinary conceptual scheme'. This conclusion may seem hardly surprising, but it needs to be established and borne in mind when we recall the long tradition in which God is spoken of as substance, and spoken of as substance either in one of these senses or in a sense which is an illegitimate derivation from one of these senses. Indeed, in an Appendix I shall be arguing that in some of the writings of the Greek Fathers we encounter such illegitimacies.

It might be said that, whilst 'God' as an item of discourse

can be subject to the kind of inquiry conducted above, *God* cannot, and even if it is shown that 'God' cannot exhibit those features which substance terms do, this does not show that *God* is not substance. I cannot understand the first part of this remark; if it is simply the point that God is not an item of discourse, then it is trivially true and to no avail; but if it implicitly suggests that what God is can be separated from the use 'God' has and the roles it can perform, then such a remark is misguided. Concerning the second part of the remark one must ask 'What kind of inquiry *would* settle the issue as to whether God is substance?'—and one must comment that no inquiry as to whether *x* is or is not substance (in any philosophical sense of that word) could adopt a procedure which would yield substantial information about *x*, for to decide whether or not *x* is substance is not itself a *substantial* inquiry but a conceptual one, or if you prefer it, an ontological one. It is precisely such a conceptual inquiry which I have been pursuing.

NOTES

p. 59 For some further discussion on Geach here and for an objection to the point made in my article, cf. my 'The Logical Status of "God"' in *New Studies in the Philosophy of Religion*, ed. W. D. Hudson, London, Macmillan, 1972, Chapter 3, pp. 59ff. and pp. 53–4.

Appendix A

Aristotelian influence in the Greek Fathers

A. (1) ORIGEN, *De Oratione*, 15. 1.
Ex Homiliis in Epistolam ad Hebraeos
In Joannem Commentarii, X, 21.
(2) ST BASIL, *Epistles*, 38, 2; 361 and 362; 235, 6; 214, 4. *Ad Eunom.*, 2, 9; 1, 23; 1, 19.
(3) ST ATHANASIUS, *De Synodis*, 34; 53.
(4) HIPPOLYTUS, *Refutatio*, 7, 18.
(5) ST JOHN OF DAMASCUS, *De Fide Orthodoxa*, 1, 8.

B. WOLFSON, H. A., *The Philosophy of the Church Fathers*, vol. I, Cambridge, Mass., Harvard University Press, 1956, Chapter XV.
PRESTIGE, G. L., *God in Patristic Thought*, London, Heinemann, 1936, pp. 27, 160, 163, 176, 190–1, 270.
KELLY, J. N. D., *Early Christian Doctrines* (third edn), London, A. & C. Black, 1965, pp. 12, 84, 231, 268.
WEBB, C. C. J., *God and Personality*, London, George Allen & Unwin, 1918. pp. 40–6.
QUASTEN, JOHN, *Patrology*, vol. II, London, Spectrum Press, 1943, pp. 8, 65.
Patrology, vol. III, London, Spectrum Press, 1943, pp. 200, 217, 308.

C. For evidence of Platonic influence, cf.
PATTERSON, G., *God and History in Early Christian Thought*, London, A. & C. Black, 1967, especially

Chapter 2, 'Justin—Origen'.
NORRIS, R. A., *God and the World in Early Christian Theology*, London, A. & C. Black, 1966; especially Chapters 2 and 5.
PRESTIGE, G. L., op. cit.
KELLY, J. N. D., op. cit.

Appendix B
The term 'God' in Christian usage

I earlier considered the thesis that 'God' could not be said to be an enumerable general term since in its Christian use 'God' could not take the indefinite article. I rejected this as a serious case against 'God' being an enumerable general term in the cases considered, on the grounds that it is a contingency that certain languages possess the indefinite article form. I now take this matter up again.

When it is asserted that God is the one and only true God, this cannot be taken as asserting that God is *the one and only true god of the many gods that there are*, for this would imply that God was a god—which I shall argue cannot be the case. Even though this point could not literally be made in Greek or Latin, the fact that Θεὸς always occurs with a capital Θ, and 'Deus' with a capital 'D' can be taken as at least implying that *a* god is not signified, any more than 'Man' or 'Love' in English can be taken as signifying a particular man or a particular love, where these are the abstract noun forms of 'man' and 'love'. Further, if to say that God is the one and only God is to say that God is the only true or genuine god of the gods that there are, then apart from the consideration that this would allocate God to a genus or species of a genus, which Aquinas at Ia,q3,a5 argues is impossible, such a thesis would imply that the other gods were simply false gods, whereas Christianity is committed to the contention that they are *no* gods. God, as is sometimes said, is not 'one god amongst many'; 'He' does not vie for placing amongst Zeus, Athena, Baal, or Mars and simply come out top—it is not that these other divinities start in the race and fail to make the winning post; they don't even get under starter's orders. Again, there are certain 'formal' predicates which form an integral part of the Christian concept of God which rule God out from being the type of entity which the other gods are and hence from being a god. For example, God is said to be of his essence 'outside space', that is He is *necessarily* 'outside space'; spatial predicates are not possible of Him: any proposition purportedly expressing that God were *in* a certain place, or allocating a certain spatial position to Him, would necessarily be neither true nor false, not simply false. Again, any such question as 'Where is God?' is necessarily non-askable if it is to be thought of as yielding an answer giving a spatial location. The proposition 'God is two million miles away from the earth' is not merely false, but necessarily neither true nor false; if this proposition were merely false, then it would be intelligible to suppose that it could be shown to be false by an experiment carried out by the means of an interplanetary rocket. Whether God exists however cannot be shown to be either true or false by such an experiment, for God's existence is not a matter of fact.*

In contrast, the other deities are not necessarily a-spatial; for example, Zeus, Jupiter and Mars were locatable deities, and others inhabited less majestic if perhaps a more desirable residence, that is the top of Mount Olympus. In the case of the gods, it made good sense to ask where they lived, even though a believer might not know the answer or might be told that they lived nowhere in particular. Someone might be tempted to say that God lives in heaven, treating 'heaven' as the name of some place—as in the children's hymn 'Above the bright blue sky'. If this were so, it would make perfectly good sense to say that one might get to heaven by

* Cf. D. Z. Phillips, 'Faith, Scepticism and Religious Belief', in *Religion and Understanding*, Oxford, Blackwell, 1967, pp. 63–79.

a rocket or some other conveyance. However, you cannot get to heaven in an old Ford car, not simply because an old Ford car won't get that far, but because no sense can be made of the notion of getting to heaven by the means of *any* conveyance: one gets to heaven through prayer and doing the will of God in this life and by the divine mercy.

Again, God is said to be 'outside time' in the sense of 'eternal': temporal predicates cannot be sensibly attached to Him. One cannot ask of God, as one can ask of things having temporal duration: 'When did He come into existence?'; 'How long has He existed?'; 'When is it anticipated that He will cease to exist?'; 'Is He *still* in existence?' Neither can one assert that God existed for a certain period of time and then ceased to exist or that God has ceased to exist or will cease to exist at some future time. Necessary eternity is part of the concept of God and hence a part of God's essence, as necessary existence is. As Professor Malcolm has so aptly put the matter.*

> Someone may be inclined to object that although nothing could prevent God's existence still it might just happen that He did not exist . . . I think, however, that from the supposition that it could happen that God did not exist it would follow that, if He existed, He would have mere duration and not eternity. It would make sense to ask 'How long has he existed?': 'Will he still exist next week?': 'He was in existence yesterday but how about today?' and so on. It seems absurd to make God the subject of such questions. According to our ordinary conception of Him, He is an eternal being. And eternity does not mean endless duration, as Spinoza noted.

One can expand on Malcolm here. It is not simply 'our ordinary conception of Him' which yields this truth (lest anyone should wish to query appeals to 'ordinary conceptions'): it is the biblical conception also, for the Scriptures teach us that God is Alpha and Omega; the Beginning and the End, and to be thus is part of his nature. As this is so, He cannot be *in* time or exist *through* time—as natural existences can and do—unless we make the error of supposing that 'beginning' and 'end' are themselves periods of

* 'Anselm's Ontological Arguments', reprinted in *Religion and Understanding*, ed. D. Z. Phillips, p. 49.

time as opposed to limits. Indeed, when God says 'I am Alpha and Omega' this cannot be construed in any straightforward sense without sheer nonsense arising, for whilst it makes sense to speak of 'the beginning' in relation to any activity which takes place in time or to any time period, it makes no sense to precede *time* by 'the beginning'—for to to do so would be to make the nonsensical assumption that time itself was a period of time or a set of periods of time (a nonsense I think Zeno sought to expose). One can only make sense of God being Alpha and Omega in that God is *not* in time, but eternal. It might be said: 'But God has existed from the beginning' or 'God has existed from *before* time'. Both propositions are nonsensical if taken at their face value. The first is so, since it assumes that 'the beginning' is itself a period of time as opposed to a limit; the second is so, since it employs a temporal notion of 'before' to apply to time itself thus assuming that time itself is *in* time. This is not to say these propositions are nonsensical however—for their authors, in their use of them, may precisely intend to convey the very truth that God cannot be spoken of in temporal terms, and the use of what in other contexts would be strictly nonsensical propositions has the function of bringing this home to the reader. A nonsensical proposition may well, in some employment, have the function of bringing home an important truth–for example, Parmenides' assertion that το ὄν is one. It is unfortunate that some modern theologians (such as Paul Tillich) have taken this as expressing a straightforward and serious truth. By contrast, the gods of the Greeks and of the Old Testament were not eternal—let alone necessarily eternal, in the sense in which God is. As Professor Geach has pointed out, the Homeric gods 'forever are'—that is they have endless duration.*

Further, as Malcolm has pointed out (op. cit., p. 50), the notion of 'contingent existence' or 'contingent non-existence' can have no application to God: necessary existence is a property of God, it follows from the very concept of God; but the heathen deities did not so necessarily exist, for they

* 'Form and Existence', reprinted in *God and the Soul*, p. 58.

were thought of as having endless duration. And again, as Malcolm has said, necessary omnipotence is a property of God, and so is necessary omniscience; in contrast, the heathen deities are contingently omnipotent and omniscient in so far as they are thought of as exhibiting these characteristics. It would have made perfectly good sense to say of Zeus that he might not have been all-powerful: indeed Zeus was to be overthrown.

Finally, if 'God' is to be construed as 'The one and only god', there would be no *need* to talk of God as a 'supreme being'; 'He' would simply be a supreme *god* and that would be the end of the matter.

Consider the following extracts from Emil Brunner's 'The Name of God',*

> (1) The phrase, 'The Doctrine of God' must sound strange to an unprejudiced person. How can *man* undertake to formulate a doctrine of God? If there is one point which is clear from the very outset it is this: that God is not an 'object' which man can manipulate by his own reasoning: He is a mystery dwelling in the depths of 'inaccessible light'. On the contrary, the gods of the Greeks and the Heathen *were* 'objects' which man could manipulate by his own reason; as Tatian (*Ad Gr.* 21:3) comments, the gods of the heathen, such as Hera or Athene, were not, in the opinion of Metrodorus of Lampsacus, in the least what those people thought who had established temples in their honour, but were mere allegories, ὑποστάσεις of Nature and decorative representations of the elements. (p. 117.)

> (2) *this* precisely is the knowledge of God and the doctrine of God, that he is incomparable and that he cannot be defined . . . It is precisely this fact which distinguishes the God of the Biblical revelation from the gods and divinities of paganism. The gods of the heathen are not really mysterious because they can be 'known' within the sphere of that which is natural and given whether in the process of the world of nature or in the mind of man. (pp. 117–18.)

By contrast, one might comment: God cannot be known within the sphere of that which is natural and given in the *same sense* as the heathen gods, for God is not either something within nature (for He is said to be the Creator), neither is God an *explanatory hypothesis*. If God *were* such a hypothesis, then there might be a time at which such a

* In his *The Christian Doctrine of God—Dogmatics* vol. I, tr. O. Wyon, London, Lutterworth Press, 1949.

supposed hypothesis ceased to have a use or value; if this were possibly the case, then it would be possible to say that God, at some future time, *might not exist*, which is not so possible.

> (3) Holiness is of the nature of God ... to be holy is the distinguishing mark peculiar to God alone, it is that which sets the being of God apart from all other forms of being ... Even the etymology of the Hebrew word for 'holy' (*gadosh*) suggests this: it contains the idea of 'separation' as a fundamental element in the conception ... the gods and divinities of the other religions outside the bible are most certainly not 'Wholly Other'. (p. 158.)

God is 'wholly other' than natural things and contingent existences in that the set of 'formal' predicates which set forth their 'internal qualities' in Wittgenstein's sense (*Tractatus*, 2.01231)—the set of formal predicates which set forth their 'grammar' are in antithesis to the set of 'formal' predicates which apply to God, which set forth the 'grammar' of God. For example, any natural entity as commonly understood—such as trees, plants, rivers, beasts, men—can be meaningfully said to come into existence, exist through a period of time, go on existing, cease to exist and no longer exist. As pointed out above, God cannot be so meaningfully said. God is ἀγγενήτος and necessarily so; one cannot sensibly ask 'Who created God?', 'What generated God?' God cannot sensibly be said to be destroyed—only that which can be said to be created or generated can be said to be destroyed; and only that which can be said to be generated can be said to suffer corruption.* On the contrary, the gods and divinities of the heathen are such that they *can* be spoken of as 'coming into existence', 'going on existing', 'ceasing to exist'—even though it may be held by their worshippers that it is false that at a certain time they have ceased to exist. In this way they are not 'wholly other': they are contingent existences as opposed to eternal, immanent as opposed to transcendent. The notion of 'transcendence' may be a thorn in the flesh of the more hard-headed; there is nothing suspicious about saying that God

* For some further comments concerning contingent and necessary existence, cf. my paper 'St. Thomas' "Third Way"' in *Religious Studies* vol. 4, pp. 229–43.

is transcendent if in so saying we mean that God exhibits those formal characteristics I have set out.

> (4) The whole conflict between Yahweh and Baalim of the Near East raged round this essential transcendence of God: the conflict raged between the God who is the 'Wholly Other' and the nature-gods, who were only the hypostasised forces of nature. That is why the commandment forbidding the worship of graven images was of such decisive significance. It emphasised the transcendence of God. (p. 159.)

I draw the following from this—that to worship a graven image or to worship Baalim was idolatrous in that it showed a fundamental *misunderstanding* of God: it was to treat that of which it would make *no sense* to attach those predicates which signify the essence of God, as that of which it *would* make sense; thus, in rather more old-fashioned language, to confuse the immanent with the transcendent. It is for this reason that Christianity, following the Hebrew tradition, *has* to be intolerant towards religions which express belief in such deities—as Brunner comments. (p. 178).*

Support for my contention that God cannot be regarded as a god can also be found in the writings of Karl Barth:

> (1) He proves himself in Jesus Christ to be the One to whom no-one and nothing is to be preferred or even compared. 'Cuius neque magnitudini neque maiestati neque vistati quidquam, non dixerim praeferri, sed nec comparari potest' (Novatian: *De Trin.* 31). Because He manifests himself thus, He makes himself knowable to us not through revelation of some sort of other, but through the fact of His self-revelation. On this Paul has based the knowledge of God as the one and only God, *in contrast to the many 'gods'* (Barth, op. cit., p. 21) (my italics).
>
> (2) We must be clear that when we are speaking of God in the sense of the Christian faith, He who is called God is not to be regarded as a continuation and enrichment of the concepts and ideas which usually constitute religious thought in general about God. In the sense of Christian faith, *God is not to be found in the series of gods* . . . When we Christians speak of 'God' we may and must be clear that this word signifies *a priori*, the fundamentally other . . .†

* Cf. also Peter Geach, 'On Worshipping the right God', in *God and the Soul*, pp. 100–16; Karl Barth, *Knowledge of God and the Service of God*, London, Hodder & Stoughton, 1938, p. 21.

† Karl Barth, *Dogmatics in Outline*, tr. G. T. Thompson, S.C.M., 1940, pp. 35–6 (italics mine); cf. also his *Credo*, London, Hodder & Stoughton, 1936, pp. 14 ff.

In the light of these considerations, I contend that it is not possible to say that God is *a* god, or that He is *one* god. To say that God is the one and only true god is to say that 'god' is only properly used when it is used to signify a nature which is unchangeable, immutable, immortal, eternal; it presents us with a re-definition of 'god', not with a purportedly true statement about *a* god. If you use the term 'god' to signify a nature which is not of this kind, as the heathen do, then 'god' simply becomes a nature which is an extended version of man's nature—which is why the 'old man in the sky' conception of God, ridiculed by the then Bishop of Woolwich in *Honest to God* (London, S.C.M. Press, 1963), if any Christian has seriously held it, is an idolatrous conception.

The account I have attempted to present would imply that when the heathen says that for example Zeus is God, he is not simply making a false predication, as I think is Professor Geach's contention,* but showing a *misunderstanding*; in saying that 'Zeus is God' he has not grasped the proper concept of God, he is in *darkness*, not simply in the error of falsely predicating 'God' of Zeus. Zeus could not possibly be God, but it can be maintained that it is *true* that Zeus is *a* god. Indeed the worshipper of Zeus cannot be shown that Zeus is simply a false god—what would show it? Although what Zeus and the God of Christianity conceived of as a god can meaningfully be said to do is determined by their respective theologies, such that we cannot say outright that the worshipper of Zeus believes that Zeus can do exactly the same as the God of Christianity, there is no way of showing that Zeus is simply a *false* god, for granted that it makes sense within both theologies to say that God or Zeus did O, then nothing will be allowed to count against Zeus doing O or in favour of God doing O in the eyes of the Zeus worshipper. That is, for any occurrence O, concerning which it would make good sense to say God (conceived as a god) or Zeus did O, there is no way of showing to the worshipper of Zeus that God did O, as opposed to Zeus doing it. Say it is held by party A that a thunderbolt which caused the

* In *God and the Soul*, p. 57.

destruction of a dwelling-house H inhabited by unbelievers in both God and Zeus, was sent by God and by party B that it was sent by Zeus. Granted that it makes sense to both parties to say that if *x* is God, then *x* can send thunderbolts to destroy the unbelievers, there is no means of deciding which party is *right*. The destroyed dwelling-house can offer support for both parties equally. There is nothing to choose between the accounts; the facts of the matter support both parties equally—or neither if we do not believe that the gods can send thunderbolts. The believer in Zeus will accept as evidence that his god did O, whatever the believer in God (thought of as a god) accepts as evidence. It might be thought that the story of Elijah on Mount Carmel provides a counter-case. The worshippers of Baal, it might be pressed, were confounded: the God of Israel was shown to be the true God in that in spite of the piling up of adverse conditions, He caused the sacrificial fire to be lit in the 'crucial experiment' situation. The point to be made in answer to this is that the worshippers of Baal should not have allowed this to count as a 'crucial experiment'; they should have argued that there was no set of conditions which could constitute conditions for a decisive experiment of this kind. They would have been correct in so arguing, for there was no guarantee that there would be circumstances in which Baal would answer their prayers—let alone this situation. The reply of the Baal worshippers should have been that the 'experiment' did *not* show that their god was false, only that he chose not to hear them on that occasion, or that he heard them but decided not to answer, for instance on the grounds that this was a real test of their faith or that he decided not to answer in that it was better for them to suffer, etc. The lighting of the sacrificial fire on Mount Carmel no more shows conclusively that Baal is a false god than the death of Christ on Calvary shows that the God and Father of Our Lord is not God. Further, if the Mount Carmel episode is conceived of as showing that it is false that Baal is God in the Christian sense, there would be no place for the concept of *conversion* in the change from believing in Baal (or in a parallel situation, Zeus) to believing in God. Yet the heathen has to be converted. If all the worshippers of Zeus or Baal had to do in order to believe in God was to acknowledge another entity of the same *kind*, but more powerful and more dreadful, there would be no place for the concept of conversion. All such a worshipper would have to have for such a change of belief would be more *evidence*—evidence that this god was a more powerful and hence more dreadful god than the god he had previously worshipped.*

To refer back to Professor Geach's comments in his paper on Aquinas, which I previously mentioned†—'Aquinas rejects the idea that "God" is necessarily used equivocally by polytheists and by monotheists: he holds that the polytheist *may* be using the word "God" in the same sense when he says his idol is God, as the missionary when he says that the idol is not God but a senseless block.' When the missionary says that the idol is not God, he cannot be taken to mean, as I think Geach takes him to mean, that it is simply false that the idol is God. For if it is simply false that the idol is God, then it is possibly true that the idol is God—which is impossible on the Christian understanding of God. It is logically impossible that an idol can be spoken of as having those formal predicates attributed to it which are attributable to God, for instance 'eternity', 'immortality'. The missionary must be construed as saying: 'If your conception of God is such that you think it true that *this* is God, you are under the gravest delusion'—and this is why the idol-worshipper is in darkness and needs converting. It is in this sense that he is *lost*. On what I take to be Professor Geach's account, not only is there no place for the concept of conversion, but none for the concept of a change from darkness into light or for the concept of Christ as being a light to lighten the gentiles. On this account there is no need for *light*—only for evidence of the same kind for the belief in a more powerful god of the same kind as the idol.‡

* This does seem to be Geach's conception. Cf. *God and the Soul*, p. 127.

† *Three Philosophers*, p. 109.

‡ Cf. also his comments in 'The Moral Law and the Law of God', in *God and the Soul*.

I thus conclude that God, in the Christian sense, cannot be spoken of as *a god* or as *one* god. From this consideration it does not follow that 'God' is a proper name: neither does it follow that 'God' cannot be sensibly prefaced by 'one' or 'many'. This latter, however, I contend can be shown. Consider the contrary view: someone says, 'To say there is only one God is to say there is only one entity which is such that it is necessarily a-spatial, eternal, ungenerated, indestructible, incorruptible and so on for all the list of formal properties which comprise God's essence; to say there are many Gods is to say there are many entities exhibiting these properties.' To which it must be replied: 'Only one *what*?'; 'Many *what*?' We have to supply a value for 'entity (entities)' here and precisely this is impossible since:

(a) Any such value must be a term which can supply a criterion of continued identity and a principle of individuation for individuals, but the introduction of such a term *would* place God in a genus, which is impossible (*Summa Theologica*, Ia,q3,a5).

(b) Any such term would render it impossible for God to be 'simple' (cf. Ia,q3).

(c) The whole formulation assumes that to say that God is necessarily a-spatial, eternal, etc. is to say that God has certain *non-formal* properties, such as a house for example has, which other individuals may have or fail to have. Whereas to say that God is necessarily a-spatial, eternal, etc. is to say that God has certain *formal* properties; such a remark is a 'grammatical' one. It shows the category to which God belongs: it does not allocate God to a class. Yet it is only on the assumption that such remarks allocate God to a class that the formulation 'one God', 'many Gods' is possible. One cannot qualify categories 'formal concepts' with number, as Wittgenstein pointed out in the *Tractatus*.*

(d) If someone is tempted to say that we can supply

* *Tractatus* 4.1272. The whole of this section is relevant here, but I shall cite only the central points for my present purposes: 'one cannot say "There are objects" as one says "There are books". Nor "There are 100 objects" or "There are N objects". And it is senseless to speak of the *number of all objects*. The same holds of the words "Complex", "Fact", "Function", "Number" etc.'

'individual' as a value for 'entity' in the above formulations, this commits the error of treating 'individual' as the name of a sort of thing, whereas to say of something that it is an individual, is to reveal the ontological status it has; it is to show the category (formal concept) to which it belongs.

Granted then that 'God' introduces a category and hence cannot sensibly be prefaced by a number, it becomes necessary to offer some explanation of how the phrase 'The one and only God' comes to have a use in Christian theology. My explanation of this is that it is a remnant of former days when the concept of God, whilst being distinguished from that of a god, was still thought to introduce a class of things even though that class only had one member, it not being realized that the requirements of necessary existence, eternity, etc., entailed that 'God' introduced a category. The justification for such a phrase being retained in contemporary Christian thought is that it might be regarded as a heuristic device through which people may be led to the truth.

Appendix C

οὐσία *and* ὑπόστασις *in the Greek Fathers*

Introduction

I introduced the above discussion on the various senses of οὐσία in Aristotle's writings and those purportedly inherited from his philosophical forerunners as forming an essential background and framework against which the Greek Fathers of the Church were writing and ultimately as a prelude to St Augustine's invocation of οὐσία. I shall not labour the reader with complex details of the various edifices which were constructed within that framework: to do so would be too vast an enterprise in the present context and in any case I do not regard myself as competent to do so. What I propose to do in this Appendix is:

(1) Produce a list of those uses of οὐσία cited by scholars in this field in which we seem to have genuine descendants of one or more uses of οὐσία as discussed above;

(2) Produce a list of and a discussion of those uses of οὐσία and its correlative ὑπόστασις cited by scholars in this field which are not genuine uses in that they present us with illegitimate concepts of οὐσία for various reasons which I shall introduce and discuss, which concepts present us with a fundamental misinterpretation of the framework in terms of which they were introduced. Where οὐσία is employed in any of the senses I have discussed above, then *vide* my above arguments there is, to say the least, no clear sense in which God can be said to be substance or spoken of in such

terms. Where οὐσία is employed in a sense which gives rise to an illegitimate and impossible concept, thus far to say that God is substance or can be spoken of in the language of substance rests on a mistake or series of mistakes.*

A. It can be contended, with certain reservations to be specified, that οὐσία is employed in one of the senses above discussed in the following writings. To indicate which sense is being employed, I list the senses as follows:

(1a) Something *not said of a subject* in the sense of a 'simple' body

(1b) Something *not said of a subject* in the sense of an individual such-and-such

(2) τὸ τί ἦν εἶναι

(3) τὸ τί ἐστι (second substance)

(4) Matter

(5) Form (εἶδος)

(6) Formal explanation (αἴτιον)

(a) Origen, *On the Proverbs*, vii, 22 (Origenes, vol. VII, c. 185)

In this passage the Wisdom of God is said to be οὐσία—οὐσία οὖσα ἡ τοῦ θεοῦ σοφία. We might say that the sense of οὐσία here is (1a), but even this is problematic, for the 'internal' properties† exhibited by the Wisdom of God are those of 'coming into existence before the ages and before creation' and of being 'eternal'—internal properties not exhibited by the 'simple' bodies but only by the body which moves in a circle—the primary body (cf. *De Caelo*, 270a1ff., 270b1ff., 270b20ff.). If someone were tempted to say that the Wisdom of God is substance in sense (1b), then he would have to say the kind or sort of thing the Wisdom of God is—yet this question is not raised in the context under discussion.

(b) Origen, *St. John*, Fragment 37

The Holy Spirit is said to be substance. Parallel difficulties

* All the Greek texts provided are taken from Migne, *Patrologia Graeca*, Paris, Garnier Fratres, 1857–1912, save as otherwise specified. 'c' refers to the column in Migne.

† In the sense introduced by Wittgenstein at *Tractatus*, 2.01231.

arise here, for whilst it might be contended that the Holy Spirit is substance in the sense of an individual, the Holy Spirit cannot clearly be said to be οὐσία in either senses 1a or 1b above. Not in 1a, for the Holy Spirit exhibits the 'internal qualities' of *ekpempsis* (proceeding from) or *ekporeusis* (cf. Gregory of Nazianzus, *Orationes* 25.16; pseudo-Cyril, *De S.S.Trinitate* 9) and τὸ αἰτιατόν 'being caused' (cf. Gregory of Nyssa, *Quod non sit*), which 'internal' qualities are not exhibited by Aristotelian simple bodies. Not in sense 1b, for the very reason that it is not specified what kind or sort of thing the Holy Spirit is: indeed there is a major problem as to whether this is specifiable.* Thus even in these potentially clear-cut cases, which are cited by scholars as unproblematic, one is met with difficulties—yet Prestige† says quite cheerfully, as if there were no problems, that the most important meaning of ὀυσία in relation to theology is that of 'individual substance'.

(c) Origen, *De Oratione*, 15.1. (Origenes, I,c.465)
'The son is different from the Father according to οὐσία and ὑποκείμενον.' Here it seems that we have senses (3) and (1b) at work respectively. Even this is unclear, however, since the notion of 'according to substance' suggests that substance in sense (3) is something the Son might *have*, as opposed to giving an account of what He is, which is its proper use. (Cf. also Wolfson's peculiar account in relation to this passage; I say the account is peculiar for he introduces the quite *un*-Aristotelian notion of 'proximate ὑποκείμενον', understanding it to be Aristotelian.)‡

(d) Origen, *Ex homiliis in Epistolam ad Hebraeos*
(Cited by Wolfson, op. cit., p. 322.) According to Wolfson, ὁμοούσιος seems to mean 'the same second substance' (3). I cannot trace this fragment and so have to accept a secondary authority.

* Cf. Chapter 5.
† Prestige, op. cit., p. 191.
‡ Wolfson, op. cit., p. 318.

(e) St Basil, *Epistle* 361 and 362 (St Basileus IV, c.1101), In these letters it may be claimed we get οὐσία used in sense (4) above. ἡμεῖς μὲν γὰρ ὑπειλήφαμεν, ὅπερ ἂν εἶναι καθ' ὑποθεσιν τοῦ πατρος οὐσία ληφῇ 'For we have supposed that whatever by way of hypostasis the substance of the Father is taken to be . . . (this must by all means be assumed as also that of the Son).' But even this is not clear, for what can constitute ὕλη here is not what would constitute ὕλη in sense (4).*

(f) St Basil, *Adversus Eunomium*, (St Basileus, I c. 588) Here St Basil is commenting on Aristotle's statement at *Categories*, 8b21 and 8a30–1 that no ὀυσία is relative in character. It is substance in sense (3) which is referred to here (cf. also Wolfson, op. cit., p. 341).

(g) St Basil, *Epistle* 362 (St Basileus, IVc. 1101, 1104) Wolfson (op. cit.) suggests that the reference to γένος here implies that Aristotle's 'second substance' is in operation when Apollinarius says: οὐσία μία οὐκ ἀριθμῳ μόνον λεγεται . . . ἀλλὰ καὶ ἰδιῶς ἀνθρώπων δύο καὶ ἄλλου, ὁτουοῦν τῶν κατὰ γένος ἑνιʒομένων '(Things) are not only said to be one substance in number (in this way) . . . but also in a special sense as when two men or anything else are subsumed under a class'. All is not clear however, since Apollinarius continues: ὥστε ταύτῃ γέ καὶ δύο καὶ πλείονα ταὐτον εἶναι κατὰ τὴν ὀυσίαν . . .

'So that in this sense both two and more are said to be the same according to substance', which suggests that being an individual is separate from being a substance, which is certainly not Aristotle's doctrine. (Cf. also: ταύτῃ γέ τοι καὶ ἓν εἶναι γένος ὑπερκείμενον, ἢ μιάν ὕλην ὑπο κειμένην . . .)

'(In this way it will be thought that) there is one underlying γένος, or one underlying material' (in the case of the Father and the Son).'

(h) Origen, *In Joan.* X. 21 (Origenes, IVc.376) In this passage Origen is criticizing those who deny any

* What constitutes ὕλη here is φῶς νοητόν, αἴδιον, ἀγεννητον 'mental light, eternal unbegotten'. 'Matter' in sense (4) cannot taken on such predicates as 'eternal' and 'unbegotten' (cf. *De Caelo*, III, 6).

real distinction between the members of the Trinity; he says that the Father and the Son are not only one in οὐσία but also in ὑποκείμενον. The use of 'one' in ὑποκείμενον is queer, but the context certainly suggests that by οὐσία is meant (3) above, though *which* second substance is left unspecified.

(i) St John of Damascus, *De Fide Orthodoxa*, I.8. (St John of Damascus, I c.828)
In this passage it is said that, whilst Peter is judged to be distinct from Paul (Πράγματι γὰρ ὁ Πετρος τοῦ Παύλου κεχωρίσμενος θεωρεῖται . .), they are judged to have a common nature and to have the same nature and to be one in thought and speech ('Η δέ κοινότῆς καὶ ἡ συνάφεια καὶ τὸ ἓν λογῳ καὶ ἐπινοίᾳ θεωρεῖται . . .). . . for each of them is a rational and a mortal animal. In the light of this we might think that the sense of 'nature', which is synonymous with οὐσία here, is substance in the sense of (3) above. This is not clear when we take the following sentence, which occurs a little later, into consideration: Αὕτη οὖν ἡ κοινή φύσις τῳ λογῳ ἐστι θεωρητῆ. . . . 'It is, then, by reason that the common nature is observed', for this use of κοινὴ φύσις suggests the doctrine that Peter and Paul are individuals *period* which partake of a common nature in thought, so that we have not a genuine occurrence of second substance after all, for on Aristotle's account individuals do not 'partake in' second substances, and Aristotle has no such doctrine of simple individuals. This fear is borne out by a later passage (*De Fide Ortho.*, III, 4. 997a ff.).* The emphasis here that οὐσία signifies the common form of the similar hypostases—and we have as examples 'God' and 'man'—and that the hypostases are ἄτομα which are the bearers of the names

* ὅτι μὲν οὖν ἕτερόν ἐστιν οὐσία, ἕτερου ὑπόστασις πλειστακις εἰρήκαμεν και ὅτι ἡ μὲν οὐσία, τὸ κοινὸν και περιεκτικον εἶδος τῶν ὁμοειδῶν ὑποστασεων σήμαινει, οἷον Θεος, ἄνθρωπος, ἡ δὲ ὑποστασις, ἄτομον δῆλοΐ, ἤτοι Πατέρα, Υἱὸν . . . Παυλον (Now we have often said already that 'essence' is one thing and that 'hypostasis' is another and that 'essence' signifies the common and generic form of 'hypostases' of the same kind, such as 'God', 'man', whilst 'hypostasis' indicates the individual, viz., Father, Son . . . Paul).

'Father', 'Paul', etc. strongly suggests that οὐσία is treated as a common *characteristic* or form of many individuals (unspecified) which are the bearers of proper names, and hence that we have not an occurrence of οὐσία in the sense of second substance.

I have mentioned the above passages as passages in which one or more of the senses of 'substance' introduced in the last chapter might be thought to have application; but as we have seen, strong reservations have to be made and even from these *prima facie* cases doubt can be cast on Prestige's assertion above.

B. That all is not clear concerning οὐσία and the correlative notion of ὑπόστασις in the writings of the Greek Fathers is indicated by passages which I now cite from Dr Prestige's classic *God in Patristic Thought.*

> (1) To the mind of the Fathers, down to the time at which the terminology became fixed and technical, the practical meaning of these terms (ousia and hypostasis) was substantially identical. They both indicate, to take the inevitable physical metaphor, the particular slab of material stuff which constitutes a given object and neither term is used in a generic sense. (p. 168.)

> (2) The sense of hypostatis to which we shall now turn, the emphasis lay not on the content, but on the externally concrete independence, objectivity . . . in relation to other subjects. Thus when the doctrine of the Trinity finally came to be formulated as one ousia in three hypostases, it implied that God, regarded from the point of view of internal analysis, is one object, but from the point of view of external presentation three objects. (pp. 168–9.)

As regards (1), it must be noted that, if 'hypostasis' is going to represent at any stage what Aristotle meant by ὑποεκείμενον, then at least at the early stage alluded to by Prestige, it is not clear that 'hypostasis' in the use of the Fathers is Aristotle's use of ὑποκείμενον, for Aristotle does *not* solely mean by ὑποκείμενον 'the particular slab of material stuff which constitutes an object', if he means this at all. Agreed, he does sometimes mean 'this particular lump of gold' or, in general, this particular lump of matter (cf. *Physics*, 190b24; 191a3), but (a) this is not the sole candidate for ὑποκείμενον—a particular man might be (cf.

Physics, 190b24; 191a3)—and (b) although, for instance, 'this lump of gold' is ὑποκείμενον, such a lump of gold does not *constitute* the statue. The statue is *of* gold, and is made out of a particular lump of gold which can be independently identified, but such a lump of gold does not constitute the statue, as can be seen by the fact that Aristotle will not allow a matter term like 'gold' to enter into the λόγος of τὸ τί ἦν εἶναι of *x*, where *x* is an artefact (cf. *Metaphysics*, 1043b1), and this is surely correct, for it is an accident of any given statue that it is made of gold. In the light of this it is difficult to see how Wolfson* can simply claim that hypostasis and ὑποκείμενον are equivalent.

The real trouble lies in the second passage I have cited from Prestige. It is difficult to follow his talk of 'internal analysis' and 'external presentation'. One wants to ask: 'Why contrast analysis and presentation?': 'How does one set about producing an "internal analysis"?' Some account must be attempted and I construe the point Prestige is making as follows. Consider the propositions:

'This (lump of) gold is the statue of Joan of Arc.'

'This (piece of) silver is a cigarette box.'

In such propositions the expressions 'This (lump of) gold', 'This (piece of) silver' are logically analysable into two elements, 'This' and 'gold', 'This' and 'silver' respectively; we have not one unanalysable element in each case. On this construction 'gold' in the expression 'This (lump of) gold' refers to the *content* of what is referred to by the complete expression, and the demonstrative here refers to the *particularity* of what is referred to, as opposed to the content. Hence we get Prestige's statement '. . . the emphasis lay not on the content, but on the externally concrete independence . . .'

This is an impossible construction of such phrases. They are not so logically analysable into two elements such that one can introduce a dichotomy between 'content' and 'externally concrete independence'. That such an analysis is possible supposes that it is possible for a demonstrative to refer to an individual without any completing predicate being

* Wolfson, op. cit., p. 319.

attached to the demonstrative. This is not possible. Demonstratives of themselves are incomplete expressions: they are not names. One cannot ask what is referred to by a demonstrative on a given occasion, for nothing *can* be; they do not contain the means whereby identification of an individual could be secured. For any use of a demonstrative which has in fact no completion we must always either (i) already know what the implicit completion is or (ii) be able to provide a completion which answers the question 'This (That) *what*?' (Aristotle's τί ἐστι question). Unless such a completion is supplied there is no possibility of identification being made by a hearer and no possibility of reference being made by a speaker. As this is so, the phrase 'This (lump of) gold' is *not* logically analysable into two elements as the above construction supposes. This can also be shown from a consideration of the second supposed element here, 'gold', 'silver'; for as occurring in the phrase 'This (lump of) gold', (for example), 'gold' is incomplete in sense—it has the form '— gold'; it occurs here as a predicate and not as the name of some metal. To produce an analysis of the phrase 'This (lump of) gold' in terms of two distinct elements, one would have to treat it as a complex of two names, which would be a perversion of the function of such a phrase, namely to refer to a given lump of gold.

We may also consider a further passage from Prestige which shows that he is misguided in his discussion. He says at the bottom of p. 168 (op. cit): '*Ousia* means a single object of which the individuality is disclosed by the means of internal analysis . . .' Now it *could be* that what he has in mind is that *ousia* can mean an individual denoted by a phrase such as 'This man' in a given use, and if this *is* what is being put forward there is nothing to object to. But to introduce his talk of 'internal analysis' and 'individuality', Prestige must think that the phrase 'This man' is a logically complex phrase divisible into two distinct elements, which is misguided for the reasons given above.

Thus the situation at this point is that if the concept of οὐσία or one concept of οὐσία as introduced by the Greek

Fathers is dependent upon the distinction between *content* and *externally concrete independence*, such that by οὐσία is meant 'content', such a concept of substance is illegitimate. From what Prestige has to say it looks very much as if the concept of ὑπόστασις as opposed to ὑποκείμενον, was introduced to cover what he calls 'externally concrete independence' and that οὐσία then covered 'content': if this is so, then both 'hypostasis' and 'ousia' in this use must be rejected as being illegitimately introduced as the result of an impossible dichotomy. What support there is for this impression will be investigated later.

That there is an illegitimate dichotomy present in the writings of the Greek Fathers is also suggested by the writings of Professor C. C. J. Webb on the subject. Webb's comments (*God and Personality*, pp. 40–3) reveal a misunderstanding of Aristotle and, if he is correct in his interpretation, the Greek Fathers likewise misunderstood Aristotle. Commenting on Aristotle's οὐσία, Webb says '*Ousia* meant the characteristic nature of a thing' (op. cit., p. 40). On this view a second substance term indicates, not *what* a thing is, but 'the characteristic nature' of a thing, hence a second substance term gives us a *description* of something already referred to by a demonstrative—a view which I have rejected in my last chapter; and in the light of what I have said above, it is impossible for demonstratives to refer on their own accord. Hence *this* concept of *ousia* must be rejected as being based on an impossible dichotomy. That there is such an illegitimate and impossible dichotomy in Webb's thought, and by implication that of the Fathers, can be seen by further quotations from Webb:

> Thus it is that ὑπόστασις came into use as a philosophical term, often equivalent to οὐσία which for Aristotle is most properly used of a concrete individual of a certain kind: but of Aristotle's two notes of real being, its intelligible character and its concrete independence, emphasising the latter as *ousia* emphasised the former (op. cit., pp. 41–2).

From this one can glean that by *ousia* is meant 'the intelligible character of an individual' such that a second substance term imposes an intelligible character on an individual referred to by a demonstrative; this is Mackinnon's position referred to earlier (p. 55), and, as I have argued, is impossible to maintain. And again '*Ousia* . . . was obviously more readily applicable to something which was shared by several concrete actualities but was not itself actual apart or outside them' (op. cit., p. 43). This again suggests the impossible dichotomy between (i) 'concrete actualities', that is entities denoted by demonstratives and (ii) 'characteristics' *shared* by such concrete actualities. Aristotle's second substances (rightly) are not 'characteristics'; nor can they be spoken of as being 'shared by': Aristotle gets nowhere near positing 'Forms' which might be 'shared in' by particulars; on the contrary he steers very clear of any such notion.

Kelly* is no help in easing the confusion which seems to prevail in this area. He says (op. cit., p. 253): 'Every alert reader must have noticed, and been astonished by, the extent to which theological divisions at this time were created and kept alive by the use of different and confusing theological terms', but he makes no attempt to relieve the confusion, for he continues:

> Thus the formula 'three hypostases' hitherto suspect to the Nicenes because it sounded to their ears painfully like 'three *ousiai*' i.e. three divine beings, was pronounced legitimate provided it did not carry the Arian connotation of 'utterly distinct, alien hypostases, different from each other' in other words 'three principles or three Gods' but merely expressed the separate subsistence of the three persons in the consubstantial Triad (pp. 253–4).

Kelly sets out what Origen, Eusebius, Hilary, etc. *said*, but offers no explanation or exposition (pp. 255–7).

B.1 What evidence have we that in at least some writings on οὐσία this notion is illegitimate in that it supposes the impossible model of 'pure' particulars (individuals) on the one hand and 'characteristics' on the other?: or, to use the language of Prestige, a model of 'external concrete independence' on the one hand and 'content' on the other, οὐσία being construed as 'characteristic' or 'content' respectively? I submit that the following passages present us with such evidence.

* *Early Christian Doctrines.*

(a) Eusebius, *De Ecclesiastica Theologica*, 2.23, 1. (Eusebius, VI 960d, 961)
Eusebius is here expressing orthodox doctrine; he says that the Church of God does not profess two gods, or two 'unbegottens' or two substances, but one principle (ἀρχή) and one god. He then continues: τὸν αὐτὸν Πατερα διδάσκουσα εἶναι τοῦ μονογενους καὶ ἀγαπητοῦ Υἱοῦ, ὡσαυτως δὲ και μίαν εἰκόνα τοῦ θεοῦ τοῦ ἀοράτου, τὴν αὐτην οὐσιαν τῷ μονογενεῖ και ἀγαπητῳ Υἱῷ αὐτοῦ. Here Eusebius seems to be asserting that the same substance, namely the substance of the invisible god, is present in both the Father and the Son; that is, that these two individuals *share* the same substance and this is why it is taught that the Father and the Son are the same so that we have one form (image) of the invisible god. In that the same substance can be said to be *present in* the two individuals, the Father and the Son, and in that they can be said to *share in* the same substance, οὐσία here is treated as something *separate from* individuals, a *characteristic* of individuals, and thus we are faced with the impossible dichotomy discussed above. Indeed Prestige in a gloss on this passage says: 'the whole ousia of the Father became by derivation the whole ousia of the Son, according to the old metaphor, as the radiance is derived from the light' (op. cit., p. 194).* Granted this gloss, talk of 'the whole ousia of the Father' certainly implies that the ousia of *x* is something which attaches to *x*, is a characteristic of *x*, which I have argued is radically misguided. Further, granted Prestige's gloss, *ousia* here is treated as *a* substance; only on this assumption can one introduce 'the whole'.

(b) Athanasius, *Ad Epictum*, 4 c (Athanasius IIc.1056)
Here Athanasius says that the Son was born out of the *ousia* of the Father and out of the body of Mary (. . . και τουτου μεν ἐκ τῆς οὐσιας του Πατρος, το δέ σωμα ἐκ Μαριας). That the Son can be said to be born *out of* the *ousia* of the Father

* Kelly, op. cit., p. 226, does not give this gloss, but says that Eusebius is of the view that the Son is only God as the image of the one true God. I do not see how he gets this from the above cited passage.

implies that the *ousia* of the Father is something of the Father *possesses*, as opposed to what He *is*.

(c) Athanasius, *De Synodis*, 34 (Athanasius, IIc.753)

> If when in naming the Father or in using the word 'God' one does not mean substance nor think of him who is as he is according to substance but according to something else relative to him . . . then one should not write that the Son is out of the Father, but that he is out of what is related to the Father or what is in the Father.*

Here the use of 'ousia' implies that God's ousia is something God, albeit 'essentially', *has*, as witness the condition of saying that 'the Son is out of the Father'; 'being God' is something the Father 'essentially' possesses—as opposed to what He does not 'essentially' possess, such as what is related to Him or what is 'in' Him. So once again we are faced with the doctrine that τὸ τί ἐστι of an individual or οὐσία of an individual is a *characteristic* of that individual. It does not help matters to say with Prestige (op. cit., p. 195) that the Father's ousia is the Father himself, for this way of speaking necessarily implies that there is some further identifiable entity which is the Father himself and with which the ousia of the Father is identical: but the specification of this further entity is impossible, since the only way in which it *could* be specified is by specifying the ousia of the Father with which it is asserted to be identical! If we follow Prestige and say that the point of St Athanasius's argument is that the Father's ousia is the Father himself, St Athanasius is still committed to an impossible dichotomy of individual/ousia which he tries to get out of if we construct his argument *à la* Prestige. He cannot so get out of the dichotomy, since the assertion that the Father's ousia is the Father himself is certainly nonsensical both for the consideration mentioned above and on the following consideration—How can 'What-it-is-to-be *x*' (the ousia of *x*), where *x* is what is named by a value of an individual variable, say Socrates, *be* the individual named by the name Socrates?

* Εἰ μὲν οὖν τον Πατερα ὀνομαζοντες, ἢ το "θεὸς" ὀνομα λεγοντες, οὐκ οὐσιαν σημαινετε, οὐδε αὐτον τον ὀντα, ὅπερ ἐστι κατ'ουσιαν, νοεῖτε, ἀλλα ἑτερόν τι περὶ αὐτον . . . ἔδει μὴ γραφειν ὑμας ἐκ τοῦ Πατρος τον Υἱον, ἀλλ'ἐκ των περι αὐτον ἢ τῶν ἐν αὐτῳ.

(d) St Basil, *Epistle* 236.6B (St Basileus, IVc.884)
'Substance and hypostasis bear the same relation of common to particular as animal does to the particular man' (Οὐσία δέ και ὑπόστασις ταὐτόν ἔχει τὴν διαφοράν, ἣν ἔχει το κοινὸν πρὸς τὸ καθ' ἕκαστον. Οἷον ὡς ἔχει τό ȝῶον πρός τον δεῖνα ἄνθρωπον). This passage clearly treats ousia as something which is common to a number of individuals; in this way it is something a number of individuals can be said to *share in* or *have* and thus we get an impossible dichotomy set up. Contrary to the position expressed here, the particular men Plato, Plutarch, Socrates, for example, do not have 'animal' in common: for them *to be* animals is *not* for them to possess something, namely the characteristic of animality. That there is an impossible dichotomy at work in St Basil's thought here can also be seen in the passage: 'Χρὴ οὖν τῳ κοινῷ τό ἰδιάȝον προστιθέντας, οὕτω τὴν πίστην ὁμολογεῖν' (We must therefore add the particular to the common and so confess the faith).

(e) St Basil, *Epistle* 214.4 (St Basileus, IVc.789)
'But if we are to state briefly our own view, we shall reply as follows—*ousia* bears the same relation to hypostasis as the common bears to the particular'.* The same comments apply here as to the above passage, and one must further note that on this view (i) *ousia* is a mere characteristic of a hypostasis; (ii) hypostasis is *itself* regarded as a particular thing; (iii) *ousia* is *itself* regarded as a type of characteristic.†

(f) St Basil, *Adversus Eunomium*, 1.19 (St Basileus, Ic.534)
'If therefore that which substance has in common is thus said to be thought of as being that which is out of an antecedent matter divided up and distributed in some way . . .' (Εἰ μεν οὖν το κοινόν τῆς οὐσίας οὕτω νοήσας εἶπεν, ὡς ἐξ ὕλης προυπαρχούσης διανομήν τινα και καταδιαρεσιν) I construe 'substance' here as 'individuals', for I do not see how the Greek

* εἰ δέ δεί και ἡμας τὸ δοκοῦν ἡμιν ἐν βραχει εἰπεῖν, εκεῖνο ἐρουμεν, ὅτι ὃν ἔχει λόγον τὸ κοινόν πρός τό ἴδιον, τοῦτον ἔχει ἡ οὐσία πρός τὴν ὑπόστασιν.

† Cf. also the next sentence but one: 'οὕτω κάκεῖ ὁ μεν τῆς οὐσιάς λόγος κοινός, οἷον ἡ ἀγαθοτης, ἡ θεότης, ἤ εἴ τι ἄλλο νοοῖτο'. (So even here the concept of *ousia* is something which is common, like 'goodness', 'divinity', or any other abstract concept.)

can be construed otherwise. So taking it, we are once again faced with the impossible dichotomy of individuals and what they have in common, such that what an individual *is* is a characteristic of that individual, even though what such individuals have in common is not to be thought of as an antecedent matter divided up and distributed among such individuals. Indeed, St Basil later says that it is as great a blasphemy to say that what the three 'persons' of the Trinity have in common is to be thought of as an antecedent matter divided up in some way as it is to say that they are unequal. The reason for this, I suggest, is that God cannot exist in separation from the persons of the Trinity. That is, for God to exist is for the function (__is God) to be true when the names of the persons of the Trinity are arguments. However, in so far as the persons of the Trinity are each said *to be* God, then God *cannot* be regarded as some characteristic they *have* in common, any more than in so far as Plato, Aristotle, Socrates are said *to be* men, can they be regarded as having the 'characteristic' ***man*** in common.

(g) St Basil, *Adversus Eunomium*, 2.4 (St Basileus, Ic.577)
'Again . . . the fact that the names differ does not imply any necessary variation in substance: Peter and Paul have different names . . . but there is one substance of all mankind' (και τοι . . . ὅτι ὧν τα ὀνοματα ἐστι διάφορα τούτων παρηλλάχθαι καὶ τὰς οὐσιας ἀναγκη: Πέτρου γὰρ και Παύλου . . . οὐσια δέ πὰντων μία). Here again we have a dichotomy set up between individuals which are the bearers of different proper names and *ousia* construed as a characteristic which such individuals have in common.

(h) Gregory of Nazianzus, *Orationes*, 42.15. (Gregory of Nazianzus, IIc.476)
'There is one nature (God) in the three individuals (the persons of the Trinity)' (φυσις δέ τοις τρισὶ μία, θεος).

Here too we have the 'individual/nature', 'individual/substance' dichotomy. The nature or substance of something is thought to be *in* that thing, as opposed to being what that thing *is*.

I shall not cite any more passages in detail as evidence to support the above thesis, but would refer the reader to the following as further evidence:

St Irenaeus, *Haer.*, 5.36.1. (Migne, St Irenaeus 1221–2)
St Basil, *Epistle* 189.6. (by Gregory of Nyssa) (Migne, St Basileus IV 692)
St Basil, *Epistle* 38.8. (Migne, St Basileus IV c.336) (cf. Kelly, op. cit., p. 264)
St Athanasius, *De Synodis*, 359 (as mentioned by Kelly, op. cit., p. 253)
Didymus, *De Trinitate*, 1.16
St Athanasius, *De Synodis*, 53,B,C. (Migne, St Athanasius IIc, 788) (This case is somewhat problematic)

B.2 We have an illegitimate concept of οὐσία present in the writings of some of the Greek Fathers as explained above, but there are other grounds on which their use of 'substance' is suspicious. For example, in some uses οὐσια, which is a category, is treated as an ordinary predicate, for example Eusebius, *Eccles. Theol.* 2, 23.1 discussed in B.1a above for here *ousia* is treated as *a* substance which can be ***shared in***; Athanasius, *Ad Epict.*, 4 (B.1b above) where the substance of the Father is treated as *a* substance, like the body of Mary; cf. also St Basil, *Epistle* 214.4 (B.1e). Again, in other uses to talk of *ousia* is to talk of an ultimate subject of predication which cannot itself be characterized such a use of *ousia* seems to be present at St Athanasius, *De Incarnatione*, 18. 'Would not anyone who saw the substance of the water transformed into wine, understand that he who did it was the lord and maker of the substance of the entirety of waters?' —that is the lord and maker of that of which all (separate) waters were predicated.*

C.1 I now turn to the correlative notion of ὑπόστασις. It is my contention that in at least some uses of this term we have an illegitimate notion on our hands, since in the cases cited below by ὑπόστασις is meant 'simple individual' and not 'individual of a certain sort or kind'. In these cases

* τίς δέ, ἰδών και τὴν ὑδατων ἀλλασσομενην οὐσιαν, και εἰς ὀἶνον μεταβαλοῦσαν οὐκ ἐννοει τὸν τουτο ποιήσαντα κυριον εἶναι κατα κτίστην τῆς τῶν ὁλων ὑδατων οὐσιας.

ὑπόστασις corresponds to Prestige's 'external concrete independence' and supposes the impossible model discussed above. I shall only discuss those cases cited by scholars which have not been previously mentioned or discussed under the treatment of *ousia*, where I have contended that such a notion is illegitimate.

(a) St Gregory of Nyssa, *Non Tres Dei* (Gregory of Nyssa, IIc 120)

Thus there are many who have shared in the nature—many disciples, apostles or martyrs, but the man in all of them is one. For, as has been said, the term 'man' does not belong to the nature of the individual as such, but to that which is common. (Ὥστε πολλοὺς μὲν εἶναι τοὺς μετασχηκότας τῆς φύσεως, φέρε εἰπεῖν μαθήτας, ἢ ἀποστόλους ἢματυρας, ἕνα δὲ ἐν πασι τον ἄνθρωπον. Ἐπείπερ, καθὼς εἴρηται, οὐχί τοῦ καθ' ἕκαστου, ἀλλὰ τοῦ κοινοῦ τῆς φυσεὼς ἐστιν ὁ ἄνθρωπος.)

In this passage τὸ καθ' ἕκαστον goes proxy for ὑπόστασις, and by the former is meant an individual which takes on the characteristics of being a man and accidentally the characteristics of being for example a martyr. It is clear from this passage that St Gregory subscribes to the false doctrine that there is no nominal essence of individuals.* Cf. also the earlier passage at Migne (op. cit.) 117, beginning τί δήποτε τοίνυν ἐν τῇ καθ'ἡμας συνηθείᾳ καθ' ἕνα τοὺς ἐν τῇ φύσει . . . ('What then is the reason that when we count one by one those who are exhibited to us in one nature, we ordinarily name them in the plural and speak of them as "so many men" instead of calling them all one?'). Further, if we were to accept Prestige's account of *Non Tres Dei* (Migne, 125c–d): 'In men each individual acts separately, so that it is proper to regard them as many' (Prestige, op. cit., p. 260) we should have further grist for this particular mill, but Prestige's translation is open to question.

(b) Origen, *Contra Celsum*, VIII. 12 (Origenes, Ic 1533)

'The Father of truth and the Son, who is truth, are two facts

* Cf. P. T. Geach, *Reference and Generality*, pp. 43–4.

in hypostasis' (θρησκεύομεν οὖν) τον Πατέρα τῆς ἀληθείας και τον Ὑιον τὴν ἀλήθειαν ὄντα δυό τῇ ὑποστασει πράγματα).

I construe this as saying that the Father and the Son are two entities as regards hypostasis, that is individuality, namely two individuals *period*.

(c) Origen, *De Principis*, 1.2.
'The pre-existent Christ is a hypostasis.'* Wolfson (op. cit., p. 320) gives this as an example of ὑπόστασις in the sense of 'individual existence'.

(d) Origen, *In Joan.*, X. 21 (Origenes, IVc376)
Οἷον τὸ ἐκ τούτων παρίσταθσαι μὴ διαφερειν τῳ ἀριθμῷ τον Ὑιον τοῦ Πατρος, ἀλλ' ἕν, οὐ μόνον οὐσιᾳ ἀλλα και ὑποκείμενῳ τυγχανοντας ἀμφετερους, κατα τινας ἐπινοίας διαφορους, οὐ κατα ὑποστασιν λεγεσθαι Πατερα και Ὑιον . . .

Here Origen is arguing that those who consider the Father and the Son as not numerically distinct, but *one* not only in substance but also in ὑποκείμενον, must also deny that they are distinct κατα ὑπόστασιν. So we have a distinction in operation between (i) ὑποκείμενον and (ii) ὑπόστασις and the only way I can construe this is as follows:

(a) distinct according to *ousia* means that the Father and the Son are two individuals of different sorts or kinds.

(b) distinct according to ὑποκείμενον means that the Father and Son are distinct individuals of the *same* sort or kind.

(c) distinct according to ὑπόστασις means that the Father and the Son are distinct individuals *period*, hence we have an illegitimate notion on our hands.

(e) St Cyril of Jerusalem, *Catechesis*, VII 5b (St Cyrillus, c. 609)
'God enjoyed the title of "Father" and the existence of his Son before all hypostasis and before sensation and before time. . .' 'the relevant Greek reads: ἀλλὰ πρὸ πάσης ὑπόστασεως

* Origenes, *De Principiis*, in *Die griechischen christlichen Schriftsteller der ersten drei Jahrunderte*, ed. Paul Koetshau, 'Origenes', vol. V, Leipzig, J. C. Hinrich'sche Buchhandlung, 1913.

καὶ πρὸ πάσης αἰσθήσεως, πρὸ χρόνων ...) Here ὑπόστασις naturally interprets as 'all individual things *period*' as opposed to 'all kinds of thing'.

(f) St Basil, *Epistle*, 38.5 (St Basileus, IV c. 336)
A problematic and interesting case is presented here.

> Faith teaches us to understand that which is separated in hypostasis but united in substance. Since therefore reason has distinguished an element common to the 'hypostases of' the Holy Trinity as well as an element peculiar to each, what reason shows is common relates to the substance and the hypostasis signifies the individuality of each member of the Trinity.*

Whilst it can be maintained that what ὑπόστασις signifies is that which makes each member of the Trinity an individual —namely a 'pure individuality', which is what is signified by a proper name—which makes nonsense of the notion of ὑπόστασις, another interpretation of ὑπόστασις is certainly possible here, namely that it signifies the uniquely differentiating nature of each individual. This interpretation is suggested by an earlier passage in the letter cited (Migne, c. 328): 'This then is our statement of the matter—that which is specifically referred to is an hypostasis ... (for example) if you say "Paul" you have indicated by that name the nature subsisting in the individual object' (τουτο ... πράγματι ὑφεστῶσαν τὴν φύσιν). But even on this account ὑπόστασις cannot retain its status, for there cannot be such uniquely individuating or differentiating 'natures'. Even if it can be maintained that the meaning of a proper name was the set of definite descriptions which uniquely distinguished the bearer of such a proper name from other members of the same class, such a set of definite descriptions cannot constitute the statement of a nature, for they are all definite descriptions of something or other—for instance some *man*, which is itself the nature. To be correct, we should rewrite St Basil's point to read: ' "Paul" does not

* '... ἡ πίστις και το κεχωρισμένον ἐν ὑποστάσει, και τὸ συνημένον ἐν τῇ οὐσίᾳ διδάσχουσα. Επει οὖν τό μέν τι κοινὸν ἐν τη ἁγίᾳ τριάδῖ, το δἓ ἰδιάȝον ὁ λόγος ἐνεθεωρησεν, ὁ μεν τῆς κοινοτητος λόγος εἰς τῆν ὀυσιαν ἀναγεται, ἡ δέ ὑπόστασις τό ἰδιάȝον ἐκαστου σημειον ἐστιν.'

indicate the nature subsisting in an individual object, but some individual object uniquely differentiated.' In short, on this account of ὑπόστασις as an 'individuating nature', it is only possible for this concept to be sensibly introduced if it is possible to introduce the notion of an individuating element which is *not* the individuating element of something or other, but the notion of 'individuating element' necessarily implies 'individuating element of something or other'.

Also in support of the above contention I should cite the following passages discussed in B.1 above: St Basil, *Epistle*, 236:6; *Adversus Eun.*, 1.19.

C.2 We also have an illegitimate concept of ὑπόστασις on our hands in cases where this term is intended to designate an 'underlying substrate', a necessarily unspecifiable subject of predication which is the subject of any and every predication. This concept can be found in the following writings:

(a) Eusebius, *De Laudibus Constantini* 1.5. (Eusebius II c.1333–40)
In this passage Eusebius uses the phrase 'before the entire hypostasis of visible objects', the 'hypostasis of a visible object' in this context referring to that ultimate element of which the name of any visible object is predicated, such element itself being unspecifiable (cf. also Prestige, op. cit., p. 171).

(b) Philo, *De Somniis*, I. 188
'The intelligible world has an hypostasis though it is only discernible by the intellect' (ὁ δέ νοητῆς ὑποστασεως κοσμος ἄνευ ἡστινοσουν σχημάτων ὄψεως, μόνης δὲ διὰ τῆς ἀρχετύπου ἰδέας . . .)* (cf. also Philo, ibid., 1.32).

(c) Philo, *De Aeternitate Mundi*, 17, 87 (Wendland, op. cit., vol. IV, p. 100)
At this passage Philo says that coal and all the elements would have no hypostasis (μηδὲν ὑφεστάναι) if they were

* *Philonis Alexandrini Opera*, vol. III, Berlin, Paulus Wendland, 1898, p. 245.

assumed to be destructible; 'hypostasis' here indicates that indestructible element of which 'coal', etc. are predicated, such element itself being unspecifiable.

Cf. also Hesychius of Jerusalem, *In Psalmo*, CV. 16.

C.3 We also have an illegitimate introduction of ὑπόστασις in the following cases:

(a) St. Cyril of Alexandria, *Commentary on St John*, 859E. (St Cyril Alexandrini, vol. VII, c 337).
'The godhead is one substance truly and by nature in three intelligible hypostases' (Μιᾶς δέ οὐσίας, τοῦτ' ἐστι, τῆς ἀληθοῦς και κατα φυσιν θεότητος ἐν τρισίν ὑποστασει νοουμένης).

My objection to 'hypostasis' here is that there is no mention of the *sort* of which we have three hypostases; 'hypostasis' here must mean 'intelligible individual *period*'.

(b) St Cyril of Alexandria, *De Trinitate*, 1, 408 c. (St Cyril, vol. VIII c 697)
'The Son is his own hypostasis' ((The Son) ... ἐν ἰδίᾳ δὲ ὢν ὑποστασει). Even taking 'hypostasis' to mean 'individuality' it is impossible for a given individual *to be* its own individuality.

I also mention the following passages in which the use of ὑπόστασις is suspicious and problematic:

(c) St Gregory of Nazianzus, *Orationes*, 31. 6 (St Greg. Naz., IIc149)

(d) St Methodius, *De Resurrectione*, 3, 6. 4.*

C.4 Special consideration needs to be given to the notion of οὐσία ὑποστατή as introduced by St Hippolytus. At *Refutatio*, 7, 18, 1–2, he writes:*

> Ἐπειδὴ ⟨δέ⟩ ἐστιν ἡ οὐσία τριχῇ ⟨διῃρημένη⟩, ὡς ἔφην, γένος, εἶδος ἄτομον, καὶ ἐθέμεθα το γένος εἶναι ζῷον, τον δέ ἄνθρωπον εἶδος τῶν πολλων ζῴων ἤδη κεχωρισμένον, ⟨ἔτι⟩ συνκεχυμένον

* *Die griechischen christlichen Schriftsteller der ersten drei Jahrunderte*, ed. Paul Koetshau, 'Methodius', p. 397.

* *Hippolytus Werke*, Dritten Band, Wendland, Leipzig, 1916, p. 192.

δὲ ὅμως ἔτι και μήπω μεμορφωμένον εἰς εἶδος οὐσιας ὑποστατης, οναματὶ μορφωσας τὸν ἀπό τοῦ γενονς ληφθέντα ἄνθρωπον ὀναμαȝω Σωκρατην ἤ Διογένην ἤ τι των πολλων ὀναματων ἐν, και ἐπειδαν ὀναματι καταλαβω τὸν ἀνθρωπον εἶδος γενους γεγενημένον ἄτομον καλῶ τῆν τοιαυτην οὐσιαν . . . . . ταυτην 'Αριστοτέλης πρωτως και μάλιστα και κυριωτατα (οὐσιαν καλεῖ) . . . *

Here Hippolytus says that we may distinguish substance under three divisions, as the heretic has said—genus, species, and individual. 'Animal' is an example of a genus, 'man' of species. 'Man', whilst distinguished from all other types of animal, but still as yet unindividualized, is not yet transferred into οὐσια ὑποστατή. From what he goes on to say (ὀναματι . . . οὐσιαν) an οὐσία ὑποστατή is a particular man called by a proper name, and such an entity Hippolytus calls an ἄτομον, claiming that this is what Aristotle primarily and most importantly meant by οὐσία. From this, two accounts of ὑπόστασις are derivable, both of which reveal it to be an illegitimate notion. On the first account, since what St Hippolytus means by ἄτομον is (for example) the particular man and οὐσία ὑποστατή is an ἄτομον, then what is meant by ὑπόστασις is the individual *without* the οὐσία, such that it is only a contingency that an individual is an individual of a certain kind or sort. It is perfectly correct for Hippolytus to maintain that οὐσία at least in the *Categories* primarily meant ἄτομον, but Aristotle never introduces the notion of οὐσία ὑποστατή, neither could he, granted his thesis that to be is (primarily) to be of a certain sort or kind. On the second account it could be argued that by ὑπόστασις here is meant 'what makes an individual *x* the individual *x* it is'. But on this account too the notion is illegitimate—for here it means an individualizing element which is *not* the

* 'Since the threefold "essence" is, as he says, genus, species and individual (atom), and we have granted "animal" to be genus and "man" to be species already differentiated from the multitude of animals, but at the same time commingled with them and not yet transformed into a species of particular beings, I, when I give the form to the man taken apart from the genus, call him by the name of Socrates or of Diogenes, or of any one of the many names that there are, and when I (thus) restrict with a name the man who from genus has become species, I call such a being an individual . . . and this is what Aristotle primarily, most importantly, and properly called "substance" . . . '

individualizing element of something or other. (For a parallel case on this interpretation cf. C.1 (f) above.) The only account which can be offered of οὐσία ὑποστατή which would not render it illegitimate on the above grounds would be one in which it was to be treated as a complete and unanalysable notion, not interpretable as οὐσία plus ὑπόστασις. Even on such an account the notion is open to objection, for it carries with it the implication that an individual is itself to be regarded as a sub-species of the species to which it belongs, such that no distinction can be made between class membership and class inclusion and a proper name is itself treatable as a kind of predicate. However, such an account would at least not lay Hippolytus open to the charge of introducing an illegitimate and impossible notion, and it is with the possibility of this account in mind that I have given separate consideration to St Hippolytus's notion.

C.5 That scholars in this field are also open to the charge of perpetrating an unintelligible notion of ὑπόστασις can be seen as follows. Prestige (op. cit., pp. 177–8) says: 'Instances could be multiplied but those which have been quoted* are sufficient to show that what the word hypostasis really means when it comes to be applied to the prosopa of the triad . . . it implies that the three prosopa possess a concrete and independent objectivity.' On this account, by 'hypostasis' is meant 'individuality', which is something the prosopa *possess*. The prosopa are individuals, but not of any kind or sort; they are individuals since they possess *individuality*—which is an absurd thesis. Webb (op. cit., p. 39) claims that there was a close approximation in meaning between ὑπόστασις and οὐσία, but offering some account of the development of the former from Aristotle† he says that the introduction of the term ὑπόστασις probably arose in the following way (p. 41). 'ὑποκείμενον is used by Aristotle to mean "a subject" or (as he puts it) a "substratum"; but was also used by Aristotle . . . to mean ὕλη in the sense of in-

* The instances quoted are: St Iraeneus, *Haer.*, 1.5,4; St Cyril of Jerusalem, *Cat.*, 6,13; Origen, *De Princ.*, 3.1.22; *Cont. Cels.*, 8, 12.

† Aristotle has no such notion.

determinate matter.'* Then Webb continues:

> Now it was, I take it, because this word ὑποκείμενον might be thus used, and so could not be restricted to the concrete individual thing in which some form or nature describable in general terms which are applicable to more things than one, is realised in this or that instance, this or that man, this or that horse, that there was felt in the post-Aristotelian period of Greek philosophy to be a word appropriated to this last signification only, such a word was found in ὑπόστασις . . .

Webb's position is at least ambiguous; is he saying that by ὑπόστασις is meant for instance *this man* (Socrates), *that man* (Aristotle), namely particular men, or is he saying that by ὑπόστασις is meant 'concrete individual things which take on the character of (for example) being man' or 'concrete individual things in which some form or nature is realized'? From his use of the term 'concrete independence' in contrast to 'distinguishable nature' earlier on this page, and his point that ὑποκείμενον meant 'concrete independence', together with his points on p. 40 that the answer to Aristotle's 'what-is-it?' question is a *description* or *characteristic* of a thing, I conclude that on his view ὑπόστασις means 'simple individual' in the impossible sense discussed earlier. (Cf. also Prestige, op. cit., p. 168–9, discussed under my treatment of οὐσία above.)

Confusion pervades Wolfson's comments also. He remarks to the effect that for the Fathers there is a real distinction between the three members of the Trinity; they are each real individual species, but they are to be regarded as one:† 'But inasmuch as there is only one of these members and inasmuch as each of them is a real being each of them also is an individual; each member of these Trinities is therefore an individual species'.‡ (Cf. also p. 315.) The concept of an 'individual species' is a gross confusion. It is necessarily true that any individual is an individual of some sort or kind, and in so far as sorts or kinds are amenable to

* This is a highly contentious thesis; I should argue that Aristotle *never* meant his: indeed this is what he throws out in *Metaphysics*, z.3.

† Op. cit., p. 310.

‡ Ibid., p. 309.

the genus–species division, then it is likewise necessarily true that any individual is an individual *of* some genus or species, and any genus or species is such that some individual can fall under it, but there cannot be an *individual species* as opposed to an individual *of* some species or other. The doctrine of 'individual species' I suggest arises from treating proper names as mini-predicates or descriptions. In so far as the Fathers are open to Wolfson's interpretation, they can likewise be said to be guilty of such a gross confusion in the notion of ὑπόστασις.

D. This is not to say that ὑπόστασις never has a legitimate use in the writings of the Greek Fathers; sometimes it does refer to an individual of a certain type or sort or to that which can be a genuine subject of predication or has a special sense which does not give rise to difficulties (cf. Tatian, *Ad Graec.*, 21.3: 5.1; Athenagoras, *Suppl.*, 24.4; Irenaeus, *Haer.*, 5, 13.3; Prestige, op. cit., p. 170).

From the foregoing discussion it has, I hope, been made clear that not only have we a number of senses of οὐσία and ὑπόστασις in operation in the writings of the Greek Fathers, but that also in central cases cited by scholars in this field these concepts are themselves illegitimate for the reasons offered.

It might be objected that my discussion does not treat of the questions for which the kind of theological formulations I criticize were intended as answers, the controversies which it was hoped they would resolve and the perplexities which it was believed they might help to clarify.* My general answer to this is that if the formulations are such that, in any given writer's use of them, such a use makes fundamental logical errors or erroneous assumptions, then such formulations cannot furnish possible answers, possible resolutions or clarifications, hence there is no need to pursue the particular questions, etc. for which these formulations were intended as answers, etc. Of course one has to illustrate the use of these formulations and this I have attempted to do in the particular extracts I have cited from the writings of the Fathers; but

* I owe this objection to Professor MacKinnon.

the need to supply a detailed account of the particular problems, controversies, perplexities, etc. it was hoped such formulations would resolve only arises if one subscribes to the thesis that one can only decide whether such formulations have sense if one understands the problems, controversies, etc. for which they were to constitute answers, namely, if one understands the role such formulations were intended to play. I claim that this thesis is false; such formulations can only play some role if the use of such formulations in the writings of the Fathers is such as to indicate that such formulations are logically in order. It is my case that in many of the 'classic' passages cited or referred to there is a strong case for maintaining that this is not so. When, therefore, St Augustine claims that God is οὐσία in the use of the Greek Fathers, it is not clear what is being claimed or whether a possible claim is being made. I shall investigate St Augustine's argument that God is 'substance' to see in what sense or senses this multifarious concept is employed and whether a possible claim is being made. In my later discussion of St Augustine's treatment of 'one substance'; 'in one substance'; 'of the same substance', it will also be necessary to keep one's eyes open for any illegitimate concept of οὐσία stemming from earlier illegitimacies in the writings of the Fathers; I surmise that we shall find echoes of these and sometimes more than echoes.

3

St Augustine's Argument that God is Substance

1. St Augustine's explicit argument for saying that God is *substantia, essentia* runs as follows:

(i) 'For as "wisdom" is called from "to be wise" and "knowledge" from "to know" so from "to be" is that which is called *essentia.*' (Sicut enim ab eo quod est sapire dicta est sapienta ab eo quod est scire dicta est scienta, ab eo quod est esse dicta est essentia.)

(ii) 'And who is there that is, more than He who said to his servant Moses, "I am that I am" and "Thus thou shalt say unto the children of Israel, He who is hath sent me unto you"?' (Et quis magis est, quam ille qui dixit famulo suo Moysi: Ego sum qui sum; et dices filiis Israel, Qui est misit me ad vos?)

(iii) 'But other things that are called essences or substances admit of accidents, whereby a change whether great or small is brought about in them' (Sed aliaequae dicuntur essentiae sive substantiae, capium accidentia, quibus in eis fiat vel magna vel quantalumque mutatio).

(iv) 'But there can be no accident of this kind in respect to God and therefore He who is God is the only unchangeable substance or essence, to whom most certainly being itself, whence comes the name of essence, most especially and truly belongs.' (Deo autem aliquid ejus modi accidere non potest: & ideo sola est incommutabilis substantia vel essentia, qui Deus est, cui profecto ipsum esse, unde essentia nominata est, maxime eu verissime competit.)*

2. To consider this argument in detail: (i) might be construed as simply a point as to how 'sapienta', 'scienta' and 'essentia' are formed from the stems of the present infinitives of the respective verbs; but if (i) is to be taken simply as a grammatical point about the formation of abstract nouns in Latin, it can have no reference to the rest of the argument, which is certainly not about formations in Latin grammar. In order to be of relevance, the first part of the sentence 'Sicut . . . est essentia', namely 'Sicut . . . scienta', must be construed as saying that there could be no concept of wisdom or knowledge unless there were the concepts of 'being wise' or 'knowing', namely unless there were these capacities and activities in our culture, there could be no such thing as knowledge or wisdom. In general, there could not be a people who could be said to have the concepts of wisdom or knowledge, if there were no such capacities as being wise or knowing in that culture. As thus construed, St Augustine can be taken as making a conceptual point about the conditions for the sensible introduction of abstract concepts, and his point is surely correct. However, Augustine now moves to saying that from being (*esse*) comes that which we call *essentia*. If he is to be construed as making a purely grammatical point here, his point is correct and harmless enough, but in that case it is difficult to see how what he says is relevant to the rest of the argument. If he is to make a parallel point to the construction I have put on his point above—namely that there could not be the concept of *essentia* unless there were that of *esse*, then difficulties arise. The argument runs 'For as . . . *so* . . .' which implies that there is a strict parallel between the cases of 'to be wise' ('being wise'), 'to know' ('knowing') and 'to be' ('being'), whereas an objector will point out that there is no such parallel. The objector's argument runs as follows:

(a) whereas both 'being wise' and 'knows' are 'first order' predicables such that, when conjoined with a referring

* *De Trinitate*, V, 2.

expression (in Professor Strawson's sense) or a name (in Professor Geach's sense)* they can, on at least some occasions of use, yield a true or false proposition about what is referred to or named, 'being' ('is'; 'exists') is not such that when combined with such a referring expression or name it can on any occasion of use yield a true or false proposition about what is referred to or named. Indeed, treating 'is' (sc. 'exists') as such a first order predicable would precisely commit St Augustine to treating 'ousia' as a characteristic of individuals, and hence set him firmly in that impossible conception of '*ousia*' which I argued was present in the writings of the Greek Fathers.† That St Augustine is committed to such an impossible conception will be shown later.

(b) Both 'to be wise' and 'to know' are verbs which imply capacities, even though it cannot be maintained that they are analysable in terms of capacities, whereas to say that *x* exists does not imply attributing a capacity to *x*.

(c) It is illegitimate to introduce *essentia* on the argument Augustine produces, since it will look (on this argument) as if in *essentia* we have a parallel to wisdom and knowledge, but we have no such parallel, for whereas it makes perfectly good sense to say 'wisdom exists', 'knowledge exists' it is nonsensical to say '*essentia* exists', for in so saying the fallacy of self-predication is committed. In connection with this the following point will be made: 'wisdom exists' is exponible as 'Some *x*s (people) are wise' or 'is wise' is truly predicable of some *x*s (people); 'knowledge exists' is exponible as 'Some *x*s (such as people) know' or 'know' is truly predicable of some *x*s (e.g. people); but what could be the parallel exposition of '*essentia* exists'—'Some *x*s *are*?'—what could one supply as replacements for *x* here? We cannot supply 'beings' without obvious absurdity. As Aristotle rightly commented: 'There is no such class of things as the class of things which simply *are*'‡ Thus we cannot *begin* to formulate an account

* Cf. P. F. Strawson, 'On Referring', *Mind*, 1950; P. T. Geach, *Reference and Generality*, Chapter 2.

† Chapter 2, Appendix C, Section B.1.

‡ *Posterior Analytics*, 92b13–14.

of '*essentia* exists' in the way in which we can for 'wisdom exists' or 'knowledge exists'.

3. Can these objections be answered in any way such that Augustine's argument can at least get off the ground? It might be replied that at least objection (a) can be answered in that, contrary to much post-Kantian and recent disquisitions, there is a sense in which *esse* (sc. exists) is a first order predicable which in a given use operates as a first order predicate.

We must distinguish at least three kinds of existential proposition. It will not do simply to wave the banner 'Existence is not a predicate'; one has to investigate the kind of existential proposition a person has in mind. Professor Geach* has enlisted three kinds of existential proposition:

(i) 'There is no such thing as Cerberus': 'Cerberus does not exist' (this illustrates the case of '__does not exist', where the blank is replaceable by a putative proper name).

(ii) 'There is no such thing as a dragon': 'Dragons do not exist' (this illustrates the case of '__ does not exist (do not exist)', where the blank is replaceable by a general word, *not* a proper name).

(iii) 'Joseph is not and Simeon is not' (this illustrates a case of the use of 'is'/'is not' where the blank in '__is' '__is not' is replaceable by a genuine as opposed to a fictitious proper name).†

For my present purpose I shall be investigating *iii* only, for Geach makes no claim as regards the other types of case that what we have is a sense of 'is' (*esse* in Aquinas) in which 'is' and its negation is a proper and genuine predicable of individuals; indeed he purposively distinguishes between *i*, *ii* and *iii*. Geach comments that in *iii* we have that sense of 'exist' in which we say that an individual came into existence, still exists, no longer exists, goes on existing. What can be made of his case here? First, he is surely correct in pointing out that in *this* use of 'is'/'is not' (sc. 'exists'/'does not exist'), we are not referring to the use of names as in the 'Cerberus'

* In 'Form and Existence', *Proceedings of the Aristotelian Society*, vol. LV, 1955.

† The parentheses and expositions are mine.

case; *however*, even though in this use of 'is' (sc. 'exists') we have a genuine and proper predicate of individuals in a given use, 'is' ('exists') in such a use is a *redundant* predicate of individuals. To expand. To say 'Joseph is (exists)' in this sense is exponible as 'Joseph is a __' or 'Joseph is __', where the blank here is filled out by some predicate, more particularly by some predicate which will secure identity of reference for the continued use of the proper name. Aristotle's 'second substance' words are particularly appropriate here. To say 'Joseph is not' in this sense, is, as Geach himself points out, to say that Joseph is no longer alive—viz., that Joseph is no longer a man. This sense of 'exist' in which we say that an individual came to exist, still exists, no longer exists, etc. is always, I contend with Aristotle, exponible in terms of some predicate falling under one of his 'Categories'. Thus to say 'Socrates no longer exists' is to say that Socrates is no longer alive; to say that Socrates still exists is to say that Socrates is still alive; to say that the law against driving an automobile without being preceded by a man waving a red flag exists, is to say that the law is still in force. Hence in such a use of 'is' (exists)—Aristotle's use of τὸ ὄν καθ' αὑτὸ which he says is πολλαχως λέγεται (used in many ways)__'is' is replaceable by 'is__', where the blank takes an ordinary predicate.*

4. Will the sense of 'exists' discussed above help us to get St Augustine's argument off the ground? I think not, since whilst it must be agreed that here we have a use of 'exists' which is a predicate of individuals, that sense is precisely redundant—always exponible in terms of some predicate; whereas for St Augustine's case to be a starter here, *esse* must not only be a predicate of individuals, but a genuine predicate, that is a non-redundant predicate of individuals. This is not of course to say that one cannot validly introduce the concept of *essentia*, for one might be able to do so on other grounds, but one certainly cannot so introduce it on the grounds Augustine produces in (i).

* Cf. G. E. L. Owen, 'Aristotle on the Snares of Ontology', reprinted in *New Essays on Plato and Aristotle*, ed. Renford Bambrough, London, Routledge & Kegan Paul, 1965.

I now turn to the other objections raised above in 2. Even granted the sense of 'exists' in (iii), objection (b) above still holds, for it cannot be said that for instance 'to be alive' or 'to be a man' implies capacities in a parallel fashion to the way in which 'to be wise' and 'to know' imply capacities. A man may *have* capacities, but to be a man is not itself a capacity of something or other, nor does being a man imply that there is something or other which has this capacity: on the contrary, 'being wise' and 'knowing' do imply that there is something or other which has the capacity to be wise or to know. Objection (c) needs thorough scrutiny. It may be replied that the proposition 'Essentia exists' is not necessarily nonsensical in the way primarily asserted in the objection. It is not necessarily the case that we have a case of the fallacy of self-predication on our hands. We only have such a case if the sense of 'exists' contained in the notion of *essentia* is (i) the same sense as that expressed in such propositions as 'wisdom exists'; 'knowledge exists' and that (ii) that the sense of 'exists' in '*essentia* exists' is the same sense as that contained in the notion of *essentia*. Someone may deny that this is the case. He may argue that one can give sense to '*essentia* exists', if by *essentia* is meant 'things which can be said to "come into existence", "continue to exist", "still exist", "go on existing", "cease to exist"', so we might have the formulation: 'There are entities which are such that they can be said to come into existence, continue to exist, go on existing, cease to exist.' To this it must be replied as follows:

(i) From my investigation of passages from the writings of the Greek Fathers, no such concept of *essentia* emerges.

(ii) Even if this formulation is possible, we have no parallel with 'wisdom exists' or 'knowledge exists', and hence as such it cannot help St Augustine's argument, for he clearly does think that *essentia* is like knowledge or wisdom.*

(iii) We have an impossible formulation in any case. To

* As St Basil did before him; cf, Chapter 2, Appendix C above, p. 99, second footnote (†).

say that such and such can be said to come into existence, go on existing, cease to exist, etc., for example to say that men or horses or houses are such, is to pass a remark of logical grammar. It declares what it is possible to say in relation to any given (for instance) man, horse, or house; it determines what *can* be true or false predications of such entities. In this way such a remark sets up possibilities; it allocates to a category, not to a class. Yet it is only on the assumption that such a remark allocates to a class that it is possible to use the formulation 'There are . . .' $(\exists x)\ Fx$. *Essentia*, as above understood, is a category and categories cannot be said to exist or fail to exist; on the contrary they determine what *can* be said to exist or fail to exist.*

5. It might be contended that even though St Augustine's argument has broken down in so far as it depends for its validity upon the strict parallelism between 'wisdom' and 'knowledge' on the one hand and '*essentia*' on the other, this is not to say that the introduction of the latter here is bogus or that no argument parallel to that which St Augustine offers might be put forward. It might be said that we can reformulate St Augustine's argument as follows: granted that by *esse* is meant that sense of 'exists' expounded above, then we can introduce the category of *essentia* (οὐσία) in the sense of the category of those things which can be said to come into existence, continue to exist, etc. Thus St Augustine might argue (by analogy, but not in the same sense as his formulation suggests) that, *as* we could not have the concept of 'wisdom' without that of 'being wise' (in the way explained earlier), *so* too we could not have the concept of *essentia* unless we had that of *esse* in the sense I have been discussing.

This can only be a plausible reconstruction of Augustine's thought if it can be maintained that he had the above discusses concept of *esse*, and if by *essentia* is meant the category of those *x*s which can be spoken of as coming into existence, going on existing, etc. A clear case for saying that

* Cf. Wittgenstein, *Tractatus*, 4.1272 and my earlier discussion in Chapter 2, Appendix B.

he had the above sense of *esse* in mind could only be maintained if at this point he were to introduce Aristotle's sense of τὸ ὄν in the sense of τὸ ὄν καθ' αὑτὸ, which he does not. A clear case for saying that he construed *essentia* as above can only be made out in so far as the Greek Fathers so construed it. However, in the light of my arguments earlier there is a very strong case against saying that the Greek Fathers so construed it. As I there argued,* far from it being the case that they regarded οὐσία as a category, they treated it as a characteristic which individuals could be said to *possess* and *share in*. In so far as St Augustine is following in the footsteps of the Greek Fathers here, as he acknowledges, the above reconstruction is not one that can be seriously put forward.

6. I now turn to St Augustine's second premiss: 'And who is there that is, more than He who said to his servant Moses "I am that I am" and "Thus shalt thou say unto the children of Israel, He who is hath sent me unto you." '

An objector will say that this premise clearly relies on the thesis that 'existence' is a predicate of individuals, but as it is not, we have a piece of nonsense on our hands. However, as there is at least the serious possibility† that St Augustine is using 'is' in the sense discussed in 3 above, even though one cannot produce a clear-cut case for this as I argued above, this objection is not a decisive one. Even so, we are not in smooth waters for, as I pointed out earlier, that sense of 'is' (sc. exists) which is a genuine predicate of individuals is a redundant sense, always replaceable by some predicate. As this is so, the phrase 'And who is there that is' must be construed as: 'And who is there that is__', where the blank is filled out by some predicate and the problem arises as to what can provide the filling here. Someone might suggest 'god', but this would not further Augustine's argument. Further, granted the sense of 'is' under consideration, the much discussed passage 'I am that I am' would have to be construed as 'I am__that I am__', and any filling here would

* Chapter 2, Appendix C, Section B.1.

† There is such a serious possibility in that he does regard *esse* as a first order predicate.

yield nonsensical results. Professor Geach* has said that when God says 'I am who am' it *is* this sense of 'exists' which is intended. This account is open both to the difficulty of providing a completion for the blanks in 'I am__who am__' and that of being forced to say that God is in the category of those things which can sensibly be said to come into existence, go on existing, and cease to exist. It might be replied here that we can and must draw a distinction between someone saying 'I am__', where the blank can take a predicate as above expounded, and *God* saying 'I am who am', for the whole point of this odd phrase is that it is intended to convey that God belongs to the *category* '*x*s which can be said to come into existence, etc.', *not* that God is *something or other*. Hence, it will be pressed, the objection about the completion for the 'is' in 'is__' does not arise. This reply does not eradicate my second objection to Geach above; indeed it explicitly invokes it. Further, this distinction is bought at too high a price, since accepting this account of the 'God' case, we no longer have a use of 'exists' which purports to be a genuine predicate of individuals and so we certainly do not have a parallel between 'God is not' and 'Joseph is not' or between 'God is' and 'Joseph is'. I conclude therefore that we cannot take the sense of 'exists' here as that redundant sense which is a genuine predicable of individuals and that if we construe God saying 'I am who am' in the above way, we allocate God to the category of contingent existents, which is an impossibility on the Christian concept of God, as I argued earlier. Indeed, if we do construe God saying 'I am who am' in the above way, we shall have to charge Augustine with the error of thinking that one can have paradigm instances of categories, for his second premiss begins: 'And who is there that is more than He who said . . .' But there cannot be paradigm instances of a category, since to say that x belongs to the category φ, is to indicate what can be sensibly said about x and what questions can be sensibly asked of x. If God does fall under the category of *essentia* then 'He' cannot belong to it *more than* anything else; 'He' either can be

* 'Form and Existence', op. cit.

spoken of in a certain way or He cannot. The only possibility that remains here is to say that Augustine does, after all, treat 'exists' as a genuine non-redundant predicate of individuals, treating it as a property individuals may have or fail to have and which God supremely possesses. As has often been argued however, there can be no such property. It is my case that Augustine's argument completely breaks down at this point, but I shall examine the rest of his argument, since it will help us to see how Augustine took over an illegitimate concept of *essentia* from the Greek Fathers. The next premiss in his argument brings this out.

7. At 1 (iii) above we have: 'But other things that are called essences or substances admit of accidents whereby a change great or small is brought about in them.' This commits Augustine to the view that to say that *x* is substance or essence is to *call x* something, namely to attribute a *characteristic* or *property* to *x*; this reflects that illegitimate concept of substance I traced in some writings of the Greek Fathers according to which (a) a second substance term or a term falling under the category of τί ἐστι designates a property or characteristic of some individual and (b) οὐσία *itself* is regarded as a characteristic or property which in-viduals or kinds of thing can have or fail to have.* Contrary to Augustine's contention, it must be maintained that to say '*x* is substance', for example 'Man is (a) substance', is not to *call x* or man anything or to attribute any characteristic or property, but to allocate to a category, namely the category of those things which can be sensibly said to come into existence, go on existing, still exist, cease to exist, etc. Further, Augustine's treatment of substance as a characteristic which individuals or types of thing may have or fail to have leads him to imply that it is a contingency and hence a deficiency that substances admit of accidents. On the contrary, it is no contingency that anything falling under the category of substance admits of accidents; indeed it is part of the very concept of substance that anything which falls under this category *should* admit of accidents. It is no

* Cf. Appendix C above, pp. 99–101.

deficiency therefore that any such thing should admit of accidents; indeed the question of a deficiency cannot be raised. Since however it is part and parcel of saying that *x* is substance that *x* admits of accidents in terms of which a change in *x* can be explained, as God does *not* admit of accidents of this kind (premiss 1 (iv) above), far from it being the case that God is the example *par excellence* of substance, God cannot be substance *at all*. It is necessarily the case that God does not admit of accidents whereby a change in 'Him' can be explained, for it is necessarily the case that God is not subject to change; hence it is necessarily the case that God is *not* substance. The idea of an unchangeable substance, that is the idea of a substance which cannot sensibly be spoken of as being subject to change (premiss 1(iv) above) is a nonsensical one, hence to say that God is an unchangeable substance is itself nonsensical. I thus contend that, far from it being the case that St Augustine has established an important truth, he has engrossed himself in a nonsense.

It might be countered that the above criticism assumes that the only sense of substance with which Augustine could be working is that expounded above, but that this is not the only possibility here; he might be using 'substance' in the following sense: to say that *x* is substance is to say that *x* *cannot* be spoken of as coming into existence, as existing in time or through time, as ceasing to exist or as being subject to accidental predications. After all, for Plato, to say '*x* is' either is to say or at the very least entails saying:

(i) *x* is intelligible (as opposed to sensible)
(ii) *x* is changeless
(iii) *x* is not qualified by contrary predicates.*

Using *this* concept of substance, can we not give an intelligible account of St Augustine's argument, and is not God substance in precisely this sense? The difficulties involved in this suggestion are as follows:

* Cf. Gregory Vlastos, '*The Third Man argument in the Parmenides*', reprinted in *Studies in Plato's Metaphysics*, ed. R. E. Allen, London, Routledge & Kegan Paul, 1965.

(a) on this interpretation, Augustine could not draw his parallel between 'to be wise' and 'to know' on the one hand, and 'to be' on the other, for on this account 'exists' could not be a predicate of individuals at all. Whilst it is not necessarily the case that if x is an individual then x is sensible, it is certainly true that individuals are not necessarily intelligible entities, like the 'Forms'.* Further, whilst it is not necessarily the case that if x is an individual, then x changes, it is not necessarily the case that if x is an individual then x is changeless. Finally, individuals can be qualified by contrary predicates and remain one and the same. It might be contended by a supporter of Plato here that those things which we include under the category of 'individual', such as individual men or tables, are only *deficiently* so included in that it *is* necessary to the concept of an individual that if x is an individual then x is at least not subject to change or the subject of contrary predicates. This contention seems wrong-headed, for if it is necessary to x being an individual that x be such, then the individual men, such as Socrates or Aristotle, are not simply 'deficient' individuals, but no individuals at all. If St Augustine were to follow this supporter of Plato seriously, he would have to deny that there were any genuine uses of 'wise' or 'know' in this world and hence deny the basis of his opening premiss.

(b) On this interpretation of 'is', God cannot be said to be *more than* anything else in this world, for on this interpretation things in this world cannot be said to be at all, not simply that they cannot be said to be 'deficiently'.

(c) The things in this world, on this interpretation, would not simply be *called* substances by derivation, they *could not* be substances at all; the very concept of 'substance' put forward here would rule them out.

(d) To say that there could be no accident of the kind pertaining to 'things called substances or essences', premiss 1(iv), in respect to God would simply be to utter a tautology. Further, on this interpretation, for x to be substance *is* for x to be unchangeable, thus the concept of an unchangeable

* Indeed Plato precisely distinguishes between individuals and Forms.

substance becomes an empty tautology, and to say that God is an unchangeable substance becomes valueless.

On this interpretation of 'substance', St Augustine cannot be thought to be producing an argument for the thesis that God is substance, for this interpretation renders any such argument futile. Yet there seems little doubt that he did conceive himself to be producing an argument. On these grounds I conclude that the earlier interpretation of substance is the correct one and that the objections raised to his argument on this interpretation stand, forcing one to the conclusion that, far from it being the case that God is the example *par excellence* of substance, God cannot be substance at all. God is only thought to be the example *par excellence* of substance on the basis of that impossible doctrine of substance which I earlier traced in the Greek Fathers.

4

On 'Of the Same Substance'; 'In One Substance'

Introduction

In this chapter I shall be examining St Augustine's use of the phrases 'of the same substance', 'in the same substance', 'in one substance', with subsidiary reference to 'in respect of substance', 'in respect to substance' and the notion that the substance of the Father is the Father Himself. A detailed examination of these phrases is required, for it will be my contention that such concepts as they express cannot have any place in talk about the persons of the Trinity. Their use in this context is nonsensical, and what is of interest is that such a use is necessarily nonsensical. These concepts have only been thought to be employable in such a connection on account of certain errors which I shall attempt to expose.

1. I open my discussion by considering a passage from *De Trinitate*, V, 8. 'Wherefore let us hold this above all that whatever is said of that most eminent and divine loftiness in respect to itself (ad se) is said in respect to substance (substantialiter) but that which is said in relation to anything (ad aliquid) is not said in respect of substance (substantialiter) but relatively (sed relative).'

Treating 'in respect to substance' renderable as 'in respect to (Aristotle's) τὸ τί ἦν εἶναι', which interpretation seems to be the natural one here, we get: 'Granted the form of proposition "God is__", where the blank is replaceable by a predicate falling under the category of "in respect to itself" (καθ' αὑτὸ: *per se*), then when we have a proposition formed from this schema, the predicate in such a proposition is a predicate falling under "τὸ τί ἦν εἶναι" such that what is yielded by the whole proposition is a necessary truth expressing a definition.'

On this account if we substitute 'good' for the blank in 'God is __', then the resulting proposition is a necessarily true one expressing a definition. The objection to this account is that 'good' is not a predicate which can of itself form part of τὸ τί ἦν εἶναι of anything, as witness Aristotle's account of τὸ τί ἦν εἶναι as discussed earlier. In order for 'good' to so function, it must at least be the case that there is some completion for 'good' offerable, for 'good' has no sense on its own, it must be taken as an integral part of an expression of the form 'good *x*'. As Professor Geach has argued,* it is not possible to analyse '*x* is a good man' into '*x* is good' and '*x* is a man': 'good' is an attributive adjective, as opposed to a predicative adjective like 'yellow'. Further, following my previous account of τὸ τί ἦν εἶναι, it is not simply the case that in order for 'good' to be part of τὸ τί ἦν εἶναι of *x* that it must take a general term as completion, but that type of general term exhibited by Aristotle's concept of 'form'† which would at least require that it should take as completion an enumerable general term. The problem here is to specify what the completion *could be* in the case under consideration. If we say that the completion is 'god', then we have 'God is a good god', which implies that God is a god—a position I have argued against earlier. If we say that the completion is 'God', then we have 'God is a good God', which implies that 'God' can be prefaced by the indefinite article, which is not possible *vide* my earlier argument.‡ Indeed *any* completion for 'good' which we could offer would seem to be impossible as concerns 'God is

* In 'Good and Evil', *Analysis*, vol. 17 (1956), pp. 33–42. Cf. also Notes.

† Cf. *Metaphysics* H 3, 1043a34; Z 8, 1033a25ff.

‡ Appendix B to Chapter 2.

good', for any proposition of the form '*x* is good' is writable as '*x* is a good *y*'.*

This is only the first of our difficulties, but it is an important one since it reveals that St Augustine cannot sensibly employ the notion of substance in the sense of τὸ τί ἦν εἶναι here; yet this *is* the sense of substance which is relevant, for there is the explicit contrast with 'said relatively'. It is important to note that as *any* completion for 'good' which comes under the category of 'Form' will fail in this case, then it is necessarily impossible for Augustine to employ *this* notion of substance here. I have, of course, only used 'good' as an example of a predicate falling under the category of καθ' αὑτὸ (*per se*) concerning God, but the same point will hold for any other *per se* predicate, such as 'merciful', 'wise', 'loving', 'glorious', for all these viewed as predicates in the sense of 'said of a subject' *do* require completion in the above way. This is *not* to say that for *any* use of such terms, such completions must be supplied in order for sense to be made; such completions are only necessary where such terms function as and are intended to function as predicates, as in the above case, and not as for instance part of the *grammar* of something or other.†

2(a) St Augustine's second comment here (*De Trin.* V, 8) raises more problems: 'And that the effect of the same substance in the Father, Son, and Holy Spirit is that whatever is said of each of them in respect to themselves is to be taken, not in the plural in sum but in the singular. For as the Father is God, the Son is God, and the Holy Spirit is God which no one doubts to be said with respect to second substance, yet we do not say that the very supreme Trinity is itself three gods but one God.'‡

* Which would be relevant here. Someone might press that for some uses of '*x* is good' we can re-write in terms of '*x* is good for *y*': '*x* is good from the point of view of *y*.' This is to be acknowledged without detriment to the point made.

† 'part of the *grammar* of something or other'. What I have in mind is the situation in which someone construes (for example) 'God is glorious' as a remark on the *character* of God, i.e. that it is part of our understanding of God that He is glorious, as opposed to construing it as expressing a subject–predicate proposition.

‡ Tantamque vim esse ejusdem substantiae in Patra et Filio et Spiritu Sancto, ut

Now granted that the Father, Son, and Holy Spirit are *of* the same substance or *in* the same substance, namely that they are three individuals of a certain sort having the same τὸ τί ἦν εἶναι, does it follow that whatever is said of each in respect to themselves, that is in respect of their being individuals of that type, is to be taken, not in the plural in sum, but in the singular? Certainly this does not hold as a general principle for all such types of predicate. For, granted three individuals of a certain sort, say three animals having the same τὸ τί ἦν εἶναι, namely 'rational animal', it does not follow that *all* of what is said of these three animals in respect of themselves is to be taken in the singular. For some predicates this works, for instance 'having the ability to argue' or 'having the ability to operate with number'; for some not, that they are men is said of them in respect of themselves, but here the plural is certainly used. Thus the general principle breaks down and in order for the thesis advocated to hold, an independent argument must be produced.* Indeed in order for Augustine's point to have application to the 'God' case, he must conceive the predicate 'God' to be logically parallel to, for instance 'rational' or 'intelligent'; if 'God' is so parallel, then it is the case that we speak in the singular and not in the plural; if three individuals are each intelligent, then we do not have a case of 'three intelligents' or 'three intelligences'. Such a construction of 'God' brings its own general and special difficulties. The general difficulty is that on such a construction 'God' would have to be exactly renderable by 'divine' and it is certainly not clear that for all uses of 'God' we can substitute 'divine' or even the abstract form 'Divinity': 'Jesus Christ is God' and 'Jesus Christ is the son of God' are cases in point. The specific difficulty it brings in relation to St Augustine's account here is that he wants to speak of 'not three Gods' but 'one God', which talk is impossible granted such a construc-

quidquid de singulis ad se ipsos dicitur, non pluraliter in summa, sed singulariter accipiatur. Quemadmodum enim Pater Deus est et Filius Deus est et Spiritus Sanctus Deus est, quod secundum substantiam dici nemo dubitat: non tamen tres Deos, sed unum Deum dicimus eam ipsam praestantissimam Trinitatem.

* Cf. 3 below.

tion of 'God'. 'One' cannot preface 'divine' any more than it can preface 'rational' or 'intelligent': neither can it preface the abstraction 'Divinity'. In so far as Augustine wants to invoke the notion of 'not three Gods but one God', then he cannot construe 'God' as parallel to 'rational' or 'intelligent', but as parallel to 'man' or 'animal', namely as parallel to a term which can be used as a unit of counting as he does later on (*quod secundum substantiam dici nemo dubitat*), but in so far as he does *this*, his point about speaking in the singular and not in the plural falls to the ground, subject to an independent argument being produced.

These difficulties have resulted from taking the appropriate sense of substance here to be τὸ τί ἦν εἶναι; other interpretations for 'substance' must now be considered. Consider substance in the sense of ὕλη. We can reconstruct as follows: 'The effect of the same ὕλη in the Father, Son, and Holy Spirit is that whatever is said . . .' We shall have here a purported parallel with Aristotelian 'statue' cases—'Granted three lumps of metal bearing particular proper proper names, say A, B, C, are of the same ὕλη, for instance of the same gold, then whatever is said of each in respect of themselves, for example that they are malleable, is to be taken of them, not in the plural, but in the singular'. This reconstruction will not work however since 'malleable' is not enumerable, whereas 'God' in Augustine's use is.

Again, if we consider 'substance' interpreted as 'second substance' the appropriate reformulation breaks down. In this case we should have: 'The effect of the same second substance in the Father, Son, and Holy Spirit is that whatever is said of each in respect of themselves is to be taken, not in the plural in sum, but in the singular.' This reformulation breaks down since in Augustine's use of 'God', 'God' itself is a second substance term, as I cited above. Further, one could press that this reformulation cannot even *begin*, since it is necessarily the case that there can be no second substance 'in' God in any sense, for a second substance necessarily implies the existence of matter and there can be no matter in God.*

* Aquinas: *Summa Theologica*, Ia,q3,a2.

We might try to get an account of St Augustine's point here by *not* taking 'Father', 'Son', 'Holy Spirit', or their equivalents, as the names of individuals of a certain sort, which is the assumption of my initial interpretation above. Someone might object that the Father, Son, and Holy Spirit are not individuals of a certain sort, but are *prosopa* in the sense of 'aspects', 'faces' or 'roles'* of one and the same individual and that the names 'Father', etc. are the names of such *prosopa*. Even this account presents insuperable difficulties. We must ask (a) What is the one and the same individual of which the Father, Son, and Holy Spirit are the 'aspects', 'faces', or roles'? If we reply 'One and the same God', this commits us to saying that God is an individual as any given man is an individual or more generally as a τόδε τι is an individual, which is impossible granted the Christian concept of God as that which is outside space and time. Further, 'God' cannot provide an answer to the question 'One and the same *what*?' here, since in Augustine's use 'God' is *said of* the Father, Son, and Holy Spirit in respect to substance, so cannot itself *be* substance in the first sense here. Again, if we answer the question raised above by saying 'One and the same *spirit*', we imply the possibility of non-substantial individuals and, apart from the inherent difficulties of this notion, the argument that there could be such individuals which is relevant to *this* context, is based on error. Such an argument would be based on the assumption that to say that God is a spirit is to say *what* God is, which necessarily implies saying that God is of the genus 'spirit' or in the genus 'spirit', whereas it is denied that God is in any genus.† To say that God is a spirit must therefore not be construed in this way; rather it must be construed as a remark of grammar concerning God—namely that God cannot be spoken of as a body. Indeed, it is plausible to say that this is what Aquinas's argument at *Summa Theologica*, 1a,q3,a1, to the effect that God is not a body, amounts to.

* Cf. Webb, op. cit., pp. 36–7, pp. 44–7; Prestige, op. cit., pp. 157–62. For further discussion of this, see Chapter 5.

† Cf. *Summa Theologica*, Ia,q3,a5.

However the formulation 'One and the same spirit' as set out above precisely supposes that 'spirit' can have the role of identifying and re-identifying individuals, that it can provide an answer to Aristotle's τί ἐστι question.

2(b) Each relevant interpretation for 'substance' in Augustine's statement 'And that the effect of the same substance . . .' is fraught with difficulties. With regard to the phrase 'the effect of the same substance', it is important to point out that this phrase only has a proper use, only has sense, if we can specify what could constitute a substance term, but this is precisely what Augustine cannot furnish us with here. I have argued above that there is no formulation with regard to 'the same substance' which will allow what is said of each of the persons of the Trinity to be taken of them in the singular, but a requirement of even getting a formulation going is that one can provide a replacement for 'same substance', since in order to sensibly talk of 'the same substance' being 'present in' the persons of the Trinity, or 'the same substance of the Father, Son and Holy Spirit', we have to be able to say *what* it is. 'Substance', in this use, both here and elsewhere, can only have a genuine use if we can provide a filling for the blank in the phrase 'same substance, namely . . .', and this is impossible here. We can say that three statues are of the same substance, namely of the *same gold*, or that three pipes are of the same substance, namely of the *same lead*—but not simply 'of the same substance', for this calls forth the question 'Namely, *what*?'

What, we must ask, has happened here such that Augustine thinks that it is perfectly possible to say 'of the same substance' and yet does not see the necessity of providing a filling as above required? My explanation is that he has taken 'substance' in the phrase 'of the same substance' as *itself* a term designating a substance; he has committed a category mistake in that he has taken a formal concept (substance) itself to be a non-formal concept like 'gold' or 'man'. He has confused the formal concept of 'substance' in any one of the four senses above considered with something or other which may be said to be substance in one of those four senses. There are precedents for this mistake in the writings of the Greek Fathers.* Indeed, this is precisely the suggestion of the formulation 'of the same substance' left unexpounded and uncompleted, and likewise the formulation 'The same substance in the Father, Son and Holy Spirit', left unexpounded and uncompleted. This latter formulation presents us with difficulties equally as grave as the former does. 'Substance' in the sense of τὸ τί ἦν εἶναι cannot be said to be *in* something—how can what is signified by a definitional λόγος be *in* something, for τὸ τί ἦν εἶναι of *x is* what it is *to be x*. 'Substance' in the sense of ὕλη, for example gold or silver, cannot be said to be *in* the individuals which are golden or silver, for these individuals are precisely *of* gold or silver; and in any case to say that for instance gold was *in* the statue would be to say that the (lump of) gold concerned necessarily required for its identification a reference to the statue, which is not the case. We can identify the lump of gold which is the statue irrespective of its being the statue—as witness the fact that it is possible to say that one and the same lump of gold was first a statue and then the molten gold in a certain ladle. 'Substance' in the sense of 'second substance' cannot be said to be *in* anything: 'man', 'animal' are not *in* individual men and individual animals; they are what individual men and individual animals *are*. Again, 'substance' in the sense of an individual *x*, where *x* is a variable for a term which is able to be used as a unit of counting, cannot be said to be *in* anything, namely any given man or animal cannot be said to be *in* some further individual or set of individuals. Further, even if we were to take the interpretation of 'persons' as 'aspects', there is no clear sense in which for instance the aspects of a building are *in* the building or that the building is *in* the aspects; indeed the aspects of a building are how the building looks from a number of positions, but 'how the building looks from position A, B, C, etc.' can in no sense be spoken of as *in* the building and again the building is in no sense *in* its aspects, for its aspects are in no sense parts or constituents

* Cf. Chapter 2, Appendix C, p. 101.

of the building. Similarly, construing 'persons' as 'roles', the roles a person might play are in no sense *in* that person and the person who plays various roles is certainly not *in* those roles, that is part of those roles; they are the roles which he plays or performs.*

2(c) The only account which I can produce which explains how St Augustine came to say (simply) that the same substance was in the Father, Son, and Holy Spirit is as follows: taking τὸ τί ἦν εἶναι as the appropriate sense of 'substance', you then say that substance can be 'in' a number of individuals. This account immediately introduces one into that framework of talk of 'individuals', which are not individuals of a certain sort or kind, on the one hand, and 'universals' which characterize such particulars, on the other, and hence commits one to the view that substance, in the sense of τὸ τί ἦν εἶναι, is a *characteristic* of individuals which such individuals 'share in'. Hence on this account the Father, Son, and Holy Ghost become individuals (necessarily of no kind or type) partaking in the *character* τὸ τί ἦν εἶναι, which is a grossly misguided position to maintain.† Not so grossly misguided however as the position which the full account of Augustine's statement would commit him to, for the full account would have to read that the Father, Son, and Holy Spirit were 'simple individuals' in the sense of ὑποστάσεις‡ which partake in the same τὸ τί ἦν εἶναι—but since no specification of τὸ τί ἦν εἶναι can be given here, they partake in τὸ τί ἦν εἶναι *itself*, which involves the category error of thinking that τὸ τί ἦν εἶναι is itself a specific τὸ τί ἦν εἶναι. It may be said that this account of St Augustine's position is too crude. I plead in mitigation that my examination of the Greek Fathers at least provides support for such an account. The positions attributed in this account have their historical antecedents.§ It might be counteracted here that Augustine is not, after all, committed to speaking of the same substance

* For further discussion of this cf. Chapter 5, pp. 181–3.

† Cf. Chapter 2, Appendix C, pp. 92–6.

‡ pp. 102–3 above.

§ p. 101 above.

in the Father, Son, and Holy Spirit without supplying a 'namely' rider, for he does go on to say in the passage above cited that the Father, Son and Holy Spirit are said to be God with respect to second substance. This counteraction will not help matters here, for 'God' is an instance of what is said of each of the persons of the Trinity *in respect to themselves* and is the *effect* of the same substance in the persons of the Trinity and hence cannot provide the 'namely' rider for 'same substance'.

3. In the light of the above discussion, my provisional conclusion is that no intelligible account can be offered of the phrases 'of the same substance' or 'in the same substance'; however, one important point must be returned to at this juncture. I said earlier that in the absence of an independent argument, Augustine's contention that the effect of the same substance in the Father, Son, and Holy Spirit is that whatever is said in respect to themselves is to be taken not in the plural in sum but in the singular, could not be maintained. It might be held that such an independent argument is to be found at the end of *De Trin.*, V, 8, an argument which is repeated at VII, 4, 1—namely that, 'inasmuch as to God it is not one thing to be and another to be great, but to him it is the same thing to be as to be great, therefore as we do not say three essences (tres essentias) so we do not say three greatnesses, but one essence (unum essentiam) and one greatness.' A contender might press that from this we can glean that we can speak of the Father, Son, and Holy Spirit being one God, since 'in' God *to be* and *to be God* are the same. Augustine does not formally present this argument here, but it might be claimed that it certainly is hinted. However, there are objections to regarding this as a possible argument *here*, for whatever is being got at in the saying that in God there is no difference between *to be* and *to be x* (where *x* can be replaced by a predicate falling under a category other than the Aristotelian category of 'second substance'—as witness Augustine's own examples of 'great', 'wise', etc.), it cannot be of relevance in this context, since what we need here as a replacement for *x* in 'to be *x*' is *not* a predicate falling

under any *other* category than that of second substance, but precisely a second substance predicate. We need the formulation as above set out—that in God there is no difference between *to be* and *to be God*, and 'God' in this context is a second substance predicate, as can be seen from Augustine's earlier use cited above (p. 129). To this point a contender might rejoin that Augustine would not emphasize the difference between predicates falling under the category of 'second substance', or more generally, between predicates falling under the category of 'sortal universal'* and those falling under the other Aristotelian categories, as can indeed be seen in the Platonic metaphysics later exemplified at VII, 6, 11. Further, he does say (V, 8): 'Whatever, therefore, is spoken of God in respect to himself, is both spoken singly of each person, that is, of the Father, of the Son, and of the Holy Spirit: and together of the Trinity itself not plurally, but in the singular.'† So, our contender might continue, Augustine *could* argue that the persons of the Trinity are not to be spoken of as three Gods, since 'God' is spoken of God in respect to himself and in God there is no distinction between to be and to be God. One objection to starting on this line of thought is that the sense in which God, that is the Holy Trinity, is spoken of as God is a different sense from that in which the persons of the Holy Trinity are spoken of as God. In the latter case, to say (for instance) that the Holy Spirit is God, is, it might be argued, to say what the Holy Spirit is, but to say that the Holy Trinity is God is not to say what the Holy Trinity is but to assert an identity. Hence this line of thought is only a starter if one confuses a proposition propounding what something is with an identity proposition. At this point someone might interject as follows: 'It is to be denied that to say that the Holy Spirit is God is to say what the Holy Spirit is; rather to so say is to issue a rule of "grammar" to the effect that the Holy Spirit is to be

* Cf. Strawson, *Individuals*, p. 168.

† Quiquid ergo ad se ipsum dictum Deus, de singularis personis singulariter dicitur, id est, de Patre et Filio et Spirito Sancto et simul de ipsa Trinitate, non pluraliter, sed singulariter dicitur.

spoken of as God; it is to comment on the *character* of the Holy Spirit to the effect that whatever predicates are proper to any individual falling under the category of "God" are proper to the Holy Spirit, and similarly with respect to the other persons of the Trinity. Thus, although each person of the Trinity is said to be God, it does not follow that we have to say that there are three Gods, since in each case we are not making a predication of an individual but making a "grammatical" remark.' The objections to this interjection *here* are:

(i) To construe such sentences as 'The Holy Spirit is God' as 'grammatical' would go outside the scope of St Augustine's own framework. He is clearly working within the context of taking such sentences as expressing subject–predicate propositions.

(ii) It is not clear how the 'grammatical' construction of such sentences would illuminate or even tie in with the point that 'in' God to be and to be God are the same, whereas an account of what is being got at in this contention can be given if we supply the context of ordinary predication as I shall later argue.

(iii) If we do indeed offer such an account, then we cannot conclude with St Augustine that the persons of the Trinity are not to be spoken of as three Gods but one, since on such a construction we should be allocating the three persons to a category and, as previously argued, category terms do not admit of number.

As a last resort someone might say: 'Surely we can say that God is a god', intending the phrase 'is a god' as a predication telling us what God is. To take this stand commits an error parallel to saying that Man is a man, namely that of supposing that 'Man' is the name of a particular man; in our present case it is the error of supposing that 'God' is the name of a particular god.

4. I mentioned above that at VII, 6, 11 Augustine exhibits Platonic metaphysics. I shall now substantiate this claim and attempt to show how subscription to such metaphysics gets him into the impossible position of saying that the substance of the Father is the Father himself.

At VII, 6, 11, Augustine says: '. . . Wherefore as the substance of the Father is the Father himself . . . so also the person of the Father is not anything else than the Father himself.'* Granted the context here, the relevant sense of 'substance' is that sense which answers the question 'What is it?' (Aristotle's τί ἐστι;) when asked of an individual. In this case then, the τί ἐστι of the Father is the Father himself, namely the individual. Thus in this case the *individual* and *what the individual is* are one and the same. This paradoxical conclusion is the result of a false dichotomy—that of individual on the one hand, and what an individual is on the other; a dichotomy which derives from the earlier writings of Plato. Plato, prior to the *Parmenides* at any rate, had made a radical distinction of type between particulars and 'Forms'. Particulars were the particulars they were by being named after the Forms. This theory demands, for its very articulation, that one introduces the idea of a particular which is not necessarily a particular of a certain sort or type, for if one maintains the contrary thesis the theory is rendered a non-starter. On the contrary thesis, one cannot begin to raise the question 'Why is any particular the particular it is?', for example 'Why is any particular which is a man, a man?' Yet Plato certainly wanted to raise the general question here and answer it by reference to a Form.† This dichotomy between an individual and what an individual is we have seen to be present in the writings of the Greek Fathers. Were Augustine not committed to this dichotomy he would not have the distinction: 'the substance of the Father/the Father himself', for this distinction is only possible if you allow that there can be individuals without substance in the appropriate sense, namely individuals which are not of a kind or sort; the impossibility of the distinction gives rise to the paradox of the identity asserted by Augustine. It might be thought that Augustine, by this paradoxical assertion of identity, might

* Quo circa ut substantia Patre ipse Pater est . . . ita persona Patris, non aliud quam ipse Pater est.

† *Phaedo*, 78b8–99b6; *Laches*, 191c10; *Euthyphro*, 5d15; *Phaedo*, 102a11; *Meno*, 72c6.

be trying to make the point that for the Father *to be* is for the Father *to be something or other*, and from the section immediately prior to the one I am investigating, the replacement for 'something or other' would be 'person'. The difficulty with this thought is that it is not a peculiarity of the Father that for Him to be is for Him to be something or other—for Socrates to be is for Socrates to be something or other and the same goes for any individual whatsoever. Granted the framework within which Augustine is working, he is prohibited from making this point and it is clear from earlier considerations in VII that for him 'person' answers the question 'three what?' when asked, *not* of three something or other but of three individuals *simplicter*.*

I thus finally conclude that no intelligible account can be offered of the phrases considered above in relation to their use concerning the persons of the Trinity. That an intelligible account can be offered has only seemed possible since, at the worst, substance has been itself thought to be a substance; at the best it has not been appreciated that such phrases can only operate intelligently in circumstances where they can be completed by what I have termed a 'namely' rider.

5. The Trinitarian formula reads 'Three persons in one substance' (τρεῖς ὑποστασεις ἐν μίᾳ οὐσιᾳ); I now turn to the question of whether the phrase 'one substance' has sense in this context. I have previously argued that God cannot be substance in any of the senses deriving from Aristotle's list at *Metaphysics*, Δ8, and I have rejected Augustine's argument that God is substance, hence it might seem that there is no need to raise this question; the answer must clearly be in the negative. However, an objector may point out that all that I have argued so far, prior to this chapter, is not inconsistent with the thesis that God is three persons in one substance, since to say that God is three persons in one substance is not to say that God is a substance, but to offer some account of what God is and offering an account of what something is is not to be taken as saying what that

* Cf. Chapter 5, pp. 150–2.

this is. I take heed of this objection and hence raise the above question.

Now it is clear from *De Trin.*, VII, 4; 7, 8 that Augustine regards substance (substantia) and nature (natura) as genera—higher genera in the same scale as ordinary genera and species. Thus, according to him, to say that an ox, a horse, and a dog are three animals can be to subsume them under the 'higher' genera of substance or nature, such that 'substance' becomes a 'higher' genus than 'animal'.* This cannot be right. To specify that *x*, the bearer of some proper name, is a man or an animal is, as Aristotle correctly observed, to specify *what x* is. From such a specification a person has, provided he knows and understands the use of the word 'man' or 'animal', the possibility of identifying the individual concerned. Of course, simply on this information alone he cannot identify or even, in some circumstances, set out to identify the individual concerned; what Strawson calls an 'identifying description' would have to be provided.† However, to be told that *x* is a substance cannot tell one *what x* is, since one range of answers to this question falls under the category of second substance. Further, the possibility of identifying an individual is not provided in the assertion that *x* is a substance. Such a possibility is not provided since, in order for such a possibility to be provided, 'substance' would itself have to be a term which could furnish a unit of counting for particulars, or which could provide a criterion of continued identity for particulars as for instance 'man' or 'animal' can. This, however, is not possible. One cannot be asked to count the number of substances in one's present field of vision; there is no way of deciding how one could

* 'And yet again, when we say that an ox is not a horse but that a dog is neither an ox nor a horse, we speak of a three: and if anyone questions us what three, we do not speak now by a specific name of three horses or three oxen or three dogs because these three are not contained under the same species, but by a generic name, three animals; or if a higher genus, three substances or three creatures or three natures . . .' Again, later on we have: 'So three several laurels we also call three trees: but a laurel and a myrtle and an olive, we call only three trees or three substances or three natures.'

† *Individuals*, pp. 20 ff.

begin this procedure. In order for 'substance' itself to be a possible unit of counting or a criterion of continued identity, it must be regardable as an ordinary predicate of individuals; but it is not so regardable for, as I have previously argued, to say of *x* that it is a substance is to allocate *x* to a category and one cannot preface category terms with numbers or, without elucidation or qualification, with phrases such as 'the same' or 'different'. It might be objected that one could count the number of substances in, say, this field in that one can count the number of animals, plants, rocks in this field; this however does not tell against the 'uncountability of substances' thesis, for all this objection can be construed as saying is that to count the number of animals, plants, rocks in this field is all that can constitute counting the number of substances, namely, as concerns substances there is nothing to count. There would only be a case against the 'uncountability of substances' thesis if it could be shown that to count the number of animals, plants, etc. in this field were simply a *means* of counting substances, but this cannot be shown. If *x* is a means to counting *y*, then (i) *y* is countable by another independent means, (ii) *y* is specifiable and identifiable independently of *x*. Here however one can provide *no* independent way of counting substances other than by counting the animals, plants, etc., and substances are only specifiable and identifiable in that one specifies and identifies what items are said to fall under the category of substance in a given case—in this case in that one specifies animals, plants and rocks.

An observer of the above discussion might acidly comment that the suggestion that one *could* count the number of substances in one's field of vision on a given occasion implies that substances are things which *are*—which, he might add, is a sure nonsense, for whilst second substance terms are amenable to quantification by the existential quantifier, 'substance' itself is distinctly not so amenable—which is a way of highlighting the point that to allocate to a substance is to allocate to a category.

A further argument showing the impossibility of 'substance' as a unit of counting is as follows. Although there is a sense in which we can speak of the *same* substance, to ask whether *x* is the same substance as *y*, is to ask whether *x* is the *same F* as *y*, where F here is replaceable by some predicate falling under the category of second substance or, at least, some predicate falling under the category of substance in the sense of 'matter'—for instance whether *x* is the same metal as *y*, or whether *x* is the same man, horse, or animal as *y*. Such terms as 'metal', 'men', 'horses', 'animal' provide us with a criterion of continued identity:* 'substance' does not and cannot. If someone *were* to employ the formulation 'one and the same substance', this would only be intelligible in a context in which he could supply a 'namely' rider, as I mentioned above,† that is, in which he could express his thought as follows: 'one and the same substance, namely one and the same F; where "F" is replaceable by a "second substance" term or at least a "matter" term, which terms can supply us with at least a criterion of continued identity.'

It might be retorted to all this that whilst 'substance' cannot itself be sensibly prefaced by 'one', cannot itself furnish us with a unit of counting, Augustine is not necessarily committed to thinking it *can*. I contend that the passages cited from VII, 4 show that he is so committed, but to meet this retort I shall express it as follows: 'Granted your contention that there is a use for "the same substance" provided we supply a "namely" rider, why cannot St Augustine do precisely this?, that is, say that the Father, Son, Holy Spirit are three persons in the same substance, namely god or that they are three persons in the same substance, namely God? Agreed, the reformulation here is in terms of "the same substance" and not "one substance", but it would be pedantic to raise this point.'

To comment. It is not mere pedantry to raise the point of reformulation, since what can sensibly complete 'the same —' cannot necessarily complete 'one and the same —'. Further, 'god' cannot supply the 'namely' rider here, since

* As expounded by Professor Geach, *Reference and Generality*, p. 39.

† See p. 131.

'god' as signifying an enumerate entity cannot be something the three persons can be said to be *in*; 'persons', in whatever sense this is taken, cannot be said to be *in* an enumerate entity. For example, a person cannot be said to be in a man, though a man may be said to be a person; the reason for this will be set forth in the next chapter. An aspect, role, face or character may be the aspect, role, etc. *of* a man, but they are in no sense *in* a man. In order for a 'namely' rider to be supplied here, one would have to introduce a term parallel to 'gold', that is a term which could only be prefaced by 'the same' and not 'one and the same'. Again, 'God' cannot supply the 'namely' rider here for, apart from difficulties which would arise about prefacing 'God' by 'the same', the brief for our present discussion is that to say that God is three persons in one substance is to offer some kind of account of what God is, hence 'God' itself cannot occur as part of that account.

One final way may appear open in which it is possible to speak of 'one substance'. Someone might press that, as it is possible to speak of 'the same substance' provided that we can supply a 'namely' rider, is it not possible to speak of *one* substance provided that we can supply a 'namely' rider? I should argue against such a possibility on the following grounds. For example, to say 'Socrates is a substance' is exponible as 'Socrates is an *x* such that it makes sense to say that he came into existence by generation, continues in existence, will cease to exist, etc.'; but we cannot re-phrase 'Socrates is a substance' as 'Socrates is *one* substance' for, whereas the question 'One or many?' makes no sense in connection with saying that Socrates is a substance, it necessarily does make sense in connection with the use of 'one'. Even if this argument fails, such that it is, after all, possible to speak of 'one substance' provided that we can supply a 'namely' rider, there is no 'namely' rider which *can* be supplied in this case, for even if we sidestep the difficulties raised above concerning 'in one substance', then we have as our possibilities 'god' or 'God'. The first possibility fails, since its introduction would commit one to the view that the

Christian God was *a* god; the second fails for the same reason as it did above.

I thus conclude that no intelligible account can be offered of that part of the Trinitarian formula which reads 'in one substance', and furthermore that no intelligible account *could* be offered, since any 'namely' rider which we could supply for 'one substance, namely, —', *granted* this to be a possible formulation, would immediately commit one to the thesis that God is in a genus, which thesis is contrary to Christian doctrine. It might, however, be claimed that the 'facts' of Christianity are such as to demand an extension of the 'received' concept of substance. Thus, for instance if it is asserted that Christ is one substance with the Father, this is to say that the love which Christ manifests is not a simulacrum of the divine love, but that love itself. This position, suggested to me by Professor MacKinnon, (a) suggests the Platonic dichotomy between particulars, which are individual copies of the Forms and the Forms themselves, which dichotomy is open to well-known objections and (b) on this account we should have to say that love itself was a substance and hence that 'love' might form a unit of counting in its own right, whereas it will be rightly objected that one can only count *x*s which have or exhibit love since any love must be the love of something or other.* If a Christian employment of the concept of 'substance' requires that love be a substance, then it is not simply a case of stretching the concept but of collapsing it. It might be retorted that love, in the Christian sense, is nevertheless a substance in Plato's sense (as discussed in Chapter 3 above), but in that case, even if such a concept of substance is permissible, it cannot be used as a unit of counting and hence in the formulation 'one and the same —'; yet precisely this is required if we are to use it to supply an account of 'Christ is one substance with the Father'.

* See Notes at end of this Chapter.

NOTES

p. 126 It might be pressed that I am here relying on Geach's analysis of 'good', whereas this is by no means uncontroversial. R. W. Beardsmore in *Moral Reasoning** argues that neither Mrs Foot nor (by implication) Geach can substantiate their claim that the word which replaces the *x* in 'good *x*' yields criteria of goodness, except in a very limited class of cases, that is, where the replacement for *x* indicates a functional object. His case is that except in cases where an object or activity has some undisputed point, we have to consider external considerations which will yield the criteria of goodness, namely the point of farming (p. 19). But from the consideration that in certain cases, namely, where the point of an object or activity is in dispute or may be disputed, solely understanding what *x* is cannot yield us a criterion of goodness, it by no means follows that we can have a criterion of goodness *without* knowing what *x* is, even though knowing what *x* is may depend upon understanding the point of *x* in a given society. In this way Geach's point still holds.

p. 143 'Any love must be the love of something or other.' It might be contended that this is false. For example, one might say: 'Love (as opposed to the love of someone or other) bade me welcome.' In such a case however we can only understand or even begin to understand what is said if we already understand what it is for someone or other who is loving to bid us welcome. Love, here, is analogically treated as a person and our understanding of that analogy is dependent: we have in this example not a counter-case, but an analogically dependent case, whereas we could only seriously treat love as a substance if we had a genuine counter-case. (I owe the suggestion of this contention and the example to Professor Phillips.)

* R. W. Beardsmore, *Moral Reasoning*, London, Routledge & Kegan Paul, 1969.

5
Three Persons

I now turn to that part of the Trinitarian formula which reads: 'Three persons . . .'

1. St Augustine focuses our attention on the problem which gives rise to the answer 'three persons' at *De Trin.*, V, 9.* His problem is that when it is asserted that the Father, Son and Holy Spirit are three, the question is asked by a hearer 'What three?' or 'three what?' and it is necessary that this question be raised and answered. It is necessary that this question be raised, since it is unintelligible to introduce 'three', or any other number, into non-mathematical discourse without introducing a completion for the numerical expression. To be sure, there *are* cases in which no completing expression is explicitly provided, but these are precisely cases where the completion is understood in the context of the utterance—for example, someone may be heard to shout to another 'How many are there?' and the reply be 'three'. In such a case the person making the reply must know what the completion for the '_' in 'How many _s are there?' is, otherwise he could not possibly produce an answer at all, as opposed to a false answer. In order to produce a false answer, as opposed to no answer at all, he has to know what it is he is counting. A person could not begin to comply with the request 'Count the number here', for 'number', in this use, is an incomplete expression; in its complete form it

* Tamen cum quaeritur quid tres, magna prorsus inopia humanum laboret eloquium. Dictum est tamen tres personae, non illud diceretur, sed ne taceretur.

reads, 'number of _', where the blank here takes as a filling a term which can form a unit of counting.* Thus, to return to our present case, it is necessary that the question 'What three?' be raised if it is asserted that the Father, Son, and Holy Spirit are three, in order that there might be understanding on the part of the hearer. However, the speaker's assertion that the Father, Son and Holy Spirit are three supposes that the speaker himself has already provided the answer to the question 'three what?'; and *that* this is supposed presents a serious problem in the 'God' case, as I shall be arguing in the next section. I contend that St Augustine was very well aware of the point introduced above; he turns to the same question and problem at VII, 4 where he says that the Greeks have spoken of one essence (una essentia), three substances (tres substantiae), but the Latins of one essence, three persons (personae). The principal problem I shall deal with in this chapter is whether 'person' or 'persona' or ὑπόστασις can provide a completion of the type required for 'three' in the formulation 'three _'. This will necessitate a discussion of what terms can furnish us with units of counting; this I shall offer in Section 5. Prior to this discussion, however, it is necessary to raise several other and none the less important points, the first of which is crucial; for if my argument on the matter is correct, St Augustine cannot even get as far as raising the question 'What three?', for the conditions which must be met in order to sensibly raise the question are *not* met in the 'God' case.

2. At VII, 4, 7 Augustine says:†

> And provided that what is said is understood only in a mystery, such a way of speaking was sufficient in order that there might be something to say when it was asked what the three are, which true faith pronounces to be three when it declares that the Father is not the Son and that the Holy Spirit, which is the gift of God, is neither the Father nor the Son . . .

* Frege, *Foundations of Arithmetic*, tr. J. L. Austin, Oxford, Blackwell, 1950, p. 59 ff.

† Et dum intelligatur faltem in aenigmate quod dicitur, placuit ita dici, ut diceretur aliquid cum quae reretur, quid tria sint, quae tria esse fides vera pronuntiat cum Patrem non dicit esse Filium, et Spiritum Sanctum quod est donum Dei, nec Patrem dicit esse nec Filium. Cf. also, VII, 4, 9 'For it must be devoutly believed . . . nor the Holy Spirit the same with the Father or the Son'.

The serious problem here is on what basis 'true faith' pronounces there to be three, for the objection can and must be raised that in order to say 'the Father is not the Son', there has to be a completion for the formulation:

(i) 'The Father is not the same _ as the Son' or, to put the matter more precisely since what is intended here is that the Father is not identical with the Son,

(ii) 'The Father is not one and the same _ as the Son' and the problem which arises is that one cannot provide a filling for the '_' in this case. Hence, it will be pressed, the situation cannot even get as far as the formulation of St Augustine's problem; the real difficulty or difficulties lie *here*. We cannot get on to the question Augustine raises, since his problem supposes that we can *already* sensibly introduce talk of 'the three', which is precisely the problem. We have, in Augustine's treatment of the matter, no account as to how we are to complete 'the same' or 'one and the same' in the above formulations, or how it comes about that we can possibly introduce talk of 'the three' in the first place.

It might be thought that it is possible to introduce such talk in the following way, namely, it is possible to introduce talk of 'three individuals' here since in relation to the Father, Son, and Holy Spirit we can produce some one uniquely individuating characteristic. This move is question-begging since a uniquely individuating characteristic is necessarily a uniquely individuating characteristic of *something or other* and it is precisely *this* question which an account in terms of a uniquely individuating characteristic tries to answer. It might further be thought that we can speak of three individuals here since we are presented with three names and three mutually exclusive predicates, the γνωριστικαὶ ἰδιότητες. As a general thesis this will not suffice since even if we are presented with three names, by one criterion of 'different names', it does not follow that we have three individuals. They might all be names of the same individual or three fictitious names. Again, granted three mutually exclusive predicates, it does not follow that they apply to three different individuals—they might apply to more than three or less than three at different times or have no application at all. It might be argued that in the case of the *kind* of predicate here in question, namely, predicates which come under the heading of γνωριστικὴ ἰδιότης, for example 'ungenerated' or 'generated', such predicates cannot hold true of the same individual at different times, for if *x* is ungenerated then it is logically impossible for *x* to remain the same individual and at some future time 'generated' hold true of such individual. This point must be conceded, for to say '*x* is ungenerated' is not to make an ordinary predication of *x*, but to pass a remark of logical grammar on *x* to the effect that certain questions concerning *x* are ruled out of court and that certain predications concerning *x* are likewise ruled out of court—for example, the question of the source of generation of *x* and predicates of the form 'was generated by *y*'. Even so, this consideration does not rule out the point that three mutually exclusive predicates might apply to *more* than three individuals or have no application at all. Indeed, it seems patently false that the predicate 'ungenerated', for example, only applies to one individual.*

* St Augustine says that the uniquely distinguishing characteristic of the Father is that He is unbegotten (*De Trin.*, VII, 2, 3; XV, 26, 47); of the Son that he was begotten; of the Holy Spirit that he is of the Father and the Son. The production of three such purported uniquely distinguishing characteristics does not permit one to introduce the notion of 'three' in respect of the Father, Son and Holy Spirit, rather in that 'unbegotten', 'only begotten' and 'of the Father and the Son' are claimed to be such distinguishing characteristics it is *presupposed* that the notion of 'three' has been sensibly introduced.

Similar difficulties apply to any other attempt to say that one can talk of 'three' here from a consideration of γνωριστικαὶ ἰδιότητες (cf. St Basil, *Adversus Eunomium*, 2.29). That 'being generated' is the *proprium* of the Son and 'being ungenerated' that of the Father, cannot be a basis on which one can speak of 'the two'; the introduction of such *propria* presupposes that the Father and Son are two, namely, can be spoken of as two, which gets us back to our original problem. Again, any attempt to say that we can speak of 'Three' since we can speak of three operations (cf. St Cyril, *St John* 858B–859E), begs the question for an operation is necessarily the operation of something or other and in this case we are unable to specify what the subject of these operations is, as I argued in the last chapter. Finally, it cannot be maintained with Justin Martyr that we can speak of 'three' here since the Father, Son, and Holy Spirit are different *in number*, for if *x* is said to be numerically different to *y*, this is exponible as '*x* is not one and the same ____ as *y*' and hence we are back to the problem of providing a filling for the blank; we are back to the original problem.

3. It may be counter-argued that there is no need to expand the proposition:

'The Father is not identical with the Son'

into:

'The Father is not one and the same _ as the Son'.

The need for such an expansion is as follows. Strictly speaking, the phrases 'The Father' and 'The Son' are abbreviated definite descriptions, the full formulation being 'The Father of Our Lord Jesus Christ' and 'The Son of the Father Almighty' respectively, even though St Augustine often treats these phrases as names. Regarding these phrases as definite descriptions and definite descriptions which are not vacuous, it is necessary to specify what it is which satisfies them, for any non-vacuous definite description is necessarily a definite description of something or other. Further, any vacuous definite description is a potential definite description of something or other. Only if these conditions did not hold would it be possible to refuse to expand in the above manner. However, it is impossible that these conditions should fail to hold, for to entertain such a thesis would be to commit oneself to the impossible view that there need be no nominal essence of individuals.

Further, even if St Augustine is correct in treating 'The Father', etc. as names, then it is still necessary to specify what such putative names are the names *of* if one is to avoid the impossibility of saying that there need be no nominal essence of individuals. If there need be no nominal essence of individuals, then there can be no individuals, since we should, granted this thesis, have no possibility of introducing the concept of 'the same individual' and hence no possibility of introducing the 'one/many' distinction, for without nominal essence we should have no criterion of identity and hence no possibility of counting. Yet only if the thesis that there need be no nominal essence of individuals is a possibility would it be possible to refuse to expand in the above manner.

4. The problem above has been that in the case of 'The Father', etc. we cannot supply a filling for the blank in the

formulation 'one and the same —'. It will not do at this juncture to say that 'person' or ὑπόστασις can provide the required completion since even granted that these terms were of the kind which could provide such a completion, they could not do so in *this* context, since 'persons' or its equivalents answer the question 'What three?', *it already having been assumed* that the Father, Son, and Holy Spirit can be spoken of as *different xs*, when in fact no criterion of difference has been supplied. In an attempt to produce a parallel for the case of 'The Father', 'The Son', and 'The Holy Spirit', St Augustine later says (VII, 4, 7):*

> For when we say that Jacob was not the same as Abraham, but that Isaac was neither Abraham nor Jacob certainly we confess that they are three, Abraham, Isaac and Jacob. But when it is asked what three we reply three men, calling them in the plural by a specific name: but if we were to say three animals, then by a generic name.

Unfortunately the parallel breaks down in important ways. The supposed parallel case treats of proper names and not of abbreviated definite descriptions. Further, in the supposed parallel case, the condition of 'our confessing that they (Jacob, Isaac, Abraham) are three' is precisely that what we have here are three individuals of a certain sort, namely, three men of which 'Jacob', etc. are the proper names. *If* someone asks, as Augustine puts it, 'What three?' in regard to the assertion that Abraham, Jacob and Isaac are three, then it is *presupposed* that we who assert that they are three *have* provided the completion for 'three' in 'three —'. The inquirer is seeking an answer to the question 'What three?' so that *he* may understand what is being asserted. In *this* case the condition of 'confessing that Jacob, Abraham, and Isaac are three' is met, such that the inquirer's question is possible: in the former case it is not.†

* Cum enim dicimus non eundem esse Jacob qui est Abraham, Isaac autem nec Abraham esse nec Jacob, tres esse utique fatemur, Abraham, Isaac, Jacob. Sed cum queritur quia tres respondemus tres homines, nomine speciali eos pluraliter appellantur, generali autem, si dicamus tria animalia.

† A later parallel Augustine offers also breaks down for the same reason. 'Again when we say that your horse is not mine and that a third belonging to someone else is neither mine nor yours, then we confess that they are three . . .' (VII, 4, 7). The possibility of so confessing is precisely that we have introduced a term which

It can also be pressed that not only does the parallel break down, but that St Augustine's formulation of the parallel case is misleading, and understanding why it is misleading will enable us to see how it is that he can get to the stage of thinking that the *real* difficulty here is that of answering the inquirer's question. The passage for special scrutiny is: 'But when it is asked "What three?" we reply "three men" calling them in the plural by a specific name; but if we were to say "three animals" then by a generic name.' This account works on the assumption that to say 'Jacob, Isaac, Abraham . . . are men' is to *call* these individuals by a specific name, and likewise in the generic case, to call them by a generic name. Such a thesis is misguided. The formulation in terms of such named individuals being *called* men, or being called by a specific or generic name, immediately sets up the model indulged in by some of the Greek Fathers, namely* that of there being individuals of no kind or sort which are the putative bearers of proper names on the one hand and that in saying such putative bearers of these names are F (where F is a second substance word), one is, on the other hand, attaching a name to such individuals. Granted my above argument that for A to be a proper name is for A to be the proper name of something or other, and not (impossibly) the proper name of an individual *simpliciter*, then the model of individuals being called by specific or generic names cannot get off the ground.† Now St Augustine *can* get to the stage of thinking that *the* problem he has to cope with is that of the inquirer's question 'What three?' precisely because he is of the view, as is clear from this very example, that for a proper name to be the proper name of an individual it is *not* necessary that it be the proper name of an individual such and such,‡ and this is precisely why he could not have seen

can supply us with a unit of counting, namely 'horse': we have no such parallel in the 'God' case.

* Cf. Chapter 2, Appendix C, pp. 102–5.

† Cf. also VII, 4, 9.

‡ Cf. also VII, 6, 'For as Abraham, Isaac, Jacob are called three individuals (individua) . . . then if essence (essentia) is a genus, then a single essence (una essentia) i.e. a single individual has no species, just because "animal" is a genus, a single animal has no species.'

the difficulty in the confession that the Father is not the Son or in the confession that the Holy Spirit is neither the Father nor the Son. Together with the dichotomy 'particulars'/'calling by a common name' goes the dichotomy of 'particulars'/'universals', the latter to be understood in the sense of what is signified by a name which is common to several particulars. In the light of my points above, the dichotomy of 'particulars'/'universals' cannot get off the ground. However, it is clear that St Augustine is working in terms of such a model here for he says (VII, 4, 7): 'For Abraham, Isaac, and Jacob have in common that which is man: therefore they are called three men.' It is necessary to raise some additional points here to those raised in connection with 'calling by names', for it is not a sufficient condition of introducing the idea of 'having in common that which is man', that one should assert that to say 'A, B, C, ... are men' is to attach a name to such individuals. A Nominalist could and would hold this latter position and not be committed to the former. What has to be made clear is that the position from which *both* Nominalism and Realism *starts* is bogus, namely, a bogus dichotomy. Finally, it is of no value to say that Abraham, Isaac, and Jacob have in common that which is man, *therefore*, they are called three men. If they have in common 'that which is man', then in order for *that* to be determined it must already be known that they are *called* three men, hence no argument is offered here. Further, it is equally of no value to say: 'Abraham, Isaac, Jacob are called three men *since* they have in common that which is man', for here we are presented with no explanation. The supposed explanation simply repeats what is required to be explained. These considerations should make one wary of the metaphysics in operation here. Unfortunately Augustine's crucial question *is* set in the context of this metaphysical framework for he says: 'Of the Father, therefore, the Son, and the Holy Spirit, seeing that they are three, let us ask what three they are and *what they have in common*' (VII, 4, 7).*

* Pater ergo et Filius et Spiritus Sanctus quoniam tres sunt, quaeramus quid tres sunt et quid commune habeant ...

5(a) I now turn to the question of what terms can furnish us with units of counting. First, in order to alleviate a possible misunderstanding, a distinction must be drawn between 'one' and 'unit'. As Frege says* the word 'one' as the proper name of an object of mathematical study does not admit of a plural: whatever is to be regarded as a unit *must*. Frege's remark here is helpful, for it leads one to see that not only is it the case that 'one' as the proper name of an object of mathematics cannot be an object of counting, but that *no* proper name can. Proper names do not admit of the plural form and I cannot be asked to count the number of 'Socrates-es' or 'Aristotle-s' in the world or any given part of it: the device of 'Socrates-es', 'Aristotle-s' is purely artificial. I cannot be so asked since the question 'How many Aristotle-s?' (for instance) left unexpounded makes no sense. A sense *can* be given to such a question, granted an expansion into 'Count the number of __s which are called "Socrates" or "Aristotle" ', where the blank here is filled out by an item which can, at the least, take a plural form in its own right. For example, we might have 'Count the number of horses called "Socrates" present in this stable': *without* such an expansion we have no idea of what we are supposed to be counting and hence no possibility of starting. As it is with proper names, so it is with proper nouns, which can be regarded as proper names—for example, the names of colours or the names of genera or species. One cannot ask anyone to count the number of Greens in a given room, where 'Green' is the name of a colour, though of course one can count the number of 'greens' or 'shades of green'. 'Green' as the *name* of a colour does not admit of the plural, any more than 'one' as the name of a mathematical object does; and the same applies to 'Animal' and 'Man' as the names of a genus or species. One must not confuse 'Man' as the name of the species 'man', with 'man' as a common noun: the former can never admit of enumeration or quantification; the latter does so admit.

I have found Frege most helpful on the question of what terms can genuinely constitute a unit of counting. I shall

* Frege, op. cit., pp. 58–9.

follow his lead in laying down the list of conditions and defend him where some defence might seem necessary. For *x* to be a unit of counting the following conditions must hold:

(i) *x* must at least be a general term or *notio communis* as opposed to a proper name or proper noun. The above point concerning the necessity of expanding the request 'Count the number of As', where A is a proper name, is sufficient defence of this point. A general term, for Frege a 'concept word', is a term such that 'any', 'no', 'some' and the indefinite article can be sensibly prefixed to it.*

(ii) *x* must be such that it cannot as such be the reference of a grammatical subject, though it can constitute part of such reference.† This can be defended as follows. Consider an item which can ordinarily be spoken of as being a subject of number—'man'. Now 'man' as occurring in, 'The man in the white suit turned round abruptly', cannot be said to have a reference, as opposed to the whole phrase 'The man in the white suit' being said to have a reference. To ask for the reference of 'man' in such a context is to assume that 'man' contributes to the sense of the whole phrase as an independent unit of sense, that is, as a name, which is incorrect. 'Man' in such an occurrence must be regarded as an integral part of the whole phrase, and the whole phrase cannot be regarded as having sense in virtue of being a concatenation of names, for the whole phrase itself only has sense in the context of a proposition as both Russell and Wittgenstein saw, though Wittgenstein went further than Russell and claimed that proper names, as well as definite descriptions, only have sense in the context of a proposition.‡ If anyone thinks that such an item *can* occur as a legitimate subject, as in: 'All men have red blood', then Frege has an

* Frege, op. cit., p. 59; also Frege: 'On Concept and Object' in the *Philosophical Writings of Gottlob Frege*, tr. and ed. P. Geach and M. Black, Oxford, Blackwell, 1952.

† 'On Concept and Object', op. cit., p. 46.

‡ B. Russell, *The Philosophy of Logical Atomism*, Lecture VI, 'Descriptions and Incomplete Symbols'; *Introduction to Mathematical Philosophy*, Chapter XVI; Wittgenstein, *Tractatus*, 3.3.

answer to this.* Again, it would be incorrect to suppose that in the propositions 'Some men eat radishes', 'Some man hates Mr Wilson', 'man' refers to a man or 'men' refers to men: incorrect since such a supposition would confuse an indefinite description with a proper name.†

(iii) *x* must be such that it isolates in a definite manner what falls under it. To use Frege's own example, the concept 'letters in the word "three" ' isolates the 't' from the 'h', the 'h' from the 'r' and so on.‡ It is clear that whatever items yield units of counting must so isolate, otherwise there would be no possibility of (a) introducing items which isolate in an indefinite, that is, arbitrary manner, but which can form units of counting, (b) introducing items which are dependently countable items—for instance 'red things' (cf. below).

(iv) *x* must be such that it has the feature of being isolated from its environment and being indivisible; hence Frege says: 'Only a concept which isolates what falls under it in a definite manner and which does not permit any division of it at will, can be a unit relative to a finite number.' That this must hold true follows from assertions made by mathematicians about the unit which Frege has earlier considered in the *Foundations*; indeed it is only by taking the *concept* as the unit relative to number that one can give sense to assertions made about the unit and cope satisfactorily, or at least begin to cope satisfactorily, with the problem of how it is possible to curb the arbitrariness of our ways of regarding things which 'threatens to obliterate every distinction between one and many'. It is only by such a procedure that one can ascribe to units the two contradictory qualities of identity and indistinguishability. (For Frege's solution to this problem, cf. *Foundations*, p. 66–7.)

Not every general term, 'concept' in Frege's sense, can supply a unit of counting in its own right—colour predicates such as 'red' or 'blue' cannot. Frege comments: 'We can

* 'On Concept and Object', p. 47.

† Cf. B. Russell, 'On Denoting', *Mind* (new series), vol. XIV, 1905.

‡ Gottlob Frege, *The Foundations of Arithmetic*, tr. J. L. Austin, Oxford, Blackwell, 1950, p. 66.

divide up something falling under the concept "red" into parts in a variety of ways, without the parts thereby ceasing to fall under the concept "red". To a concept of this kind no finite number will belong' (*Foundations*, p. 66). I shall be discussing why this is so below.

In the light of the requirements of isolation and indivisibility it is necessary to divide general terms into two classes—those which do fulfil the requirements of isolation and indivisibility and those which do not. In order for a general term to be such as to meet the requirement of being isolated from its environment, it must at least be such as to supply what Professor Geach has called a 'criterion of identity',* namely it must be able to form a completion for the phrase 'the same __' in its own right. A general term such as 'red' is not able to provide such a completion. We can, of course, talk of 'the same red apple', but what supplies the criterion of identity here is 'apple' and not 'red'. The reasons why such adjectival general terms (to cite Professor Geach's category)† cannot be used as units of counting is not simply, as Geach points out, that they are vague or indeterminate (as Frege seems to have thought) and hence that you might have difficulty in making an *end* of counting, but that you cannot even make a *beginning*. You cannot make a beginning since you never know whether you have counted one already, for 'the same red thing' (for example) supplies no criterion of identity. However, the ability to serve as a criterion of identity does not provide a sufficient condition for a general term x to be able to serve as a unit of counting, as I pointed out in an earlier discussion.‡ Terms like 'gold' or 'lead' (mass terms; Aristotle's 'matter' terms), whilst supplying a criterion of identity, cannot supply us with units of counting. They cannot meet the requirements of indivisibility and 'isolating in a definite manner' required of terms which can furnish us with units of counting since (a) they do not exhibit a plural form; (b) even when they are prefaced in such a way as to produce the appearance of units of count-

* *Reference and Generality*, p. 39. I have introduced this notion earlier in Chapter 2. † Ibid., p. 39. ‡ Chapter 2, pp. 56–7.

ing—for example, when they are prefaced by such phrases as 'a bit of' or 'a piece of'* such complete terms *do* permit the division of, for example, gold or lead into parts at will. A bit of gold or a bit of lead can be divided into further bits and such a division necessarily does *not* result in one bit having several parts, but in several bits.† (c) 'a bit of gold' or 'a bit of lead' does *not* isolate in a definite manner *irrespective of context*. There may be circumstances in which 'a bit of gold' or 'a bit of lead' isolates in a definite manner such that one can be asked to count the bits of gold or lead, but such terms only so isolate if we are presented with a context in which what is to constitute a bit of gold or lead is made clear to us. Our ability to count bits of gold or lead is context dependent, and the same goes for our ability to count anything under the form 'a bit (piece, chunk, . . .) or *x*' where *x* is a mass term. On the contrary our ability to count clocks, saucepans or rings is not in the relevant sense so context dependent. (d) What constitutes a bit of gold or lead *is* an arbitrary matter depending on the context in question; on the contrary what constitutes a 'letter in the word "three" ', to use Frege's example, is *not* an arbitrary matter dependent on the context in question.

5(b) To say more on the features of isolation and indivisibility I shall use as an illustration Aristotle's examples of second substance terms, such as 'man', 'horse', 'animal'. This is not, of course, to say that *only* Aristotelian second substance terms can furnish us with units of counting; Aristotle himself does not hold this.‡ I use such terms for the purpose of illustration only. Such terms exhibit the feature of 'isolating what falls under them in a definite manner' in that, unlike 'a bit of gold' or 'a bit of silver', it is *not* an arbitrary matter what constitutes a man or a horse. There might be cases where a difficulty arises as to whether a given individual man is 'really' a man, but this does not show that what constitutes a man is an arbitrary matter, for if this latter *were*

* Cf. *Reference and Generality*, pp. 40–1.

† Since 'is a bit of gold' or 'is a bit of lead' is truly predicable of each item in such a division.

‡ Cf. Chapter 2, p. 56.

the case, then the kinds of problem case alluded to could never arise, for the question of whether a given individual man was *really a man or not* could never arise. On the other hand, one cannot sensibly raise the question of whether A, which is a piece of lead (say), is *really* a piece of lead or *not* really a piece of lead. *Anything* which is lead *can* constitute a piece of lead. Such terms exhibit the feature of 'being isolated from their environment' in the following senses:

(i) In order to understand their application you do not have to understand the application of some *other* concept which furnishes a criterion of identity, as you do, for example in the case of 'leg', 'arm' or 'tail'. A leg, an arm, or a tail are not 'isolated from their environment' in that a leg, arm, or tail are the leg, arm or tail of something or other, where the fill-out for 'something or other' is a term which *is* 'isolated from its environment'. Legs, arms, and tails cannot provide units of counting, since in order to count them we have to know, or implicitly understand, of *what* they are the legs, etc. Dismembered legs, for example, are still the dismembered legs of something or other and have their identity by reference to that of which they were the legs. On the contrary, in order for x to be a man or a horse it is not necessary that x be a man or a horse of something or other; indeed this latter formula '_ of something or other', where the fill-out for 'something or other' is a term which is isolated from its environment, has no clear sense in these cases.

(ii) In order to understand their application you do not have to understand the application of some other concept which furnishes a criterion of identity as you do in the case of Professor Geach's 'adjectival general terms'. Such terms exhibit the feature of indivisibility in that, whilst items falling under them can be spoken of as being divided up, the units so formed are still parts of a whole. One can divide up a man into a head, arms, legs, etc. and even into 'chunks of flesh', but in such a division we do not have a series of independent units: they are the head, arms, etc. of a *man* and are only identifiable and countable as such (cf. *Metaphysics*, 1030a23–5; 1035b3–12).

The following points must also be noted concerning the above types of term.

(a) One can count the number of things introduced by such a term without reference to some 'higher order' concept or some 'lower order' concept in the following sense. For example, I can count the number of men present in this room without reference to a 'higher order' concept such as 'person' and without reference to a 'lower order' concept such as 'flat-footed man'. I can count the number of horses in this paddock without reference to some 'higher order' concept such as 'sentient being' and without reference to some 'lower order' concept such as 'dapple grey'. Again, to complete the case for a genus, I can count the number of animals in this park without reference to the concept of 'sentient being' and without reference to some lower order concept such as 'cloven-footed'.

(b) To count the number of items falling under the genus *x* would be to count the number of items falling under the species of that genus, but the counting of the number of items falling under the genus *x* would not be comprised of the counting of the number of items falling under the various species of that genus, for a man could comply with the request: 'Count the number of animals (for instance) in this park' *without* knowing under which species they fell and indeed it might be the case that not all animals (for example) fall under clearly determined or yet even 'discovered' species. That is, one cannot adopt the position that to count the items falling under the species of a genus *is* to count the items falling under a genus. Counting the items falling under a genus is, logically, a separable activity. It hardly needs saying that to count the number of items falling under a species S is not to count the number of items falling under the genus under which S falls. I have inserted these points here as I shall have occasion to refer to them later when I discuss the question of whether 'person' exhibits the features which terms which can furnish us with units of counting do. I must emphasize that I have only taken Aristotle's examples of 'second substance' terms as an illustration in order to try to spell out what is involved in the requirements of isolability and indivisibility or what may reasonably be said to be involved.

6(a) I now turn to the question of whether 'person' in any of the senses possible in the context of St Augustine's discussion can furnish us with a unit of counting. St Augustine himself is very unsure about the answer 'three persons' to the question: *quid igitur tres?* He says (*De Trin.*, VII, 4, 7):* 'For if three persons then what is meant by person is common to them, therefore that name is either specific or generic to them if we regard the custom of species'.† Now the trouble with the 'God' case, according to St Augustine, is that in order to cope with it in accordance with the above principle, it is necessary that the three should have a specific name but *there is none to be found*. 'Person', he claims, is a generic name in so much that a man can also be called, although there is so great a difference between man and God.‡ One can indeed sympathize with him here since, as it has been said that there is no difference in *essentia* between the three viewed as individuals, it is necessary that they belong to the same species; yet 'person' in his view cannot fulfil the role of being the name of a specific kind, for the reason offered above.§ However, I shall argue that 'person' in Augustine's use here cannot be regarded as either a specific or generic name and cannot furnish us with a unit of counting. Augustine has commented that a man can be called a person, and it is this use and sense of 'person' which is up for consideration here. Now to say that (i) a given man, say Socrates, is a person or (ii) '(Any) man is a person' (this admittedly sounds odd) is not to allocate either (i) a parti-

* I have used the English translation by A. W. Haddan (in the translation of the works of Augustine edited by Dods, Edinburgh, T. & T. Clark, 1873, vol. VII) as a guide. The reference in Haddan for the passage mentioned is p. 191.

† Si enim tres personae commune est eis id quod persona est; ergo speciale hoc aut generale nomen est eis, si consuetudinem loquendi respicimus.

‡ Cf. the end of section 7; Haddan, p. 192.

§ For an alternative account in which Augustine does *not* regard persons as a species or genus, cf. *De Trin.*, VII, 6, 11; Haddan, p. 197. I shall be referring to this later.

cular man to a genus, like to say 'Socrates is an animal' is to so allocate or (ii) to allocate *man* to a genus, like to say 'Man is an animal' is to so allocate. Rather, to say that Socrates (for example) is a person is to allocate Socrates to a category; such a remark allocates Socrates to a category in the sense that to so speak is to make a remark of 'logical grammar' concerning Socrates. It gives us a rule to the effect that it makes good sense to speak of Socrates in certain ways—for example, that he can be spoken of as a 'thinking being', that is, predicates connoting activities which involve thought can be sensibly attached to him as a subject, in the way in which they cannot be so sensibly attached to machines, for instance, as subjects; that he can be sensibly spoken of as having intentions, desires, motives, aims and purposes, in other words that he can be sensibly spoken of as an *agent*, as opposed to being spoken of in purely behavioural terms as for instance a dog can; that he can be sensibly spoken of as possessing human virtues and vices and as having the capacity for such virtues and vices, and as having emotions—as opposed to exhibiting behavioural traits. In short, to say that Socrates (for instance) is a person is to say that what Strawson calls 'P-predicates' are sensibly attributable to Socrates.* Such a remark as we are considering does not present us with a proposition which says something true or false concerning Socrates in the sense that 'is a person' presents us with a true or false predication of Socrates; rather it presents us with a rule as to what can *meaningfully be* true or false predications of Socrates. In other words such a proposition expresses the condition of making true or false predications of Socrates; it decides what *can* be such true or false predications, hence 'is a person' cannot itself be such a true or false predication. It may be protested that such a proposition as 'Socrates is a person' *can* be true or false: false, for example, if 'Socrates' were not the proper name of a man, as has been assumed for the purposes of the above discussion, but the proper name of some mountain in South Carolina. What, however, would

* *Individuals*, pp. 104–5.

it be to say that it was false that Socrates, in this use of the name, is a person? It would be to say that it made no sense to attribute P-predicates to a mountain. This account by no means commits one to the thesis that that to say: ' "Socrates (where this is the name of a mountain) is a person" is false' is to falsely predicate 'is a person' of some mountain. Concomitantly, to say: ' "Socrates (where this is the name of a man) is a person" is true' is to say that one can meaningfully attribute P-predicates to such an entity. If anyone should say that it cannot both be maintained that the proposition 'Socrates is a person' presents us with a rule of 'logical grammar' *and* say that it might be either true or false, I reply: 'Take note of what the truth of such a proposition consists in'—for to say that the proposition is true is to say that the rule holds. Now the condition of one meaningfully attributing what can briefly be designated as 'P-predicates' to an individual is that the question 'What is A?'* where 'A' is the name of some individual, has taken a certain answer—namely 'man'. Had Aristotle's question not yielded this answer, such that 'A' in a given use was the name of a mountain or a cat, then one could not have meaningfully attributed P-predicates to the individual so named. It is for this reason that the above proposition '(Any) man is a person' or 'Man is a person' is queer, for 'being a man' in one sense, namely in the sense of 'being of the human species', is a necessary and sufficient condition of any *x* being sensibly said to be a person and in another sense, namely in the sense of 'being a male of the human species', is a sufficient condition of any *x* being sensibly said to be a person.

In this way, I contend, to say that 'Socrates is a person', where 'Socrates' is the name of a man, is to make a grammatical remark—in contradistinction to the proposition that Socrates is a man, where for 'man' we read 'male of the human species'. In this latter case 'is a man' can be falsely predicated of an individual animal so named. Again, whilst 'man' can answer Aristotle's τί ἐστι; question, 'person'

* Aristotle's τί ἐστι; question.

cannot. *Vide* my above argument, 'person' cannot tell us *what* something is. Further, the allocation of A, an individual of a certain kind or type, to a certain genus or species, is something which can be done on the basis of empirical observation in accordance with certain 'natural' laws or principles, and empirical observation can settle the issue, at least in most cases, as to whether it is true or false that A belongs to the genus or species to which it is said by a given person on a given occasion to belong. On the contrary, the allocation of an individual of a certain kind to the category of 'person' is not something which can be done on the basis of empirical observation. That an individual is a person is not an empirical matter; it is a matter settleable only by reference to the kind of status such an individual has or has had. To put the matter briefly, whether or not A can be said to be a person is determined by, not whether A plays a social role, but by whether A has or has had a social role: by whether A is a social being—not by the physical or biological attributes A has or even by A's behaviour. This can be illustrated as follows. If we were to come across an individual which had all the physical attributes of a man, such that a biologist were to state that such an individual belonged to the species 'man' and yet this individual were found in a remote part of the world where man had not previously ventured, or on some planet, then it would at least not make *clear* sense to say of such a being that 'he' was a person, for 'he' (it?) had not had a certain kind of birth or life—namely a birth and a life in the context of a human society. It would not clearly be meaningful to say of 'him' that he had intentions, motives, desires or thoughts, any more than it does of animals. It would not simply be false that such a being had thoughts, intentions, etc., for what could constitute it being true that such a being had thoughts or intentions, etc.?

It might be objected here that, even granted that the allocation of an individual of a certain kind to the category of 'person' is not something which can be done on the basis of empirical observation, but is only settleable by reference to the kind of status which such an individual has or has had, only settleable by reference to the social role such an individual has or has had, this is not unique to persons and certainly not a sufficient condition for saying that 'person' occurring in the predicate place in a proposition of a subject–predicate form allocates to a category. After all, what it is for someone to be a prime minister or a president is only settleable by reference to the social role that person has or plays and is certainly not a matter of empirical observation in the above implied sense, yet to say that some individual is a prime minister or a president cannot be thought of as allocating that individual to a category as opposed to a class. However, what I have said above does not commit me to claiming, neither am I claiming, that a sufficient condition for allocating to a category is that the term introduced by the predicate expression indicates a social role or status. That 'person', when appearing in the predicate place of a subject-predicate proposition, allocates to a category, I have argued on independent grounds. The relevant passage above was introduced to point out that allocation to a genus or species in the technical sense which St Augustine employs was something done on the basis of empirical investigation. To this it might be retorted that the crucial matter here concerns the wider question of whether 'person' as thus occurring can introduce a class, not whether it can introduce a genus in a technical sense, so how do I cope with the 'president' and 'prime minister' examples? Now whilst it is true that what it is for someone to be a president or prime minister is not settleable by reference to an empirical inquiry in the above implied sense but only be reference to the social role that person plays, there is indeed a crucial difference between saying on the one hand, 'A is a prime minister' or 'A is a president' and saying 'A is a person', on the other. For in the former cases, the issue can be settled by a form of sociological inquiry, which we might justifiably regard as an empirical inquiry in an extended sense: that A is a person however cannot be settled by any such sociological inquiry, for that there are persons, that we have this category, is a precondition of any such sociological inquiry. That there are persons, that we have this category, is not itself a sociological matter.

It might be further argued that on some occasions of use, *contra* to what was implied above, the sentence 'A is a president' or 'A is a prime minister' might be used to make a grammatical remark about A and on such occasions of use 'president' or 'prime minister' become category terms, yet on other occasions of use such sentences can be used to make statements of political or sociological fact and in such cases 'president' or 'prime minister' introduces a class, not a category. Can we not make out a case for saying that in a parallel fashion in some uses of the sentence 'A is a person', the phrase 'is a person' allocates to a category, as you have maintained, but in other case this sentence may be used to make a statement of sociological fact, such that 'person' introduces a class, not a category? It is my contention that no such parallel can be drawn since, whilst it might indeed be the case that 'A is a prime minister' states a matter of political or sociological fact, that A is a person can never be a sociological fact, as I implied above. Rather, that A is a person is a condition of there being sociological facts concerning A. If it is a sociological fact that A plays a certain role, say that of being a member of parliament, in the community of which he is a part, it is not a further or even prior sociological fact that A is a person: that A is a person, one might say, is a condition of the possibility of A playing that role. It was for this reason that I was careful to say earlier that the question of whether a given individual A is a person is determined, not by whether A plays a certain social role, but by whether A has a social role in the sense of whether A has the possibility of playing certain social roles, that is by whether A is a social being, and to be a social being is not itself a sociological fact about an individual but the condition of there being sociological facts concerning that individual.

6(b) I commented earlier on the queer nature of the proposition '(Any) man is a person' and I attempted to offer an explanation of this. An account of this proposition can certainly be given, namely, it is to say that anything which is a man can be sensibly spoken of in certain ways, for instance, as having thoughts, intentions, aims, motives, etc.—in short, P-predicates can be sensibly employed in connection with any such individual, and that true or false propositions containing P-predicates can be made concerning any such individual. What we have in this case, too, is a remark of logical grammar concerning any man, as 'Socrates is a person' gave us such a remark of grammar concerning the individual man. Hence, I contend, in both cases 'is a person' allocates to a category but, as I have argued earlier, allocation to a category is not allocation to a genus.

On this account of 'person' which I have been offering, the subject of the attribution of P-predicates is a man in the sense of a member of the human species: it is a certain answer to Aristotle's τί ἐστι; question when asked of an individual. This account differs from Strawson's account in *Individuals*, for in his account the subject of P-predicates is an entity of a *logical* type. On p. 104 he says: 'So far I have said that the concept of a person is to be understood as the concept of a type of entity such that *both* predicates ascribing states of consciousness (P-predicates) and predicates ascribing corporeal characteristics . . . are equally applicable to an individual entity of that type.' That the 'type' involved here is a logical one can be seen from pp. 103–4, where he speaks of acknowledging the *logical* primitiveness of the concept of a person and goes on to say:

> There would be no question of ascribing one's own states of consciousness or experiences, to anything, unless one also ascribed, or were ready and able to ascribe, states of consciousness or experiences to other individual entities of the same logical type as that thing to which one ascribes one's own states of consciousness.

Now if 'persons' are entities of a certain *logical* type, so that the concept of 'person' is a *logical* one, then Strawson cannot sensibly speak of picking out and identifying individuals of that type; yet this is precisely what he does do (p. 104):

> The condition of reckoning oneself as a subject of such predicates is that one should also reckon others as subjects of such predicates. The condition in turn of this being possible is that one should be able to distinguish from

> one another, to pick out or identify, different subjects of such predicates i.e. different individuals of the type concerned.

I contend that Strawson cannot make such a move. If *x* is a *logical type* then *x* can supply no criterion of identity for individuals and hence no criterion for picking out or identifying individuals. That Strawson's concept of 'person' cannot provide us with such criteria can be seen by referring to a sentence in the penultimate passage cited above, namely: 'unless one also ascribed, or were ready and able to ascribe, states of consciousness or experiences to other individual entities of the same logical type . . .' Here one must raise the question 'Other individual *what*?' or, less misleadingly, 'Other *what*?' in order to know *what* is being referred to. 'Other individuals of the same logical type . . .' cannot help us to determine reference, for being of a certain *logical* type can never furnish us with a means of identifying anything. To be of a certain logical type is to be of a certain *category*, not to be of a certain class. I thus maintain that Strawson's account contains a radical confusion and it is only by such a confusion that he can, so to speak, 'have it both ways'—namely *both* have the concept of person as a logically primitive concept that is as introducing a certain category *and* as introducing an identifiable type of entity. Persons cannot be identifiable entities or entities which are able to be 'picked out' if they are entities falling under a logical type and as falling under that type. When Strawson is strictly adhering to his thesis that the concept of person is logically primitive, then one cannot sensibly raise the question: 'How many persons are there in this room?'—in general one cannot introduce the form of question 'How many —'. 'Person', as Strawson introduces it, cannot furnish us with a unit of counting. It is only by the confusion which I have mentioned that he can think that persons are countable entities, and only by such a confusion that he can think that the *particular* subjects of P-predicates are entities of a logical type. How *could* the particular subjects of P-predicates be entities of a logical type?—for if *x* is a logical type, then *x* can supply no criterion of identity. On my account the criterion of identity for particular subjects of P-predicates is that supplied by such a term as 'man', which can indeed supply a criterion of identity.

I thus contend that 'person', when occurring in the predicate place in a proposition, allocates to a category and that the whole proposition containing such an occurrence produces a 'grammatical' remark. Someone however may still want to press that 'person', when occurring in the predicate place, can furnish us with a unit of counting. He may argue as follows. Why cannot it be said that if one produces a list of propositions in which 'person' occurs as part of the predicate, then one can sensibly be asked to count the number of persons introduced into such propositions? as for instance in the following:

'Matthew is a person'
'Socrates is a person'
'Aristotle is a person'?

Here the request to count the number of persons so introduced would be the request to count the number of *x*s which are the bearers of the proper names so introduced, but to count these would be to count the number of entities the terms signifying which could at the very least provide a criterion of continued identity, but the concept of 'person' can provide no such principle. We do, of course, talk of A being the *same* person as B or of A being *one and the same* person as B, but from this it must not be concluded that 'person' supplies a criterion of identity for individuals. To say that A is the same person as B, where A and B are proper names, is to say that A and B refer to one and the same __, where the blank is replaceable by a term signifying an entity which can be sensibly be spoken of as being the subject of actions, intentions, thoughts—in short, being the subject of P-predicates: and it is the term which can provide the replacement for the blank which supplies the criterion of identity. For example, 'Dr Jekyll is one and the same person as Mr Hyde' is writable as: 'Dr Jekyll and Mr Hyde refer to one and the same *man*.' Where A and B are definite descriptions, to say, 'A is one and the same person as B' is to say that one and the same _ satisfies both definite descriptions, where the blank here is replaceable by a term signifying that which can be sensibly spoken of as being the subject actions, intentions, thoughts—in short, being the subject of P-predicates. For example, 'The Prime Minister of Great Britain is one and the same person as the Member of Parliament for Bexley' is writable as: 'One and the same *man* satisfies both the descriptions "the prime Minister of Great Britain" and "the member of Parliament for Bexley".' If 'person' were such as to provide a criterion of identity, then we could understand such a proposition as 'Dr Jekyll is one and the same person as Mr Hyde' *without* having to understand that a *man* is being referred to here; it would thus be a contingency that 'Dr Jekyll' and 'Mr Hyde' are the proper names of a man, which is no contingency in the use of these names under discussion. I have no need to make out a separate case here for saying that 'person' cannot supply a principle of individuation for individuals, for only those terms which can supply a criterion of identity *can* supply a principle of individuation even though not all such terms can.

Since 'person' cannot supply us with a criterion of identity, it cannot exhibit that feature of 'being isolated from its environment' and neither can it exhibit the feature of 'isolating in a definite manner'. Indeed it cannot isolate at all, for it does not and cannot have the function of allocating to a class. Further, it cannot exhibit the feature of indivisibility, since in order for it so to do it must be such as to furnish a principle of individuation for individuals—as Frege's 'letters in the word three' does—which in the light of my above argument it cannot do. In the light of these considerations I see no reason to withdraw my contention that 'person', at least as occurring as part of the predicate '_ is a person', cannot furnish us with a unit of counting.

6(c) I now turn to the use of 'person' as occurring as part of a subject term. It may be pressed that, as thus occurring, it can furnish us with a unit of counting. In such a use it can be sensibly prefaced by 'any', 'no', 'some' and the indefinite article, and what it signifies can constitute part of the reference of a grammatical subject. Further, we can quite naturally introduce propositions in which 'person' as occurring as part of the subject term is preceded by a number, for instance 'Three persons were killed in the fire which ravaged Macy's department store' or 'Twenty persons were executed in Salisbury this morning'. Now granted my case above that 'person' cannot supply a criterion of identity and hence a principle of individuation for individuals, these propositions which seem to imply that 'person' can furnish a unit of counting cannot be taken at their face value. From the fact that 'person' here can be sensibly combined with a number is not to be taken to imply that it can sensibly be combined with a number in its own right. 'Person' in such a context could only furnish a unit of counting in its own right if the above-mentioned conditions of isolability and indivisibility are met. However, 'person', in such a use, cannot 'isolate in a definite manner' what falls under it, for it cannot isolate at all. This can be seen as follows. One only understands the use of 'Three persons' in my first example if one can supply a formulation of the form 'Three _s were killed in the fire which ravaged Macy's department store', where the blank takes as a replacement a general term which can provide a criterion of identity and individuation signifying an entity which can be spoken of as being the subject of P-predicates—for example, three men in the sense of three individuals of the human species. What 'isolates in a definite manner' here is 'man' in the sense of the human species, and it is likewise 'man' which furnishes us with the unit of counting. And likewise in regard to the second example above. Persons, even in this use, are not to be regarded as a genus of which man, in the sense of the human species, is to be regarded as a species for, whereas a generic term is a unit of counting which can be introduced without reference to some 'higher order' or 'lower order' concept, as explained above,* 'person' is not. One cannot count the number of persons present on a given occasion without

* See p. 159 (a).

introducing such a 'lower order' concept, namely 'man' in the sense of the human species. Again, whereas a generic term is a unit of counting which is genuinely isolable from terms denoting species which fall under it, as I argued earlier,* 'persons' in relation to *x*s which are persons is not so isolable. Whereas to count items falling under a genus may, but need not, comprise counting items falling under the various species of that genus, to count items falling under the concept of 'person', where 'person' forms part of the subject of a proposition, *is* to count and consists in counting the number of *x*s which are said to be persons. To count the number of persons killed in the fire *is* to count the number of *x*s which are said to be persons, namely to count the number of men, in the sense of the number of individuals falling under the concept of the human species. To put the matter in a Rylian way: there are not men, women and children *and* persons. This is not, of course, to say that for there to be persons is for there to be men in the sense of members of the human species, for such an account supposes that such a proposition as 'There are persons' makes sense, which it does not, any more than the proposition 'There are objects' makes sense. One can only introduce the formulation 'There are . . .' in connection with countable entities.

It follows from these considerations that 'person', even in its use as part of a subject, cannot exhibit the further features of either (a) 'being isolated from its environment' or (b) 'being indivisible'. Only a term which can furnish a criterion of continued identity can exhibit the latter feature, as I argued earlier. I thus conclude that 'person' cannot exhibit those features which are required of a term which can furnish us with a unit of counting.

It might be interjected: 'Surely we can introduce "one and the same person" ', where 'person' signifies a continued existence and is not replaceable by (for instance) 'man', 'woman', 'child' or any such phrase? Do we not want to say that it is one and the same person who is first a boy and then

* See p. 159 (b).

a man, so that it is necessary to allow that 'person' can indeed be both a term which introduces a criterion of continued identity and a unit of counting? I contend that it is not so necessary and indeed not so possible. In the first place, it is not the case that we *can* speak of 'one and the same person who was first a boy and then became a man', for it is not a person who becomes a man but a boy; in the particular case, it is not the person A who becomes a man, but the boy A who becomes the man A. There is no underlying something or other (a person) who first takes on the characteristics of a boy and then of a man, for to say of A that A is a boy is not to attribute any characteristic to A but to specify what A is; similarly to say of A that A is a man is to specify what A is. We might say: 'The boy becomes a man and the man becomes an old man and yet the same personality is retained', but this is not to say that one and the same person was a boy, became a man and then an old man, and does not, necessarily does not, commit one to saying that 'person' can introduce a criterion of identity and unit of counting in its own right. Indeed, a necessary condition of introducing 'the same personality' and hence 'one and the same personality' is that we first introduce that continued existence which exhibits that personality. The continued existence which exhibits that personality is the human animal which is a boy and then becomes a man. That is, where we want to speak of 'one and the same person', this is to speak of one and the same human animal which retains the same personality, the (numerical) identity of the personality being determined by the identity of the human animal whose personality it is. That is, in central cases, we can only speak of 'the same person' in that we can speak of the same human animal (sc. same man); 'dual personalities' are necessarily the deviant case. This is not to deny that there are problems concerning how we determine that we speak of 'the same human animal' (the same man') in relation to any individual, but this need not concern us here.

6(d) To return to the 'God' case. St Augustine has commented that a man can be called a person, and it was such a use of 'person' which was primarily up for consideration in this section. In *this* use of 'person', since it allocates to a category, God cannot be said to be three persons or any number of persons. However, this does not of itself rule out of court the formula 'Three persons in one substance'. Even so, this latter formulation *is* ruled out of court unless it is possible to produce a formulation in terms of a term which *can* provide a criterion of identity and unit of counting which is such that whatever falls under it can be sensibly spoken of as a person; yet it is just such a formulation which it is impossible to provide. Indeed the demand for an answer to the question 'Three *what*?' was precisely the worry St Augustine had had earlier under his worry about the 'specific name'.* He comments there that there is none to be found, as indeed there is none. As he is only too well aware such items as 'friends', 'sons', and 'holy spirits' will not do, although they fail for different reasons which it would be tedious to spell out. However, not only is it the case that no answer can be found to the question 'Three *what*?' but that none could be, for any such answer must furnish a principle of individuation, yet the introduction of a term which could furnish a principle of individuation in relation to God would go against the doctrine of the divine simplicity.†

7. I now turn to the question of whether 'person' in the sense of *prosopon* exhibits those features which would enable it to be regarded as a unit of counting. We may enlist the following senses of *prosopon*: 'face', 'character', 'type', 'representation', 'aspect', 'role'.‡

7(a) To take 'face' first. It seems clear that this concept cannot present us with a unit of counting in its own right, for it does not present us with that feature of being isolated from its environment which is required of such units. A face is necessarily the face of someone or other, or something or other, and the identity of the face is determined by the identity of whom or of what it is the face. This is not to say

* Cf. p. 160 above: *De Trin.*, VII,iv,7.

† *Summa Theologica*, Ia,q3,a7.

‡ Cf. C. C. J. Webb, op. cit., pp. 36–7; 44–7; G. L. Prestige, op. cit., pp. 157–62.

that we cannot count faces, but to count faces we have to count the *x*s of which (say) A, B, and C are the faces. It might be contended that this is false; it might be said that one can count the number of faces in this room (say) without knowing *whose* faces they are. True enough; but one cannot count the number of faces without knowing *of what* they are the faces, for without such knowledge one would not even know that what one was putatively counting were faces, as opposed to animated physical features which *looked like* faces. Again, I can only count the number of sad, sanguine, or wistful faces in that I can count the number of *x*s which exhibit such sad, sanguine, or wistful faces. Admittedly one and the same man or animal may now exhibit a wistful face, now a sad face, but in that we have two faces here we have two faces of one and the same man or animal. A counter-case might be pressed here. Suppose one were presented with a piece of paper on which a number of 'funny faces' were drawn; surely one can be asked, in this situation, to count the number of faces even though the question 'faces of what?' cannot arise? (The supposed answer to the question 'faces of what?' in terms of 'faces of funny men' is *no* answer: for there are no funny men here if there are no *drawings of* funny men.) This counter-case will not work, for in the envisaged situation what one is being asked to count are *drawings of funny faces*, and the criterion or criteria for whether *x* is a drawing of a funny face are not those for deciding whether *x* is a face.

Even though 'face' does not exhibit the feature of being isolated from its environment, which is required of units of counting, it might still be pressed that this is not to say that one cannot speak of three persons, in the sense of three faces, in connection with God. However, a condition of so speaking is that in connection with God we can supply a term which is such that it can furnish a replacement for the blank in the formulation: 'Three faces in one and the same __'. 'Substance' cannot furnish such a replacement, for as I previously argued, it cannot sensibly be preceded by a number. 'God' cannot so furnish, for apart from considerations raised earlier,* we are here concerned, as St Augustine is concerned, with 'Three persons in one substance' in its role as an explanation as to how *God* can be both *three* and *one*.† Finally, taking 'god' as a replacement would commit one to the thesis that God was *a* god. Thus, far from it being the case that 'person', in the sense of 'face', can provide a unit of counting in its own right and hence furnish an answer to St Augustine's question 'Three what?' it is, to say the least, problematic as to whether 'person' in this sense can be sensibly used in connection with God.

7(b) 'Character' meets with similar difficulties in one use. In that use a character is necessarily the character of someone or other, or something or other, and to count the number of characters involves a necessary reference to the *x*s which *have* the character. However, to count the number of characters, in this use, is not necessarily to count the number of *x*s which are said to have or exhibit that character. For example, whilst on the one hand, to count the number of sleazy characters on Lime Street station on a given evening is to count the number of men or women *of* such a character, on the other hand one and the same man may exhibit several different characters; *but* the several different characters exhibited are all characters of *one and the same man* and the identity of the individual characters exhibited is uniquely determined by the identity of the man. One cannot simply be asked to count the characters in this type of case; one has to be asked to count the characters a given man or series of men exhibits. Thus 'characters', in this use, does not exhibit that feature of being isolated from its environment, neither can such a term 'isolate in a definite manner', hence it cannot provide an answer to St Augustine's question. Indeed 'person', in this sense of 'character', in relation to God, can only sensibly be preceded by a number if we can produce a formulation of the form: 'Three characters of one and the same__', where the replacement for the blank can

* Cf. Chapter 2, Appendix B, pp. 85–6 above.

† In itself, without any further specification, a nonsensical question. I shall not adumbrate on this now.

furnish us with a criterion of identity and unit of counting and we meet the same difficulties here as we did in regard to 'faces' above.

There is however another sense of 'character', the sense in which we speak of characters in a play or dramatic performance, and this is the sense, it will be said, which is pertinent here, granted the origin of *prosopon*. Now whilst characters in a play are not the characters of someone or other in the way in which 'character' in the above-discussed sense is—they are not something someone *has*—even so, 'character' in this sense does not exhibit that feature of isolability required of units of counting, since in order to *begin* to comply with the request 'Count the number of characters' one has to know the identity of the play or drama in question. Hence 'characters' in this sense cannot provide an answer to St Augustine's question and once again 'character' in this sense can only sensibly be used in connection with God if one can provide a formulation of the form 'Three characters in one—', where the blank here can be replaced by a term which can furnish a criterion of identity and unit of counting.

7(c) 'Type' meets with similar objections and hence with parallel difficulties in regard to answering St Augustine's question. 'Representation' might be thought to be a more promising candidate but it turns out to be more problematic. A representation, as opposed to a symbol, is a representation of something or other, and the identity of a representation is dependent upon that of which it is a representation. A representation however presents special difficulties. To say that *x*, say a portrait of Homer, is a representation is *not* to say *what x* is; in this case we already know *that*—*x* is a portrait. To say '*x* is a representation' is to make a grammatical remark concerning *x*: it indicates the realm of discourse to which *x* belongs. It indicates to a hearer that one set of questions, as opposed to another set, make sense when asked of *x* and that one set of predicates, as opposed to another, are possible predicates of *x*. For example, saying that *x*, for instance the portrait of Homer, is a representation of Homer, precludes one from asking that set of questions which are askable of the person so represented and from using those predicates which can be sensibly employed in connection with *x*s which can be said to be persons as falling under that category. For example, to ask whether the portrait of Homer thinks, acts, or has intentions indicates a 'grammatical' mistake on the part of the person so asking. Again, to say that the portrait of Homer thinks, acts, or has intentions is not to make a series of merely false propositions, but a series of impossible ones. What are possible predicates in this case is dependent on and determined by what it is for something to be a representation: we can ask whether the portrait of Homer is a good likeness or a poor one; whether it is 'true to life'; whether it brings out his character. If Plato ever thought that works of art in the sense of portraits were 'a third remove from reality' he was gravely misguided, for it makes no sense to predicate of the portrait, as falling under the category of 'representation', what it makes sense to predicate of the man Homer, and this is what is brought out in saying that the portrait of Homer, for example, is a representation. (It must be pointed out that the same considerations do not hold in respect of pictures: a picture need not be a representation of anything or be intended to be a representation of anything.) Now it is only if 'representation' can answer the question 'What is it?' and yield substantial as opposed to grammatical information that it can supply an answer to St Augustine's question and hence enable him to start counting. We can, of course, talk of several representations of the same thing—for example, several representations of the Eastern seaboard of the United States in poetry, landscape paintings and in music (say Dvorak's 'New World' Symphony), but this does not show that 'representation' can furnish us with a unit of counting or provide an answer to St Augustine's question. If we *do* talk of 'several representations of the same thing' then we are prepared, and must be prepared, to say what *form* these representations take and we can only speak of 'several representations' in that we can introduce the several *forms of* *representation*. We cannot speak of several representations of the Eastern seaboard of the United States unless we specify the forms these representations take: 'a poem', 'a piece of music', 'a landscape painting' *and* specify that they are respectively 'a poem about the Eastern seaboard', 'a piece of music (e.g. a symphony) having as its subject the Eastern seaboard', 'a landscape painting of (part of) the Eastern seaboard'. Thus, even though we may speak of 'several representations', 'representations' even in such a use cannot furnish us with a unit of counting and hence cannot answer St Augustine's question. It might be replied here: 'Even though "representation" cannot furnish us with a unit of counting in its own right, is it not possible for St Augustine to introduce "three" in connection with the Trinitarian formula in the following way, namely, "Three representations of the same substance"?' This reply falls down for several reasons. Such a reply could only begin to be a possibility if (i) one were allowed to raise the question 'same what?' in relation to 'the same substance', which one is *not* in this case since in the Trinitarian formula we are being presented with an attempt to explain how it is possible for God to be both *three* and *one*, (ii) even if this question were allowed, we cannot provide an answer. 'Same god' would be open to the difficulties I have raised earlier, and 'same God' is not a starter here since God is the subject of the 'explanation' putatively offered by the Trinitarian formula. Again, there seems to be no answer to the question 'What *form* do these representations take?' 'Image' might be suggested here, but in order for this suggestion to be fruitful it must be possible for us to draw up a formulation of the form 'Three images of one and the same__', where the blank is replaceable by a term which can provide a criterion of identity and unit of counting, and hence we are forced back on to a former difficulty. Yet it is only if an answer to the above question can be supplied that it is possible to speak of 'one'/'many' representations and hence of 'three representations'. Thus, far from it being the case that 'representation' can supply a unit of counting, it does not seem possible to introduce the notion of 'representation' at all in connection with the Trinitarian formula.

7(d) Again special difficulties arise if we consider *prosopon* in the sense of 'aspect'. An aspect is not only the aspect of something or other and depends for its identity upon that of which it is in an aspect; it is also not something someone or something possesses or which can be said to be *in* something or someone. An aspect of *x* is *x* viewed from a certain standpoint or position. This is obvious in the case of aspects of material bodies. For example, the southern aspect of Syon House is not something Syon House possesses or which is part of Syon House, but Syon House viewed from a southerly position or standpoint. Similarly in relation for instance to the western aspect of St Paul's Cathedral: I need not prolong the examples. It might be thought that the notion of 'aspects of a person's character' would be more helpful here, since it might be suggested that we view the 'persons' of the Trinity as three aspects of one and the same character. However, aspects of a person's character are not either something a person possesses or something his character possesses, neither are they in any sense *in* a person. To speak of aspects of a person's character is to speak of a person's character from *a*, *b*, *c*, *d*, . . . points of view. For example, to say that a person's character has an honest or sincere aspect and to speak of that aspect of his character which reveals his honesty and sincerity, is to speak of his character from the standpoint or point of view of honesty or sincerity.* Viewed from the standpoint of honesty or sincerity, he is, we may say, an honest or sincere man. Now in order for 'aspect' to be a possible answer to St Augustine's question, not only must he be able to provide an answer to the question of what it is that the three persons of the Trinity are *three aspects of*,

* It might be objected that the examples of honesty and sincerity are ill-chosen since virtues characterize men, not the points of view from which we talk about them. To this I reply that my concern here is not to propound a thesis to the effect that (for instance) 'A is honest' is for all cases writable as 'A is describable as honest from the point of view of honesty', but solely to produce an account of what it is to speak of *aspects*, of a person's character, as opposed to what it is to speak of a person's character, namely what it is to say that a given person *is* honest, etc.

but he must also take it that aspects can both be *in* things and in some sense be entities and countable units. My above argument was aimed at showing that aspects cannot be regarded as being 'in' things—we cannot ask *whereabouts* in Syon House its southern aspect is, and unless we are prepared to hypostasize 'from the *x*, *y*, *z* points of view' *à la* the old 'sense data' theorists, I cannot see in what sense aspects can be regarded as entities. Indeed, in the light of what I have said above it would be grossly misguided so to regard them. Further, it may be said, aspects are not able to be the subjects of enumeration: we cannot raise the question 'How many aspects has Syon House got?' or 'How many aspects are there to St Paul's Cathedral?'; neither can we raise the question 'How many aspects are there to Mr A's character?' To this it might be countered that although one cannot raise *these* questions, one can raise the following: 'From how many points of view may Syon House be viewed?'; 'From how many points of view may Mr A's character be assessed?' and the number given in answer to these questions is the number of aspects. To this it will be rejoined that these latter questions are themselves impossible: imagine asking 'From how many points of view may Syon House be viewed?' and getting the answer 'twelve'! One cannot count points of view or standpoints any more than one can count aspects. Now whilst it is the case that we can sensibly speak of Syon House or St Paul's or a man's character being viewed from *a number of* different aspects in the sense of a number of different standpoints, it does *not* follow from this that the question 'How many?' can sensibly be raised. Speaking of a number of different aspects or standpoints does not imply speaking of a *definite* number of such aspects or standpoints, any more than saying that Syon House or a man's character may be viewed from several aspects is to say that Syon House or a man's character may be viewed from *a given number of aspects*. Yet it is only if we can speak of a definite number of aspects that 'aspect' can fulfil the role demanded of it in the 'God' case.

Even if an argument can be put forward for saying that,

after all, it *is* possible to introduce the notion of a given or a definite number of aspects, this will not alter the point that 'aspect' cannot furnish a unit of counting in its own right; it precisely does *not* exhibit that feature of being isolated from its environment. Further, if such a situation were to be brought about, there would still be the problem of whether 'aspects' can be sensibly introduced at all in connection with God, let alone furnish an answer to the 'Three what?' question. This problem arises since in such a situation one would be faced with the question of determining the *identity* of the aspects. The formula, 'Three persons in one substance' would read 'Three aspects in one substance' which in turn would have to read 'One substance viewed from three aspects, namely from three standpoints'. In order to get an intelligible proposition here it is necessary to answer the question 'Namely what?' in relation to the introduction of 'One substance'* and it is also necessary to answer the same question in relation to 'three standpoints'. I have earlier argued that it is impossible to supply the 'namely' rider in relation to 'one substance': what could supply such a rider in relation to the 'three standpoints'? 'From the standpoint of being a father'; 'from the standpoint of being a son' might be put forward as two answers. I hesitate to put forward a third in terms of 'from the standpoint of being a spirit' for this will obviously give rise to especial problems. Even so, the first two answers give rise to insuperable difficulties, for such answers necessitate that the 'persons' of the Trinity, viewed as aspects, cannot be regarded as being *in* the Godhead or as being *part of* the Godhead. And in any case, since it is impossible to supply a 'namely' rider in relation to 'one substance', it is impossible to specify the identity of such aspects or standpoints; but it is only on this condition that it is possible to sensibly introduce the concept of 'aspect' here.

7(e) I now turn to *prosopon* in the sense of 'role'. I shall not pursue the account in terms of 'role' at great length since the principal objection to saying that this concept can provide

* Cf. Chapter 4, p. 131.

an answer to St Augustine's question is that it cannot supply a unit of counting in its own right, since it cannot exhibit that feature of 'being isolated from its environment'—an objection which has held against other interpretations of 'person' discussed in this section. 'Roles' are necessarily the roles of someone or other, or something or other, or in relation to something or other, and the identity of individual roles is determined either by reference to the identity of the person or thing whose roles they are, in the sense of the roles a given person or thing has or plays, or by reference to that of which they are a part—as in, for example, the roles in a play. Special difficulties arise however in introducing the concept of 'role' in relation to the doctrine of the Trinity. In order to sensibly introduce this concept into the Trinitarian formula, it is necessary that we supply a 'namely' rider for 'substance' in the formulation 'Three roles of one and the same substance'. The difficulty, indeed the impossibility, of providing a term which can supply such a 'namely' rider has been a perpetual stumbling-block. Further, roles cannot be said to be *in* something or *part of* something, as opposed to something *x* has or plays; yet the Trinitarian doctrine is a doctrine of three 'persons' *in* one substance. There is a sense of 'role' in connection with which it makes sense to ask 'How many?' and get an answer in terms of a definite number, namely in the sense in which we ask how many roles a given actor has played either in a given play or in a given period of his life. This sense of role is not relevant to our present discussion, since the Father, Son, and Holy Spirit cannot be regarded as parallel to the roles an actor plays. It is not essential to an actor being the actor he is that he plays or has played certain roles, whereas it can certainly be argued that it *is* essential to God that there be the Father, Son and Holy Spirit. There is another sense of 'role' in which we speak of a person *having* certain social roles, such as that of a husband, father, breadwinner, political animal and so forth. In this sense, whereas it is possible to speak of a man having a number of such roles or several such roles, it does not seem possible to ask *how many* such roles a man plays. The explanation of this is not hard to find. In the former case, with the actor, an actor can take on and cast off his roles at will; his roles are distinctly something he plays as opposed to something he has. A man cannot cast off his role of a father or parent at will; he has these roles, he does not play them. We can, of course, ask *what* roles a man has in his life in a given society, but a specification is not a list, and the applicability of the 'What?' question does not entail the applicability of the 'How many?' question. It might be pressed that it is *this* sense of 'role' which is appropriate to the 'God' case; but if this is so, granted my points above, it will be a misunderstanding to speak of a definite number of roles and hence of three. But even if the question 'How many roles . . .?' is allowable, the putative answer 'Three roles of *one substance*' is not a possible one. Further, even if the difficulty about providing a 'namely' rider for 'one substance' *could* be overcome, one is not in smooth waters. In the case of the Holy Trinity we should have to reformulate as follows:

'The role of being a father'
'The role of being a son'
'The role of being a spirit'

and it will be objected that it is not possible to translate 'The Father of Our Lord Jesus Christ' into 'The role of being a father' or 'The son of the Father Almighty' into 'The role of being a son', which translations are required here. It is not possible since in the former cases, if the present concept of 'role' can be invoked at all, we have definite descriptions of some role, whereas in the latter cases (the translations) we have specifications of some role. In any case we could not get as far as construing *prosopon* as 'role' on St Augustine's *own* account, since it is a requirement of such a construction that 'Father', 'Son' be treated as descriptions and not as names: yet as I earlier pointed out, St Augustine does regard them as names.

I thus conclude that 'person' in the sense of *prosopon*, in the senses above considered, fails to exhibit those features which are necessary for it to furnish a unit of counting, and that there are insuperable difficulties in introducing this concept in connection with God.

8. It might be said at this juncture that what St Augustine intends by 'persona' is not 'person' in any of the senses above expounded, but in one of the following senses:

(i) ὑπόστασις in the sense of Aristotle's το ὑποκείμενον in the sense of Aristotle's 'first substance'.

(ii) ὑπόστασις, *not* in the sense of το ὑποκείμενον but in the sense of 'individual *simpliciter*'.

To comment on (i). In that to say 'A (Socrates, say) is a ὑπόστασις is to allocate to the category of 'first substance', and ὑπόστασις, in this use cannot be prefaced by a number: 'Socrates is *one* ὑπόστασις' is an impossible proposition. One cannot count 'first substances' as opposed to those entities which are said to fall under this category. Thus the Trinitarian formula in the form: 'One substance in three ὑπόστασεις' is not a possible formulation. Simlarly the Trinitarian formula in the form: 'Three ὑπόστασεις in one substance' is an equally impossible formulation.

As concerns (ii), I have already argued* that the notion of an 'individual *simpliciter*' is an unintelligible one, so a claim to attach a number to 'person' in this sense cannot even begin to be entertained. St Augustine considers alternatives to 'person' as an answer to his question 'What three?'—such as 'essence' (*essentia*),† but as he rejects these I shall not consider them—even though I think that he rejects *essentia* for the wrong reason, namely that the Scriptures do not speak of *essentia*. Indeed, this cannot be a reason either for or against answering the question he poses in terms of *essentia*.

9. I earlier criticized St Augustine for treating 'person', in the use he there intended, as a generic term, and there made reference to a passage in which he does not so treat 'person'.‡ The passage referred to was *De Trin.*, VII, 6, 11 (Haddan, op, cit., p. 197). Will this passage enable us to supply an answer to his question which will indeed furnish

* Cf. Appendix C to Chapter 2.

† *De Trin.*, VII, iv, 8.

‡ See p. 160 above.

us with a unit of counting? In this well-known passage, St Augustine tries to parallel the formula 'Three substances, one essence' (Tres substantias, unam essentiam) or 'Three persons one substance or essence' (Tres personas unam substantiam vel essentiam) to 'Three statues, one gold'.* Such a parallel cannot be drawn, for although, contrary to what might seem initially to be the case, 'statue' cannot furnish us with a unit of counting, since it does not meet the requirement of isolability discussed earlier, what turns 'statue' *into* such a unit *cannot* turn 'person' or 'substance' in the relevant sense here, namely Aristotle's 'first substance', into such a unit. 'Statue' does not meet the requirement of 'isolability' since it is no contingency that statues are the statues of something or other, or someone or other, for instance of men or horses or divinities, and one can only count the statues present in a given place by counting the 'statues of__', where the blank is filled out by a term which can furnish us with a unit of counting in its own right. I can of course count the statues in a particular museum or garden without knowing *of whom* they are the statues or what they are made of or by whom they were created, but if I don't know that what I am supposed to count are (for instance) 'statues of horses' or 'statues of men on horseback' or 'statues of men'—if I am just told, 'Count the statues', then I have no possibility of knowing where to *begin*. What constitutes *one* in this situation?—does a piece of stone, or a stone (bronze) leg or head so count? It will not do to say here: 'You can start counting because you can count what is physically discrete': on the contrary, what is physically discrete here is only determinable by knowing what constitutes *one* statue. Taking 'person' as parallel to 'statue', as St Augustine suggests, we shall have formulations as follows: 'person of __', 'first substance of __': yet replacements of the type instanced above make nonsense here—we should have such expressions as: 'person of man', 'first substance of animal', 'first substance of man'. Hence the parallel breaks down.

* Sicut ex eodem auro si fierent tres statuae diceremus tres statuas unum aurum, species autem statuas: nec aurem speciem, statuas vero individua.

10(a) It is my contention, in the light of all the above discussions, that there is no sense in which 'person' can provide a unit of counting and hence no sense in which this term can furnish an answer to St Augustine's question: 'What three?' Having come to such a conclusion, someone might raise the following problem: 'Granted your present case and your former case concerning "substance" and granted that the Christian faith *does* speak of the Father, Son, and Holy Spirit, how is one to avoid speaking of three gods as opposed to one? Surely you are precisely left with St Augustine's problem with no apparent means of answering it?' It is my contention that there is no problem here, for two reasons. First, I refer the reader back to that section of this chapter in which I pointed out that St Augustine could not even get as far as raising his question 'What three?'* He had, I there argued, no basis for assuming that one had the right to speak of three individuals in this context. Hence the problem posed above cannot get *started* from this point of view. Further, to raise the question 'Is God one god or three?' implies that God might be *a* god, and a specific answer in terms of either 'one god' or 'three gods' would entail asserting that God was *a* god and the question 'Is God one or three?', where no completion for 'one' or 'three' is specified, is an unintelligible question.

10(b) It might here be said: 'Even granted your arguments above, all they show is that the Trinitarian *formula* is unintelligible, *not* that the Trinitarian *doctrine* is! I do not think that anything can be gained from such a move, since the relation between the formula and the doctrine is not a contingent one, as can be seen by the fact that one cannot specify what the Trinitaian doctrine is *without* invoking the formula. Of course one can invoke the basis of this doctrine without invoking the formula, but to invoke the basis of the doctrine is not to invoke the doctrine itself. Again, one can attempt to explain the doctrine without having explicit reference to the formula, but to attempt to explain the doctrine is not to state the doctrine. Further, one can give an

* Section 2 above.

account of why it was thought necessary to introduce such a doctrine without invoking the formula, but this is not to introduce the doctrine. One cannot specify what the doctrine of the Trinity is without specifying the formula, for the issuing of the formula *was* the issuing of the doctrine of the Church and the occurrence of the formula in the Athanasian Creed *is* the statement of the doctrine. The *Quicunque vult* reads:*

> Whosoever will be saved: before all things it is necessary that he hold the Catholic Faith.
> Which Faith except everyone do keep whole and undefiled: without doubt he shall perish everlastingly
> And the Catholic Faith is this: That we worship one God in Trinity, and Trinity in Unity;
> Neither confounding the Persons: nor dividing the Substance. For there is one Person of the Father . . .'

It would be nonsense to say that one might perish everlastingly on account of a *formula*: but the doctrine only has the possibility of sense if the formula has sense. Someone might be tempted to say, following a suggestion of Wittgenstein, that if a formula or set of words has a use, then such a formula or set of words has a meaning: the Trinitarian formula clearly has a use, hence it has a meaning. This suggestion, however tempting, cannot be taken seriously here since, whilst it is true that the Trinitarian formula has a use, the sense in which it has a use is not the sense (if there is one) of 'use' which would give it meaning. The sense in which it has a use is the sense in which it has a function, namely that of 'stating' a doctrine: but having a function in this sense presupposes having a sense or meaning, hence the suggestion could only be taken seriously by playing on an ambiguity in 'use' and thus begging the issue at stake—for the whole problem *is* whether the concepts of 'person' and 'substance' *have* a use in the context of the Trinitarian formula, and simply to occur is not to have a use.

10(c) At this point someone may put the following view forward: 'What you have been doing may be of scholarly

* Taken from *The Book of Common Prayer*, 1662.

and philosophical interest, but what is wanted is not a discussion of the "old formula" but a reinterpretation in terms intelligible to modern man.' My answer to this line of approach is threefold. (i) *vide* my above argument, one cannot separate the formula from the doctrine. (ii) Unless the 'old formula' *is* understood, then what could constitute one knowing that one was indeed giving a reinterpretation of the 'old formula' as opposed to putting up something new? Indeed the problem goes deeper than this, for in order to decide that one was putting up something *new*, one would first have to understand what was involved in the 'old formula', which demands that the 'old formula' is itself intelligible. (iii) If, as I have argued, the old formula *is* unintelligible, then any supposed reinterpretation of it will itself be unintelligible. To give a reinterpretation that itself has the possibility of sense, it must be shown that that which is reinterpreted has sense. These points might be disputed. It might be countered that it is possible for an unintelligible formula to have an intelligible reformulation. There might be cases where we might understand what an 'old formula' is trying to say, even though we would say that, as it stands, it is unintelligible. Such cases would be cases where we might want to operate with it: cases where we are intending to do something with it. A reformulation in such cases would be perfectly possible if both the old formula and some further formula can be said to have been devised for the same purpose or if both can be said to fulfil the same function. In the case of possible Trinitarian formulae, it might be said, the 'old' formula was designed for a purpose: another formula could be said to be a reformulation of this same doctrine if it can be said to have been devised for the same purpose. This counter immediately raises the difficulty of *what* the doctrine *is* independently of the formula. Further, the argument presented makes it a sufficient condition of formula x_1 being a reformulation of x that x_1 performs the same function as x or is at least designed or intended to perform the same function as x. This is open to objections. 'Shut the gate' may have the function of telling you to shut the gate, but 'The bull is coming through the gate' may have exactly the same function; yet it can indeed be denied that one is a reformulation of the other. However, even if we were to allow the above as a sufficient condition, the problem still remains as to whether this counter-argument applies in the situation under discussion. We must ask: 'For what purpose was the "old" Trinitarian formula devised?' Can it be said (a) to have the possibility of fulfilling that role (b) to have fulfilled that role? I quote Wolfson (op. cit., p. 308):

> With the elevation of the Logos to the position of God in the literal sense of the term and with the elevation of the Holy Spirit first to the position of an object of worship and adoration like God and then gradually to the position of God in the literal sense of the term, the Fathers found themselves confronted with a new problem, the problem of how to reconcile their new Christian belief in three Gods with their inherited Jewish belief in one God.

It is clear from this that the 'old' formula was intended to solve a problem and effect a reconciliation. However, no unintelligible formula can solve a problem and hence effect a reconciliation; it has no *possibility* of doing so. Thus we cannot concern ourselves with (b) above. And a parallel point holds if we recast the counter-argument in terms of intention or design. One cannot intend to solve a problem with an inherently nonsensical formula, though a nonsensical formula may be used to bring out or draw attention to a problem. I thus see no reason in the above counter-argument for withdrawing my original points.

A supposed 'reinterpretation' of the 'old formula' in terms of 'a contemporary language' has recently been advocated by John Macquarrie in his *Principles of Christian Theology*.* He says (p. 176):

> But while these remarks may to some extent defend the traditional doctrine of the Trinity, it will be said that the formula of one substance and three persons constitutes an interpretation that has ceased to communicate, for it talks the language and moves in the universe of discourse of an obsolete philosophy. This does not mean the formula is to be rejected . . . what is required is a new act of interpretation that will interpret in a contemporary

* London, S.C.M. Press, 1966.

language this ancient and hallowed formula of the Church, just as it in turn had interpreted the mythological and historical material which lies behind it.

I comment on this as follows:

(a) What is the 'Three persons in one substance' formula supposed to be an interpretation of? According to what he says a page earlier, the Trinitarian formula is an interpretation of the Christian community's belief that God, who had created heaven and earth, had become incarnate in a particular man and that, furthermore, he still dwelt with the community and guided it. Apart from *saying* that the Trinitarian formula is an interpretation, Macquarrie does nothing whatsoever to even show us by what kind of criteria this formula can be regarded as an interpretation, as opposed to anything else. We are not given an inkling as to how this decision is *makeable*. In the light of this it is difficult to take Macquarrie's case seriously; indeed there is no case to be taken.

(b) The formula of 'one substance—three persons', in that it employs the notions of οὐσία and ὑποστασεις or their Latin equivalents and variants, has only ceased to communicate to those who cannot be bothered to take the trouble to explore these difficult and complex concepts, or who, having taken some trouble, find the tide too great. The philosophy of substance and essence, to invoke a crude nomenclature, may not be in vogue in some circles, but were those circles to study it seriously, they might well save themselves from a number of errors, such as, for example, treating 'beings' as a class of things or 'being' as a universal property or 'Being' as a supreme genus.

(c) How seriously the 'reinterpretation' offered by Macquarrie is to be taken may be judged by the reader for himself from the following considerations:

(i) The 'Traditional Trinitarian Doctrine' is discussed in little more than five pages (pp. 173–9).

(ii) The notion of 'persona' and ὑπόστασις are discussed in two sentences (p. 177).

(iii) The doctrine of 'in one substance' or 'essence' is discussed in fourteen lines (p. 176), with no mention whatsoever of the variety of senses possible for 'substantia' or 'ousia' and an unsupported claim to the effect that when Aquinas says that in God essence and being are identical, this allows us or at least directs us to understand God as Being.*

(iv) There is a claim to the effect that the doctrine of God as Being sums up a long history of revelatory experience, with a back reference to p. 107, where it is asserted that God has been associated with Being in theological thought—'an association that is found in the Greek Fathers, in St Augustine and St Thomas'; no evidence is provided for this assertion. Indeed it can certainly be denied that Aquinas at least held any such doctrine.†

(v) The 'reinterpretation' is covered in eight pages (pp. 179–86) and no criteria are offered as to how one would set about determining that this *is* a reinterpretation.

The actual reinterpretation itself I shall not discuss, for it is, in my view, based on certain logical errors which lead the author into sheer nonsense, for instance talk about *Being* (cf. pp. 181, 182 *inter alia*). In the light of these points I do not see how such a 'reinterpretation' can be taken seriously—most especially in the light of St Augustine's struggles in what is only one book of the *De Trinitate*, namely book VII.

11. I commented earlier that it is necessarily the case that no intelligible account can be offered of the phrases 'of the same substance', 'in the same substance', and 'in one substance' in their use in relation to God.‡ I think this is an important point to be made, and in connection with it I want to cite and discuss some of the things St Augustine says about the possibility of formulating a doctrine of the Trinity. I shall end my discussion of the Trinitarian doctrine with these remarks.

At the beginning of *De Trinitate* V, St Augustine says:§

* For a serious discussion of Aquinas's point, cf. P. T. Geach in his paper on 'Form and Existence', reprinted in *God and the Soul.*

† Cf. Geach: 'Aquinas' in *Three Philosophers.*

‡ Chapter 4 above, pp. 125–7, 131, 143.

§ Hinc jam exordiens ea dicere, quae dici ut cogitantur vel ab homine aliquo, vel certe a nobis non omni modo possunt: quamvis et ipsa nostra cogitatio, cum de Deo Trinitate cogitamus, longe se illi de quo cogitat, imparem sentiat, neque ut est eum

> Beginning as I do now henceforwards, to speak of subjects which cannot altogether be spoken of, as they are thought . . . although even our very thought, when we think of God the Trinity, falls (as we feel) very far short of Him of whom we think nor comprehends Him as He is; but He is seen, as it is written, even by those who are so great as was the Apostle Paul, 'through a glass and in an enigma'.

and again:*

> And we shall mutually pardon one another the more easily if we know, or at any rate firmly believe and hold, that whatever is said of a nature unchangeable, invisible, and having life absolute sufficient to itself, must not be measured after the custom of things changeable and mortal or not self-sufficient.

Now it appears from the first passage that I have cited that the difficulty which the writer of a treatise such as St Augustine is here engaged upon is faced is simply a practical one, though a practical difficulty of immense proportions. It is a case of our thought falling very far short of God, but that we can, in some sense or other, speak of God 'by analogy' or in terms of images. It follows from this line of thought that our speaking about God as 'substance', in any of the senses above discussed, or in using the phrases 'of the same substance', 'in the same substance', in any of the senses discussed above, is only supposed to be analogical talk. However, I claim that my investigation has shown that it is not possible to use these conceptions in connection with God *at all*—not simply not possible to use them univocally. Indeed to employ the univocal/analogical distinction in relation to these concepts would be out of place, for this is a distinction which was introduced in connection with ordinary first order predicates, not in connection with predicates signifying categories.† I am not to be thought of as contending that it is not possible to speak of God 'by analogy' at all, even though

capiat, sed ut Scriptum est, etiam a tantis quantum Paulus apostolus hic erat, per speculum et in aenigmate videatur.

* Facilius autem nobis invicem ignoscimus si noverimus, aut certe credendo firmum tenuerimus, ea quae de natura incommutabile et invisibili summeque vivente ac sibi sufficiente dicuntur, non ex consuetudine visibilium atque mutabilium et mortalium vel egenarum rerum esse metienda.

† Cf. Aristotle, *Nicomachean Ethics*, A.6.

it can be held that at least some modern attempts to make out a case for this fail.* Here I am maintaining no such general thesis, but the more particular thesis that it is not possible as concerns the items discussed. And the kind of impossibility involved here is not practical, but conceptual, granted the account of God's nature given by St Augustine himself. To say that God is a *nature* unchangeable, invisible, and having life absolutely to itself, is to make a remark on the concept of God, or to make a remark on the nature of God; it matters not which way we put it. It is not as if the nature of God is something which could be discovered or settled by an empirical investigation. To say that God is a nature unchangeable, invisible, etc. gives us what Wittgenstein calls a 'grammatical' remark concerning God. It does not give us a true predication of God, for the force of saying that God is a *nature* unchangeable, invisible, having life absolutely to itself is that, as concerns God, it is a misunderstanding to say that 'He' is the subject of our vision, in the straightforward sense that spatio-temporal objects are the subject of our vision; that 'He' is subject to change and decay; that 'He' is dependent for 'His' form of life on anything else, as men are or the gods of the heathen were. It is to be noted that St Augustine does not simply say that God is not-changeable, not-visible, etc.: indeed such 'properties' could not form part of a *nature*, they could only be 'properties' of an individual or set of individuals which *fell under* a certain nature, namely a nature that was subject to change and visible. The remark that God is a nature unchangeable, etc., is parallel to the remark that Man is a nature changeable, visible, and not having life absolutely to himself; which is to say that it makes sense as concerns any man to say that he *is* the subject of change and decay, an object of vision, that he is dependent for his form of life upon something else, for instance his parents and the human society in which he lives. Hence when St Augustine says that that nature (God) must not be measured after the custom of things visible and changeable, etc., this must not be taken as a warning to the

* Cf. my paper 'God and Analogy', in *Sophia*, op. cit.

effect that if you *do* you will get a *false* account of God, but as a warning that if you do you will get an *impossible* account. For in such a procedure you will be imposing on that which is necessarily not *either* mortal or not-mortal, changing or not changing, visible or not visible, etc., a set of categories which have their home and natural habitat in a conceptual scheme in which individuals and types of thing *can* sensibly be said to be changing or not changing, visible or not visible, mortal or not mortal. In short, a set of categories which have their home and natural habitat in what Professor Strawson has called 'our conceptual scheme'—the scheme of material bodies and persons.*

Unfortunately St Augustine does not recognize that the kind of difficulty involved here is conceptual, hence he thinks that it is perfectly possible, but highly problematic to say that God is 'as good without quality, great without quantity, a creator though lacking nothing, ruling but from no position, sustaining all things without "having" them, in his wholeness everywhere, yet without place, eternal without time, making things that are changeable without change of himself and without passion'.† An objector will be quick to point out that, for example, granted the Aristotelian categories of 'quality' and 'quantity', which St Augustine is obviously invoking here, the Greek concept and the 'received' concept of 'Creator', etc., then what we are faced with here is not a set of highly problematical remarks, but a set of contradictory ones or at least a set of inconsistent ones. For, such an objector will argue, it is logically impossible (granted the above framework) that for instance anything be said to be 'good' and what this predicate signifies *not* fall under the category of 'quality'; that anything be said to be 'great' and what this predicate signifies *not* fall under the category of 'quantity'; that anything be said to be a 'creator' and yet lacking nothing, etc.

* *Individuals*, p. 15.

† Sine qualitate bonum, sine quantitate magnum, sine indigentia creatorem, sine situ praesisentem, sine habitu omnia continemtem, sine loco ubique totum, sine tempore semperiternum, sine vela sui mutatione mutabilia facientem nihil patientem.

This is *not* to say that St Augustine's remarks here are unintelligible *period*: they only are unintelligible, in the sense of nonsensical, if they are taken as remarks *within* the received conceptual scheme: but they need not so be taken. They can be taken as remarks about the concept of 'God' or the 'nature' of God as concerns the received scheme, though I do not think that St Augustine so takes them for, taken thus, they do *not* present a difficulty. He actually has said 'that so we may understand God, if we are able and as much as we are able *as* good without quality, great without quantity . . .' and we can construe this in such a way that we do not get inconsistencies as in the former construction. Such a construction is as follows. To say that God is *as* good without quality, etc. is to say that God cannot be spoken of (a) in terms of that conceptual scheme or schemes which is (are) geared to and have their bases in our speech about spatio-temporal particulars; (b) in terms of that scheme or schemes which are geared to and have their home in the concept of a creator creating something out of a material; or the concept of a ruler, where this entails ruling from some position; or the concept of 'everywhere', where this has a necessary reference to spatial position; or the concept of 'eternity', where this has a necessary reference to time, namely continued existence in time. As thus construed, what we have in St Augustine's remarks is a series of 'grammatical' remarks about God. It is only by treating such remarks as remarks *within* the scheme which for instance Aristotle's categories reflect, that we get inconsistencies and contradictions and it is only by treating such remarks thus that St Augustine can be of the view that it is very difficult to talk about God.

12. My arguments to the effect that no intelligible account can be offered of the Trinitarian formula and hence of the doctrine of the Trinity, does not commit me to the view that it is impossible to speak of God: indeed in one sense of 'speak of God' I have already said a great deal. Neither does it commit me to the view that God is 'wholly other' in the sense that one cannot even sensibly introduce the concept

of God, let alone that it commits me to the view that God is, to use the customary quaint phrase, '*The* Wholly Other'. As Professor Geach has rightly commented: 'A man may *assert* that God is too high a subject matter for human argument: but having said this he had best keep silence, for if he *argues* the matter he at once contradicts himself.'* Neither does it follow from what I have said that that no intelligible account can be offered of any theological proposition. All that is implied in the above discussion and all that is intended to be implied is that in so far as theology takes over and uses categories which form an integral part of our discourse about that which is spatio-temporally determined (the categories of our 'ordinary conceptual scheme' as Strawson puts it)—such as substance and its correlates—then thus far theology remains and must remain unintelligible.

* *God and the Soul*, p. 105.

A NOTE ON FREGE ON 'INDIVISIBILITY'

It may be said that in the above discussion I have not taken sufficient cognisance of Frege's special sense of 'indivisibility' (cf. *Foundations of Arithmetic*, p. 66). The feature of indivisibility which terms that are to provide units of counting must exhibit, according to my central account as illustrated on p. 158, is that items which fall under such terms, if divided up, do not yield us with a number of independent units, whereas what Frege means by 'indivisible', as illustrated by his concept 'syllables in the word three' is that a concept of such a type is not truly predicable of the parts of any entity which falls under it if such an entity is divided up. Taking due cognisance of Frege's special sense of 'indivisibility' however does not affect my argument against 'person' being a unit of counting (pp. 169 ff), in spite of initial appearances to the contrary: whilst it is true that *if* 'person' is a concept in Frege's sense *then* an objector can certainly make the point that it is 'indivisible' in that '—is a person' is not truly predicable of the parts of a person, I have already produced independent arguments in favour of denying the antecedent here, viz., in favour of the thesis that 'person' is a 'Formal Concept' in Wittgenstein's sense, not a 'Proper' one, and hence not a concept in Frege's sense. It might however be pressed that lack of sufficient cognisance of Frege's special sense of 'indivisibility' materially affects my cases against 'person' being a unit of counting, where the sense of 'person' is one of the senses of '*prosopon*' (cf. pp. 173 ff.). For example, '—is a face'; '—is a character'; '—has a character'; '—has a role' are not truly predicable of the division of a face, character, or role respectively and I do not claim that such senses of '*prosopon*' introduce 'Formal Concepts'. However I contend that my case against such terms being units of counting in their own right is not materially affected by such lack of cognisance since such terms do not meet the requirement of being isolated from their environment.

Bibliography

ACKRILL, J. L. (tr.), Aristotle's *Categories* and *De Interpretatione*, Oxford, Clarendon Press, 1963.

ANSCOMBE, G. E. M., 'Aristotle', in G. E. M. Anscombe and P. T. Geach, *Three Philosophers*, Oxford, Blackwell, 1961.

AQUINAS, ST THOMAS, *Summa Theologiae*, editio Joseph Pecci, Paris, Lethielleux, 1887.

Summa Theologica, tr. by Fathers of the English Dominican Province, London, Burnes Oates & Washbourne, 1920.

ARISTOTLE, *De Anima* (Loeb Classical Library), tr. W. S. Hett, London, Heinemann, 1957.

De Caelo (Loeb), tr. W. K. C. Guthrie, London, Heinemann, 1939.

Categories (Loeb), tr. H. P. Cooke, Heinemann, 1955.

De Generatione et Corruptione (Loeb), tr. E. S. Forster, London, Heinemann, 1955.

Metaphysics, Books I–IX (Loeb), tr. H. Tredennick, London, London, Heinemann, 1961.

Nicomachean Ethics (Loeb), tr. H. Rackham, London, Heinemann, 1956.

Physics, Books I–IV (Loeb), tr. P. H. Wicksteed and F. M. Cornford, London, Heinemann, 1957.

Posterior Analytics (Loeb), tr. H. Tredennick and E. S. Forster, London, Heinemann, 1960.

Topics (Loeb), tr. H. Tredennick and E. S. Forster, London, Heinemann, 1960.

ATHANASIUS, ST, *Epistola ad Epictum*, in J. P. Migne, *Patrologia Graeca*, Paris, Garnier Fratres, 1857–1912.

Epistola de Synodis, in J. P. Migne, *Patrologia Graeca.*

Oratio de Incarnatione Verbi, in J. P. Migne, *Patrologia Graeca.*

AUGUSTINE, ST, *De Trinitate*, in *Sancti Aurelii Augustini Operum*, Editio Tertia Veneta, Bassani, 1797.
On the Trinity, tr. by A. W. Haddan, Edinburgh, T. & T. Clark, 1873.

BARTH, KARL, *Credo*, London, Hodder and Stoughton, 1936.
Dogmatics in Outline (tr. G. T. Thompson), London, S.C.M., 1940.
Knowledge of God and Service of God, London, Hodder and Stoughton, 1938.

BASIL, ST, *Adversus Eunomium*, in J. P. Migne, *Patrologia Graeca*.
Epistles 38, 214, 236, 361, 362 in J. P. Migne, *Patrologia Graeca*.

BEARDSMORE, R. W., *Moral Reasoning*, London, Routledge & Kegan Paul, 1969.

BOOK OF COMMON PRAYER, 1662.

BRUNNER, EMIL, *The Christian Doctrine of God* (*Dogmatics*, vol. I), tr. Olive Wyon, London, Lutterworth, 1949.

CYRIL OF ALEXANDRIA, ST, *Commentary on St. John's Gospel*, in J. P. Migne, *Patrologia Graeca*.
De Trinitate, in J. P. Migne, *Patrologia Graeca*.

CYRIL OF JERUSALEM, ST, *Catecheses*, in J. P. Migne, *Patrologia Graeca*.

DURRANT, MICHAEL, 'God and Analogy', in *Sophia*, vol. VIII, no. 3, October 1969.
'St. Thomas's "Third Way" ', *Religious Studies*, vol. 4, April 1969.

EUSEBIUS OF CAESAREA, *De Ecclesiastica Theologica*, in J. P. Migne, *Patrologia Graeca*.
Oratio de Laudibus Constantini, in J. P. Migne, *Patrologia Graeca*.

FREGE, GOTTLOB, *The Foundations of Arithmetic*, tr. J. L. Austin, Oxford, Blackwell, 1950.
'On Concept and Object', in *Translations from the Philosophical Writings of Gottlob Frege*, ed. P. T. Geach and M. Black, Oxford, Blackwell, 1952.

GEACH, P. T., 'Aquinas', in G. E. M. Anscombe and P. T. Geach, *Three Philosophers*, Oxford, Blackwell, 1961.
'Form and Existence', *Proceedings of the Aristotelian Society*, 1955, repr. in *God and the Soul*, London, Routledge & Kegan Paul, 1969.
'Good and Evil', *Analysis*, vol. 17, 1956, repr. in *Theories of Ethics*, ed. by Philippa Foot, Oxford, O.U.P., 1967.
'The Moral Law and the Law of God', in *God and the Soul*.
Reference and Generality, Ithaca, Cornell University Press, 1962.
'On Worshipping the Right God' in *God and the Soul*.

GREGORY OF NAZIANZUS, ST, *Orationes*, in J. P. Migne, *Patrologia Graeca.*

GREGORY OF NYSSA, ST, *Quod Non Sit Tres Dei* in J. P. Migne, *Patrologia Graeca.*

HIPPOLYTUS, ST, *Refutatio Omnium Haeresium*, in *Hippolytus Werke*, P. Wendland, Leipzig, J. C. Hinrich'sche Buchhandlung, 1916.

IRENAEUS, ST, *Adversus Haereses*, V, in J. P. Migne, *Patrologia Graeca.*

JOHN OF DAMASCUS, ST, *De Fide Orthodoxa*, I, in J. P. Migne, *Patrologia Graeca.*

KENNY, ANTHONY, *Action, Emotion and Will*, London, Routledge & Kegan Paul, 1963.

KELLY, J. N. D., *Early Christian Doctrines* (third edn), London, A. & C. Black, 1965.

MACKINNON, D. M., 'Aristotle's Conception of Substance', in *New Essays on Plato and Aristotle*, ed. R. Bambrough, London, Routledge & Kegan Paul, 1965.

MACQUARRIE, JOHN, *Principles of Christian Theology*, London, S.C.M. Press, 1966.

MALCOLM, NORMAN, 'Anselm's Ontological Arguments', repr. in *Religion and Understanding*, ed. D. Z. Phillips, Oxford, Blackwell, 1967.

ORIGEN, *Contra Celsum*, in J. P. Migne, *Patrologia Graeca.*

De Oratione, in J. P. Migne, *Patrologia Graeca.*

De Principiis, in *Die griechischen christlichen Schriftsteller der ersten drei Jahrunderte*, ed. Paul Koetshau, 'Origenes', vol. V, Leipzig, J. C. Hinrich'sche Buchhandlung, 1913.

Ex homiliis in Epistolam ad Hebraeos in J. P. Migne, *Patrologia Graeca.*

In Joannem Commentarii, in J. P. Migne, *Patrologia Graeca.*

On the Proverbs, in J. P. Migne, *Patrologia Graeca.*

OWEN, G. E. L., 'Aristotle on the Snares of Ontology', repr. in *New Essays on Plato and Aristotle*, Bambrough, London, Routledge & Kegan Paul, 1965.

PETERS, R. S., *The Concept of Motivation*, London, Routledge & Kegan Paul, 1958.

PHILLIPS, D. Z., 'Faith, Scepticism and Religious Understanding' in *Religion and Understanding*, ed. D. Z. Phillips, Oxford, Blackwell, 1967.

'Introduction' to J. L. Stocks, *Morality and Purpose*, London, Routledge & Kegan Paul, 1969.

PHILO, *De Aeternitate Mundi*, in *Philonis Alexandrini Opera*, vol. IV, P. Wendland, Berlin, Reimer, 1898.
De Somniis, in *Philonis Alexandrini Opera*, P. Wendland, Berlin, Reimer, 1898.

PLATO, *Euthyphro* (Loeb Classical Library), tr. H. N. Fowler, Heinemann, 1914.
Laches (Loeb), tr. W. R. M. Lamb, London, Heinemann, 1924.
Meno (Loeb), tr. by W. R. M. Lamb, London, Heinemann, 1924.
Parmenides (Loeb), tr. H. N. Fowler, London, Heinemann, 1958.
Phaedo (Loeb), tr. H. N. Fowler, London, Heinemann, 1914.

PRESTIGE, G. L., *God in Patristic Thought*, London, Heinemann, 1936.

RUSSELL, BERTRAND, 'The Philosophy of Logical Atomism' in B. Russell, *Logic and Knowledge*, ed. R. C. Marsh, George Allen & Unwin, 1956.
Introduction to Mathematical Philosophy (second edn), London, George Allen & Unwin, 1930.
'On Denoting' in *Mind* (new series), vol. XIV, 1905, repr. in *Logic and Knowledge*.

STOCKS, J. L., *Morality and Purpose*, London, Routledge & Kegan Paul, 1969.

STRAWSON, P. F., *Individuals*, London, Methuen, 1959.
'On Referring' in *Mind*, 1950, repr. in *Essays in Conceptual Analysis*, ed. A. Flew, London, Macmillan, 1963, and in P. F. Strawson, *Logico-Linguistic Papers*, London, Methuen, 1971.

VLASTOS, G., 'The Third Man argument in the Parmenides' repr. in *Studies in Plato's Metaphysics*, ed. R. E. Allen, Routledge & Kegan Paul, 1965.

WEBB, C. C. J., *God and Personality*, London, Allen & Unwin, 1918.

WITTGENSTEIN, L., *Tractatus Logico-Philosophicus*, with Introduction by B. Russell, London, Routledge & Kegan Paul, 1922.

WOLFSON, H. A., *The Philosophy of the Church Fathers*, vol. I, Cambridge, Mass., Harvard University Press, 1956.

Index